Industrial Revolution in America

Industrial Revolution in America

AGRICULTURE AND MEATPACKING

Edited by

Kevin Hillstrom and Laurie Collier Hillstrom

A B C  C L I O

Santa Barbara, California • Denver, Colorado • Oxford, England

Library of Congress Cataloging-in-Publication Data
Library of Congress Cataloging-in-Publication Data
Communications, agriculture and meatpacking, overview/comparison /
edited by Kevin Hillstrom and Laurie Collier Hillstrom.
    p. cm. — (Industrial Revolution in America; 7-9)
    Includes bibliographical references.
    ISBN-10: 1-85109-719-8 (hardcover : alk. paper)
    ISBN-10: 1-85109-724-4 (ebook : alk. paper)
    ISBN-13: 978-1-85109-719-7 (hardcover : alk. paper)
    ISBN-13: 978-1-85109-724-1 (ebook : alk. paper)   1. Agricultural
innovations—United States—History.   2. Packing-houses—United
States—History.   3. Communication—United States—History.   I.
Hillstrom, Kevin, 1963–   II. Hillstrom, Laurie Collier, 1965–

    S494.5.I5.C654 2007
    630.973—dc22

                                                                    2006100745

11   10   09   08   07   10   9   8   7   6   5   4   3   2   1

Senior Production Editor: Cami Cacciatore
Editorial Assistant: Alisha Martinez
Production Manager: Don Schmidt
Media Editor: Jed DeOrsay
Media Production Coordinator: Ellen Brenna Dougherty
Media Resources Manager: Caroline Price
File Manager: Paula Gerard

ABC-CLIO, Inc.
130 Cremona Drive, P.O. Box 1911
Santa Barbara, California 93116-1911

This book is also available on the World Wide Web as an ebook. Visit
http://www.abc-clio.com for details.

This book is printed on acid-free paper. ∞
Manufactured in the United States of America

Contents

Series Introduction

The **Industrial Revolution** was a transformational era in U.S. history, ushering in a host of major technological and socioeconomic changes that continue to define the nation's political, social, and environmental landscape today. Indeed, the rise of the industrial age changed all facets of American life—often in decisive and far-reaching ways. Prior to the advent of railroads, industrial factories, telegraph systems, mechanized agriculture, and the automobile, the United States was a nation with an overwhelmingly rural character and a subsistence-oriented economy. The changing of the seasons governed all aspects of daily life in the preindustrial era, and towns, cities, and states that lay a mere hundred miles distant seemed nearly as foreign and exotic as those of Europe or the Far East.

The Industrial Revolution changed all that. As railroad networks, steam shipping routes, textile factories, telegraph and telephone lines, steel foundries, and mechanized harvesting machines blossomed across the land, they transfigured American life. Major metropolitan centers sprang up across the land, even in areas of the interior that had been wholly unsettled a mere quarter century before. Subsistence economies gave way to vibrant commercial economies based on national and international trade, and the land's natural bounty was exploited with near-religious zeal. American culture and self-identity underwent similarly profound changes, nurtured by the seeming fulfillment of the Manifest Destiny doctrine, spiraling tensions between workers and employers, and dawning awareness of the nation's ever-growing influence and stature on the global stage.

In recognition of the profound impact that the Industrial Revolution had on the United States and the wider world, ABC-CLIO has created *The Industrial Revolution in America*. This nine-volume series covers all aspects of the American Industrial Revolution, from the introduction of steam-powered engines to the emergence of the automobile. In the process, the series provides a wealth of fascinating, detailed information on the historical impact of various industries on the nation's workers, families, and communities. It also casts a discerning eye on the various ways in which these industries shaped U.S. politics, corporate practices, philosophies of natural resource use and stewardship, and cultural development.

Coverage in *The Industrial Revolution in America* is broken down into the following subject-specific volumes:

Iron and Steel. These are the most formidable of all the manufacturing industries that transformed American life in the second half of the nineteenth century. Steel production provided the United States with the infrastructure necessary to transform itself into an industrial superpower.

Railroads. The rise of the so-called Iron Horse drove the nation's breathtaking economic and geographic expansion, providing Americans with the means to harvest and market the continent's remarkable bounty of natural resources. In the process, it became an iconic image of the American conquest of the frontier.

Steam Shipping. A uniquely American contribution to modern technology, steam shipping was the first major transportation innovation that facilitated economic expansion across the United States in the nineteenth century.

Textiles. When textile production began in the late eighteenth and early nineteenth centuries in the northeastern United States—boosted in large measure by abundant cotton crops from the Deep South—it marked the nation's first successful parlay of technological innovation into mass production.

Mining and Petroleum. U.S. extraction of coal, iron ore, gold, silver, oil, copper, and other minerals became increasingly sophisticated and profitable during the late nineteenth century, providing industries with the raw materials they needed to dramatically expand production.

Automobiles. The last of the great technological innovations of the American Industrial Revolution, the advent of the automobile wrought enormous changes in U.S. commerce—and even greater changes in the country's social fabric.

Agriculture and Meatpacking. As America's transportation infrastructure expanded and improved, it created an environment in which farmers could deliver goods to lucrative marketplaces that were beyond reach only a generation earlier. The existence of this network, coupled with the rapidly expanding U.S. population, turned farmers, ranchers, and meatpackers and other commodity packagers into cornerstones of the emerging U.S. empire.

Communications. The introduction of the telegraph and the telephone revolutionized the dissemination of information across the United States. This technology, which provided for the virtually instantaneous transfer of information from one end of the United States to the other, radically altered many aspects of American culture and business enterprise.

Industrial Revolution Overview. This volume provides readers with an introduction to the Industrial Revolution in general and assesses the impact of various industries on each other and on the nation as a whole.

Each of these volumes is divided into the following topical chapters:

- Origins and Development
- Innovations and Inventions
- Major Entrepreneurs and Companies
- Lives of the Workforce
- Labor Organizations and Reform Movements
- Environmental Impact
- Immigration's Impact
- Societal Impact
- Gilded Age Art and Literature
- The Modern Era

Other valuable features included in each volume of the *Industrial Revolution in America* series include:

- Attribution and referencing of primary sources and other quoted material to help guide users to other valuable historical research resources.

- Photographs of the leading figures and major events discussed in the text.
- Biographical profiles of notable individuals (indicated by **bolded** names).
- Extensive bibliography of works consulted.
- A subject index.

Introductory Note

For much of America's history, the nation's self-image has been an agrarian one—and little wonder, since farming has traditionally ranked as the most economically important of all U.S. industries and since pioneer farmers and ranchers, more than members of any other demographic group, were responsible for the settlement of the American West. Indeed, even as the industrial age roared to life in cities from New England to California, the land-clearing and cultivation activities of farmers and ranchers were permanently transforming the natural landscape and providing the nutritional staples required to sustain the fast-growing American populace.

Agriculture was the cornerstone of New England's economic vitality and culture during the colonial era, but it was in the nineteenth century that American farming truly came into its own. During that period, local, state, and federal officials all recognized that agriculture was the lifeblood of the young nation, and they made every effort to help farmers increase their yields and expand their landholdings. These efforts included major investments in transportation networks capable of delivering crops from remote fields to urban dinner tables, as well as land settlement policies explicitly designed to lure pioneering farm families to unsettled terrain. The monumental Homestead Act of 1862, for instance, was created for the express purpose of assisting the country in fulfilling its Manifest Destiny—bending the American wilderness to its will and forcing it to give up its natural bounty for the betterment of millions of Americans.

Industrialization, of course, also brought great technological change and innovation to the world of American agriculture. These developments moved the industry from an era in which primitive and inefficient hand-powered tools were the sole means of tilling, planting, and harvesting crops to a vastly more productive era of cotton gins and steam-powered threshers. Incredible surges in crop production were the result, and by the end of the nineteenth century, the United States was the world leader in the production of cotton, wheat, and myriad other commercially important crops. It was perhaps inevitable, then, that farmers would come to be regarded as the central players in the nation's economic well-being.

Meatpacking operators enjoyed no such high public regard. Americans preferred not to dwell on the bloody business of slaughtering and processing millions of cattle and hogs, even though these activities were executed to sate the appetites of the nation's rapidly expanding urban populations. In terms of national icons, they vastly preferred the image of the intrepid farmer nurturing crops to life under a vibrant blue sky over that of the blood-streaked immigrant laboring in the clamor of a Chicago slaughterhouse. But meatpacking operations were a critical element in westward settlement, too—especially after the introduction of the refrigerated railroad car in the late 1860s. This innovation gave cattle ranchers more flexibility and freedom than ever before to venture into pristine corners of the diminishing American wilderness and exploit the lands for financial profit.

Notes on Contributors

Kevin Hillstrom and **Laurie Collier Hillstrom** have authored and edited award-winning reference works on a wide range of subjects, including American history, international environmental issues, and business and industry. Works produced by the Hillstroms include the six-volume *World's Environments* series (2003), *Encyclopedia of Small Business*, 2nd ed. (2001), the four-volume *American Civil War Reference Library* (2000), the four-volume *Vietnam War Reference Library* (2000), and *The Vietnam Experience: A Concise Encyclopedia of American Literature, Films, and Songs.*

Jacob Jones, Ph.D., is an assistant professor for history and government at the University of Maryland/University College. Since 2003, he has been a member of the traveling faculty in Europe. He has contributed articles to numerous reference series and professional journals, including *American Eras: The Reform Era and Eastern U.S. Development, 1815–1850* (1998), *ALHFAM* [Association for Living Historical Farms and Museums] *Proceedings of the Conference and Annual Meeting* (1997), and *The Encylopedia of American Industries* (1994).

Leigh Kimmel holds degrees in Russian language and literature, library and information science, and history. She has studied at the University of Illinois at Urbana-Champaign and at Illinois State University and held positions as a librarian at Illinois Central College and at Moraine Valley Community College. Her articles have appeared in many ready-reference sources.

Roger Matuz writes and develops print and electronic resources on American history, literature, and popular culture. His recent books include *American Social Reform Movements: Primary Sources*

(2006), *U.S. Immigration and Migration: Biographies* (2004), *Reconstruction Era Reference Library: Biographies* (2004), and *The Handy Presidents Answer Book* (2004).

Nicole Mitchell is an independent researcher most recently employed as the assistant archivist at Georgia College and State University, where she received an M.A. in history. She has written a number of encyclopedia entries and book chapters and is also coauthor of *The Encyclopedia of Title IX and Sports.* She is a member of the Georgia Historical Society, the Society of Georgia Archivists, and the Southern Historical Association.

Jonathan Rees is an associate professor of history at Colorado State University–Pueblo. He is the author of *Managing the Mills: Labor Policy in the American Steel Industry during the Nonunion Era* (2004) and coeditor of *The Voice of the People: Primary Sources on the History of American Labor, Industrial Relations, and Working-Class Culture* (2004).

Origins and Development

Kevin Hillstrom

Farming has long been recognized as the cornerstone of America's social and economic well-being from its earliest era of colonialism to the close of the nineteenth century. In the nation's formative years, in fact, it is estimated that nine out of ten Americans made their livelihood through agriculture. This agrarian model of civilization was embraced by the first generations of Americans, and early American political leaders such as Thomas Jefferson expressed their satisfaction with this state of affairs in very self-congratulatory terms. "The small landholders are the most precious part of the state," wrote Jefferson, who extolled American farmers as the deserving beneficiaries of special dispensation from God. Writing in *Notes on the State of Virginia,* he declared that "those who labor in the earth are the chosen people of God, if ever he had a chosen people, whose breasts he has made his peculiar deposit for substantial and genuine virtue" (Jefferson 1794).

As the decades rolled by, agriculture maintained its place as the nation's most economically important industry. It not only provided the basic nutritional staples necessary to sustain the burgeoning American populace but also became the single leading force driving the settlement of the American interior. Farmers and ranchers spread to all corners of the North American continent during the nineteenth century, and their land-clearing and cultivation activities in turn spurred the creation of a vast support infrastructure. The growth of this industrial infrastructure, which featured new forms of transportation (steam-powered boats and railroads), thriving communities, and new industrial enterprises devoted to supporting agricultural activities, completed the metamorphosis of the United States from an unpeopled wilderness to a major economic power.

But even though the history of American agriculture is studded with triumphs and signal events—from the 1793 introduction of Eli Whitney's cotton gin to the emergence of the beef and meatpacking industry in the late nineteenth century—it also bears the stains of tears and blood. As the experiences of colonial settlers, Great Plains pioneers, and Dust Bowl refugees all attest, the American farmer's life was often a hard and even cruel one.

Colonial Farming

The first immigrants to the American colonies received free grants of land to farm. The exact terms of these dispersals, though, varied from one colony to another. In Virginia, for example, the governor gave each settler a 50-acre parcel as a headright, and an extra 50 acres were handed down for each additional person the settler brought to the colonies, including not only children and other family members but also servants, farmhands, and other employees. In some colonies, the allotments were even more generous. In the Carolinas, for instance, 150-acre parcels were the norm, and in Georgia, settlers who brought over at least ten indentured servants received 500-acre grants. In the northern colonies, allotments were much more modest, due to the smaller size of these colonies and their larger populations. Even in New England, however, land-grant incentives played a significant role in encouraging struggling English farmers to pull up stakes and try their luck in the New World.

These land-distribution schemes were fairly effective in giving a large number of settlers the space they needed to establish themselves. Their success was also partly attributable to a sensible orientation toward communal sharing and cooperation. Many colonial farming communities located their households close to one another so as to better defend themselves from possible Indian incursions, and town commons became ubiquitous. These commons were large grazing areas for livestock to which all farming families had access. Over time, they also became gathering spots for militia training, holiday celebrations, and other community events.

Of course, political connections and wealth enabled some early colonial settlers to establish large estates and plantations. Plantations became particularly abundant in the South, where massive tobacco-growing operations manned by slaves took root; some of these plantations were several thousand acres in size. But vast farming estates also appeared in Pennsylvania, Maryland, and New York (after the British pried that colony away from the Dutch).

Those wealthy landowners who utilized slaves and servants to tend their fields and livestock were early examples of the gentleman farmer, an individual who rarely was pressed or inclined to engage in the drudgery of planting, harvesting, or the multitude of other chores necessary to keep a farm running. But for most colonial farm families of the seventeenth and eighteenth centuries, farming was a grueling and dangerous way of life. Clearing land for planting necessitated the removal of formidable woodlands that had grown undisturbed for centuries, and the task of extracting massive stumps, boulders, and rocks from fields was taxing in the extreme. In addition, the threat of violence from Indian tribes that felt besieged by the steady influx of settlers became an ever-present fact of life in many parts of the colonies. And of course, farmers remained at the mercy of severe weather events, populations of crop-devouring insects, and other forces beyond their direct control.

Nonetheless, agrarian activity thrived in the colonies, in large part because the natural resources at the settlers' disposal were so rich and bountiful. And eighteenth-century farmers in the New World became adept at supplementing native crops such as corn (which was converted into a wide assortment of foodstuffs, from corn mush to corn bread) with fruits and vegetables brought over from Europe.

Not surprisingly, the abundance of natural wealth that surrounded colonial farm communities soon spawned an array of wasteful and shortsighted farming and land-use practices. Early American farmers turned their backs on the system that had prevailed in England, where the limited amount of land available for cultivation had forced people to husband their resources. Back in England, farmers had obeyed the dictates of the so-called three-field system, in which all of the cultivated land a farmer possessed was divided into three fields, one of which was left fallow each season in a rotating fashion. In the colonies, this prudent but financially limiting practice was tossed aside in short order. Rather than nurture their existing fields, most early American farmers simply worked them until the nutrients in the soil had been exhausted, then moved on to new tracts of land that they could clear and till. (In this regard, they behaved similarly to local Indian tribes, who often exploited the land in the same way.) Since the quality of much New England soil was marginal to begin with, it did not take long for many fields to be depleted and rendered useless for cropping.

By the early 1700s, these land-use dynamics had contributed to a growing shortage of farmland in many parts of New England, the most heavily populated region of colonial America. Farmers took a variety of steps to stave off this shortage over the ensuing decades. For example, some became more attentive to fertilizing the existing fields. They took greater care in gathering, storing, and distributing manure from livestock, and some coastal farmers began to fertilize their fields with spawning alewives that entered tidal rivers in the spring. More discerning crop selection was another option available to farmers. Many started to place a greater emphasis on planting forage for cattle and other livestock, devoting less space to corn and small grains. This shift in planting priorities became so pronounced that New Englanders were actually importing grain to make their bread by the early eighteenth century.

Ultimately, however, it was inevitable that American farmers would eventually cast their gaze deeper into the New World's untamed interior. They had depleted the nutrients in their old fields, and beyond that, their steadily growing access to plows and beasts of burden (horses, oxen, donkeys) made it possible for them to cultivate ever-larger tracts of land. Finally, an accelerating demand for revenue to pay for schools, libraries, churches, town halls, and other community resources had led numerous local governments to divest themselves of commons and other properties that had previously been utilized by the townspeople for agricultural purposes. Many of these parcels were snapped up by America's first land speculators.

The Nineteenth-Century American Farmer

American farming truly came into its own in the post-Revolution era. Policymakers at the local, state, and federal levels all recognized that agriculture was the lifeblood of the young United States, and they made every effort to help farmers increase their yields and expand their landholdings. Spurred on by national heroes and opinion shapers such as George Washington, Thomas Jefferson, and John Taylor (all of whom were Virginians who owed their wealth to their agricultural/plantation holdings), officials channeled more and more money into the construction of canals and bridges; the improvement of local roadways; the dredging of harbors and river mouths; and, from the 1830s forward, the laying of railroad tracks across the land. Until the eve of the Civil War, the main economic purpose of this sprawling transportation network was to carry agricultural products to the marketplace. Often, the marketplace in question was the nearest town, but as the century progressed and technological advances transformed the worlds of transportation and commerce, distant cities in the East and ports in Europe became the ultimate destinations for many of these products.

American officials and institutions facilitated the export of agricultural products through liberal trade policies and continued investment in transportation infrastructure. Most meat and grain produced in the United States was consumed domestically, but the overseas market for grain products became increasingly lucrative over time. By far the most important American export, however, was cotton. "King Cotton" exploded into prominence at the same time that industrialization was transforming England's textile industry, and the European appetite for cotton goods became insatiable by midcentury.

The U.S. government was an advocate for the farmer in other ways as well. During the 1840s, farsighted bureaucrats, led by Commissioner of Patents Henry L. Ellsworth, instituted policies to gather economically promising plants and seeds from around the world and to disseminate them—together with agricultural information and recommendations—to farmers across the country. These activities ultimately paved the way for the creation of the Department of Agriculture in 1862. Meanwhile, a succession of American presidents approved major expeditions into the mysterious western hinterlands to seek out and survey land, water, plants, and seeds that could be used to further invigorate the nation's growing agricultural might. These government-sponsored forays were supplemented by a variety of land acquisitions. Some of the acquisitions were marked by violence and bloodshed—as happened with the relentless and methodical seizure of Indian lands and with the Mexican-American War, which brought most of the modern American Southwest under Washington's control. Other additions to the emerging American empire

The Creation of the Department of Agriculture

During the mid-nineteenth century, the U.S. government was fully cognizant of the importance of farming and ranching to the national economy. To support those vital sectors, it made a concerted effort to obtain, import, and distribute improved varieties of seeds, plants, and livestock. A leading figure in this effort was Henry L. Ellsworth, who was appointed commissioner of patents within the Department of State in 1836. Over the next several years, Ellsworth energetically set about obtaining a wide variety of agricultural seeds and plants to be given to the nation's farmers, using Congress and local and state agricultural societies as primary conduits.

Henry Leavitt Ellsworth was instrumental in creating the U.S. Department of Agriculture. (Library of Congress)

Ellsworth was also instrumental in harnessing the federal government's resources in bolstering the nation's agrarian economy. During the 1840s, he pushed for the creation of a public depository for the storage of native and imported seeds and plants, and he was key in getting federal and state agencies to recognize the importance of tracking agricultural statistics and trends.

came about more peacefully, as with the 1803 Louisiana Purchase, which doubled the territory of the United States; the Adams-Onis Treaty of 1819, which brought Florida under the U.S. flag; and the 1848 creation of the Oregon Territory.

This steady expansion of U.S. borders gave the national government the resources it needed to pass a succession of major acts encouraging agricultural development. The first of these acts was the

In the 1850s, there was a growing awareness of the need for a separate federal agriculture agency that could oversee and direct U.S. agricultural policies. On May 15, 1862, President Abraham Lincoln signed the bill authorizing the creation of the Bureau of Agriculture, precursor to today's U.S. Department of Agriculture. This agency, which Lincoln dubbed the people's department, was charged with acquiring and disseminating agricultural information to farmers and ranchers across the country.

The Bureau of Agriculture initially did not have cabinet-level status, but its importance was unquestioned. In addition to its role as a distributor of agrarian information and resources, it served as a major proponent of the farming life and regularly exhorted farm families to add to the nation's bounty. As Isaac Newton, the first commissioner of agriculture, declared in 1863, "It should be the aim of every young farmer to do not only as well as his father but to do his best: to make two blades of grass grow where but one grew before" (quoted in Ebeling 1979).

During the 1870s and 1880s, the Bureau of Agriculture's responsibilities continued to grow. It became the primary regulator of both the importation of livestock and the manufacture of oleomargarine during that time. In February 1889, President Grover Cleveland signed a bill that finally elevated the department to cabinet-level status—a move that had long been lobbied for by various interest groups.

Sources

Ebeling, Walter. 1979. *The Fruited Plain: The Story of American Agriculture.* Berkeley: University of California Press.

Jefferson, Thomas. *Notes on the State of Virginia.* Philadelphia: Printed for Mathew Carey, November 12, 1794.

Schlebecker, John T. 1975. *Whereby We Thrive: A History of American Farming, 1607–1972.* Ames: Iowa State University Press.

Basic Land Ordinance in 1785, which was instrumental in guiding settlement of the Great Lakes region. In subsequent years, this act was revised in a number of ways to remove financial and legal obstacles for would-be settlers. The Land Act of 1800, also known as the Harrison Frontier Land Act, provided for the sale of public land at $2 per acre for 320-acre tracts. This price proved too steep for most settlers, even after the minimum purchase was reduced to 160 acres in

1804, so Congress acted again to grease the wheels of western expansion. By 1820, settlers could acquire farms as small as 80 acres for a minimum price of $1.25 per acre, and in 1832, the minimum purchase size was cut to 40 acres. In 1841, under the righteous urging of Missouri senator Thomas Hart Benton, Congress passed the Preemption Act, which gave squatters the first right to buy the land on which they had settled as soon as the federal government got around to surveying it. Under the terms of this law, the price was only $1.25 per acre for a maximum purchase of 160 acres. In 1854, the Graduation Act further lowered prices on unsold land.

Homestead Act of 1862

The single most important piece of legislation that turned America's western hinterlands into productive fields and pastures, however, was the Homestead Act of 1862. The measure was specifically created to settle the territory that was opened as a result of the passage of the 1854 Kansas-Nebraska Act. According to the terms of the Homestead Act, any American citizen or immigrant alien who was twenty-one years old or the head of a family could, by paying a $10 claim fee, take possession of 160 acres of unsettled public land. After five years of residence and "improvement" of the parcel, he or she would then receive final title at no additional cost (the act also gave settlers the option of paying $1.25 an acre to receive title after just six months of residency).

The Homestead Act was created for the express purpose of assisting the United States in fulfilling its self-described Manifest Destiny, and many of its proponents believed that it would materially better the lives of millions of Americans. And indeed, many settlers were able to take advantage of the Homestead Act to successfully establish themselves in the West. But the lenient terms of the act also lured many unprepared individuals and families to years of terrible hardship. One analysis of mid-nineteenth-century settlement patterns in the Midwest concluded that the cost of establishing an 80-acre farm in that region in 1860 was $1,700—three times what the average wage earner brought in on an annual basis at the time (Atack and Bateman 1993). Moreover, securing credit in the thinly populated and semi-lawless western regions was difficult if not impossible for many would-be farmers:

John Gast's 1873 painting *American Progress,* which depicts an allegorical female figure of America leading settlers and railroads into the untamed West. (Library of Congress)

The cost of transportation to the free lands in the West, of buying equipment and animals, of survival until the first crops were available was an impossible sum for the impoverished eastern farmer or urban laborer. There were no provisions for bringing poor families to the farms or for offering them credit or guidance. By the time the act took effect, a high percentage of the remaining land was semiarid. Speculation in western lands continued, since cash sale was not eliminated until 1891, and much of the richest land left in the public domain continued to be bought directly from the government by timber dealers, cattle grazers, mining corporations, and land speculators. (Horwitz 1980)

The federal government's love affair with railroads was another factor that denied prime western acreage to settlers. Congress gave huge tracts of free land to the railroads to encourage further development of this revolutionary industry, and the railroads were loathe to relinquish these lands once they had them in their possession. As a result, it has been estimated that settlers received only about 1 in 6 of the 80 million acres given away by the government between 1860 and 1900.

A New Age of Technology and Mechanization

The nineteenth century was an era of great technological change and innovation in the world of American agriculture. These changes moved the industry from an era in which primitive and inefficient hand-powered tools were the sole means of tilling, planting, and harvesting crops to an exciting and vastly more productive era of cotton gins and steam-powered threshers.

One of the first instruments of agriculture that received appreciable improvements in the nineteenth century was the plow. At the beginning of the century, wooden moldboard plows with a wrought-iron or cast-iron share were the norm. But these walking plows were not ideally suited to attack the dense prairie grasses and heavy soil of the Midwest. Over time, though, blacksmiths based in the rapidly developing Midwest conjured up massive beamed plows capable of breaking up the sod. An Illinois blacksmith named John Deere was a pioneer in this regard. In 1837, he unveiled an effective plow with a highly polished wrought-iron moldboard and a steel share. This plow easily cut through the tough prairie sod, and the turned-up soil did not adhere to the blade of this plow as it did to earlier models. Deere's innovation—dubbed the singing plow because it produced a high-pitched whine as it turned a furrow—became an indispensable aid for untold numbers of American farmers during the 1840s and 1850s.

Other simple but meaningful upgrades to the farmer's arsenal were also introduced in that period. In the realm of planting, brothers Moses and Samuel Pennock of Pennsylvania unveiled a grain drill that made it unnecessary for farmers to sow crops by hand or with broadcast seeders. The grain drill enabled farmers to seed their grain crops at the rate of about 15 acres a day, a vast improvement over the methods in earlier years. Then, in 1857, an Ohio inventor named Martin Robbins developed a mechanical planter that automatically dropped seeds in evenly spaced rows.

American inventors also introduced mechanical tools that dramatically increased the efficiency of harvesting operations, especially for

A horse-drawn combine works a California grain field. (Library of Congress)

wheat and other small grains. For generations, farmers had toiled with sickles or cradle scythes to harvest their grains. An individual could only harvest 2 or 3 acres a day with a cradle scythe—and even less with a sickle. In 1831, however, a Virginian named Cyrus Hall McCormick built a horse-drawn reaper featuring a blade that cut stalks so that they fell on a platform. A waiting worker then raked the grain so that other workers could bind it into sheaves. By the Civil War era, a self-raking feature had been incorporated into these reapers, enabling farmers to cut up to 15 acres a day, and in later years, the reapers were outfitted with automatic binding features (using wire and later twine).

Threshing machines also became steadily more efficient. First used in the 1830s, these machines had, within the space of two decades, been honed to the point that they could thresh 500 bushels of wheat in a single day. In the 1840s, meanwhile, the combine, an implement invented by Hiram Moore and J. Haskall that merged the functions of the reaper and threshing machine in a single implement, was unveiled. The combine required sixteen horses for draft, which made it too expensive for most planters in the East. But farther west, where large operations were more numerous, the combine became a virtual necessity for farmers hoping to remain competitive. By the 1880s, massive combines powered by as many as thirty or even forty horses were cutting and threshing 30 acres a day in the Red River valley area of North Dakota and Minnesota and other wheat fields farther west. These operations, precursors to today's industrialized farms, were known as bonanza farms in recognition of the spectacular volumes of wheat they harvested and the armies of laborers they utilized.

Yet another innovation was the Marsh harvester, a creation of Charles W. and William W. Marsh of DeKalb, Illinois, that came into production in 1861. By the 1880s, this machine had revolutionized sheafing and binding processes on countless farms across the continent. And of course, Eli Whitney's cotton gin had a transformative impact not only on southern industry but also on the region's cultural and social development.

Despite all of these innovations, however, American farming enterprises remained heavily dependent on draft animals right up to the end of the nineteenth century. Horses, oxen, and mules were among the most valuable assets of any farmer, and their feeding and care was a high priority for any sensible planter. Even the arrival of the tractor did not bring an immediate end to the widespread use of beasts of burden. Draft horses and mules remained commonplace on American farms into the late 1920s, when advances in mechanization finally led to their retirement (though some poor farmers continued to rely on draft animals for some time to come).

Symbol of America

As the single most vital—and visible—cog in the roaring American economic machine, farmers would inevitably come to be regarded as the cornerstone of the nation's economic well-being. Indeed, Americans—most of whom were still making their living off the land, despite the rapid growth of some eastern cities—would anoint farmers the leading embodiment of morality and integrity in the United States: "Living in natural surroundings and coaxing forth nature's bounty made rural people purer, more moral, and more respectful of God than their urban counterparts. Rural living also contributed to the simplicity of farmers, in the most positive sense of the word. Rural people, agrarians argued, had simple tastes, abhorred artificiality, luxury, and ostentation, and were honest and straightforward" (Danbom 1995).

By the mid-nineteenth century, however, this Jeffersonian image of the farmer as the symbolic heart of the American experiment, though true in many respects, was masking some significant erosion in the agrarian community's much-touted mantra of independence. With each passing year, farmers tilling fields and milking cows in remote parts of the South, the Great Lakes region, and the Great Plains became more dependent for their livelihoods on communities that lay hundreds of miles distant. By midcentury, the relationship between cities and agriculture had become more symbiotic, as historian David Danbom explained, than most farmers appreciated:

> Cities lived on the countryside, and the countryside thrived because of the cities. But as cities grew they achieved a degree of cultural dominance that Jeffersonians abhorred. Ironically, a dynamic agriculture facilitated the development of an urban culture that increasingly defined America and an industrial sector that would eventually dwarf it. . . . Jeffersonian agrarians continued to praise the independence of people who were, in fact, increasingly dependent on others to lend them money, carry and consume what they produced, and manufacture for them. (Danbom 1995)

This overarching trend manifested itself in different ways across the country, though. American agriculture was not a monolithic enterprise; farming and ranching developed in unique ways in every distinct geographic region, from New England to the Deep South to the Great Plains to sunny California, and their relationships to the marketplace developed in unique ways as well.

Farming in the Southland

Southern agricultural interests planted a wide variety of crops in the nineteenth century, and some of them, such as tobacco and rice, were of significant economic importance. But even tobacco sales paled next to those of cotton, a product that southern plantation owners were able to parlay into great wealth—and also a product that bound the region even more deeply to the "peculiar institution" of slavery. Had labor-intensive cotton production not become so integral to the South's overall economic vitality, say some historians, the region might even have been able to cast off slavery of its own volition, rather than have emancipation dictated to it as a result of the Civil War.

The American surge in cotton production can be traced back to Eli Whitney's 1793 invention of the cotton gin. Prior to that innovation, separating cotton fibers used to make clothing and other textiles from the plant's seeds was a tedious and time-consuming task. This was especially true of the short-staple cotton that was grown inland; this strain grew more quickly than others, but the shortness of the fibers and the large number of seeds buried in them made harvesting the cotton an exceedingly inefficient process. (The Sea Island cotton grown along the Atlantic coast and on various barrier islands was somewhat easier to process, but this strain did not prosper in the interior.)

Whitney's invention changed all that. His hand-powered machine, which used revolving drums and metal teeth to pull cotton fibers away from seeds, exponentially increased the amount of cotton that a single worker could process in a day. And as larger gins powered by draft animals, steam, and water were developed, plantation operations became even more efficient. In 1790, 3,000 bales of cotton were produced in the entire United States. (Before the Civil War, bales weighed anywhere from 400 to 500 pounds; today, they are universally 500 pounds.) By 1820, the nation was producing 732,000 bales. And forty years later, even as the nation trembled on the precipice of civil war, an astounding 3.841 million bales of cotton were generated in the South. Most of this cotton went overseas. At the beginning of the nineteenth century, cotton accounted for less than 15 percent of the total value of American exports. By 1860, though, it made up more than 60 percent of all American exports in terms of value. By contrast, wheat accounted for only 6 percent of American exports by value in 1860, largely because domestic demand for the product was surging, driven by the great waves of immigrants arriving on American shores (Danbom 1995).

After the Civil War, which destroyed the old slave labor plantation system in the South, farmers and planters in the region assumed one of four roles. The most enviable of the roles was that of the farm owner. Small farm owners were abundant. Plantation owners were in much smaller supply, but they were of great importance because, despite the fact that they had suffered serious financial setbacks during and after the war—most notably the loss of dozens or even hundreds of slaves—they still controlled large tracts of agricultural land.

With the deplorable institution of slavery finally extinguished, these large landowners arranged for three different types of farm tenancy on their property. Under these arrangements, the so-called cash tenant was the best off, for he owned his own farming tools, horses and mules, and other farming essentials. The cash tenant also had the necessary financial resources to buy seed and fertilizer himself rather than borrow funds from the landowner, and he was financially secure enough to provide for his family during the lean months before the harvest. Many cash tenants, unencumbered by massive debt, were able to eventually buy their own farms.

The share tenant operated at a greater financial disadvantage than his cash tenant brethren. This type of tenant typically had some modest resources that he could bring to the table, such as a few draft animals and a handful of farming tools. But he relied on the landowner to provide him with seed and fertilizer, and this business arrangement usually featured elements that were heavily stacked in favor of the landowner. For example, landowners typically received a significant percentage of the share tenant's harvested crop in exchange for the extension of credit. These diversions into the landlord's pocket made it very difficult for the share tenant to scrape together enough savings to acquire his own farm.

The third type of farm tenancy was sharecropping, and this was by far the most dismal and difficult of the forms. Most sharecroppers were blacks, former slaves who, because of terrible disadvantages in their economic circumstances and education levels, had no other choice but to enter into this grim life. Since poverty-stricken sharecropping families had nothing to barter but their labor, they had no negotiating power whatsoever. Plantation owners supplied these families with rudimentary shelter, field acreage, draft animals, seed, fertilizer, and other provisions; in exchange, they received half of the revenue from the cotton or tobacco raised by the sharecroppers when harvesttime arrived. Many unscrupulous plantation owners took an even greater cut than that, using bookkeeping sleight of hand to cheat already destitute families. All in all, the sharecropping system was often little more than a shadowy doppelgänger of the slave system that had supposedly been crushed back in 1865 with the Union victory.

Farming in the North

Farming operations in the Northeast became increasingly specialized over the course of the nineteenth century.

> Whereas the typical subsistence farmer of 1800 grew food for his family with a small surplus for sale or barter, the farmer of the mid-nineteenth century found that he could sell fresh vegetables, fruits, milk, butter, cheese and other perishables to city people, and with the money he earned he could buy the manufactured products for which he had developed a taste: cloth, tools, shoes, tableware, furniture, candles, soap—all formerly made at home, observed one scholar. The farmer, who had previously raised crops on the basis of family needs, became a businessman who grew crops for sale, making decisions about fruit and vegetable varieties and livestock on the basis of market demand. (Horwitz 1980)

Farther to the west, meanwhile, settlers in the Great Lakes region received a major boost with the opening of the Erie Canal in 1825. This engineering marvel gave farmers in Michigan, Illinois, Ohio, and Wisconsin the inexpensive transportation artery they needed to send their products to the big cities of the East—and it further convinced small farmers in New England that their future prosperity depended on the development of the high-demand but perishable agricultural commodities such as milk, butter, cheese, and fruits that were in great demand in New York City, Boston, Philadelphia, and other metropolises.

> Farmers living in northern Illinois or southern Michigan in 1840 probably did not think much about being part of New York's hinterland, because the impact of that great metropolis was not readily apparent in their day-to-day lives. But farmers living in the East could hardly avoid the conclusion that cities were shaping their lives. Eastern farmers who were flexible and innovative enough to do so shifted their production to fill the needs of nearby urbanites. Truck farming—the

production of fresh fruits and vegetables for market—and dairy farming became dominant in areas around growing cities. (Danbom 1995)

Indeed, by the 1810s, New York butter wagons were venturing as far as Charleston, South Carolina, to sell their wares, and by midcentury, New York State was universally recognized as the national leader in the production of dairy products. It held this distinction until the early 1900s, when it was finally supplanted by Wisconsin.

Agriculture and the Opening of the West

In the decades immediately after the American Revolution, incursions of settlers into the West were dictated by the courses of waterways. Since rivers were the best means to transport agricultural goods to markets, agricultural development was initially confined, in large part, to the valleys of the Ohio and Mississippi rivers and their assorted tributaries. Water transport became even more integral to agricultural operations in the 1810s and 1820s, when extensive canals connecting various bodies of water were built. Steam-powered vessels remained the primary means of sending goods to market until midcentury, when railroads eclipsed steam shipping as the backbone of America's transport infrastructure. Indeed, historians regard the railroad companies as the great drivers of the colonization of the Great Plains.

> All of them were eager to transport settlers to the province, to get it colonized as a matter of developing traffic. The land-grant railroads had their own areas to sell. But they also aggressively advertised the free homestead lands of the federal government. . . . Railroad companies, especially those possessing land grants, were colonizers of the Great Plains on a big scale. They carried forward on a vast scale the work that had been done on a lesser scale by colonizing companies on the seaboard in the colonial period. (Merk 1978)

The first agricultural settlements of the Ohio River valley and the upper Mississippi River valley were composed mostly of immigrants from the Northeast, whereas those of the lower Mississippi and its major tributaries were peopled with Virginians, Georgians, and Carolinians. The first generations of these pioneer farmers were largely self-sufficient due to their distance from established population centers, and they rooted themselves in the land only after conquering the same array of obstacles—hostile Indians alarmed by the white invasion of their traditional territories, thick forests, and rock-strewn fields—that had confronted their colonial ancestors back east.

These subsistence-oriented agricultural enterprises became the backbone of the expanding American empire. From 1791 to 1821, eleven new states were admitted to the Union, and all of them were almost totally reliant on agriculture for their economic well-being at the time of admission. As farming families and other pioneers poured into the West, the populations of several states experienced record-setting booms. The population of Kentucky, for example, tripled between 1790 and 1800, then nearly doubled again by 1810. Tennessee's population, meanwhile, rose from 36,000 people in 1790 to more than 260,000 a mere twenty years later. Ohio experienced an even greater surge in population, rising from 45,000 in 1800 to more than 580,000 by 1820 (Danbom 1995; Ebeling 1979).

The brisk pace of westward expansion continued unabated for the entire century, slowing briefly during the Civil War era and then gaining even more momentum after that bloody conflict concluded. Indeed, events such as the Oklahoma land rush and the enactment of the 1862 Homestead Act, combined with the intoxicating promise of a new beginning, enticed farmers to the most remote and semiarid corners of the nation. Between 1881 and 1885 alone, for example, an estimated 67,000 settlers established homesteads in the Dakota Territory. All told, approximately 430 million acres of land were settled in the United States during the last three decades of the nineteenth century.

In the 1870s and 1880s, the varying agricultural character of the individual western states and regions became clear. California, blessed with a moderate climate, extensive irrigation systems, and a cheap and abundant Chinese immigrant workforce, rose to prominence as a major supplier of wheat, citrus crops, and cattle during that time. The Red River valley region, meanwhile, staked a clear claim to being the epicenter of American wheat production, and Kansas and Nebraska became major corn-growing states. Farmers in Illinois and especially Wisconsin acknowledged the competitive advantages enjoyed by the highly mechanized bonanza crop-growing farms to the west, and so they diverted their capital resources to the production of various dairy products, such as milk, cheese, and butter. And midsized western cities such as Omaha and Kansas City joined Chicago and Cincinnati as major meatpacking centers.

The Emergence of the American Meatpacking Industry

In the colonial era, most cattle, hogs, and sheep were slaughtered and butchered for immediate consumption on the farm, though some cuts were traded for other staples. But by the early nineteenth century, the growing size of eastern cities prompted more and more farmers to drive cattle and hogs to the slaughterhouses that served these large populations. The first significant centers of meat slaughtering and processing were along the Atlantic coast and in Philadelphia, the largest city in the country during the Revolutionary era.

Meatpacking operations moved westward with the farming pioneers, though, and by the 1840s and 1850s, the nation's leading meatpacking centers were Cincinnati and Chicago. Cincinnati, which had the advantage of being perched on the shores of the commercially vital Ohio River, specialized in the slaughtering and butchering of hogs, whereas Chicago, which was fast emerging as the Midwest's leading railroad hub and the foremost gateway for trade with western states, was a major processor of beef.

Most of the slaughterhouses and packinghouses in these and other cities were established outside residential areas. In fact, slaughterhouse operations were so unsightly and smelly that they were usually based on the far outskirts of town, often along rivers that became terribly polluted by dumped waste. Packing plants, meanwhile, were normally located near transportation centers such as railroad yards and harbors.

Like all other sectors of nineteenth-century agricultural enterprise, technological advances profoundly affected the meatpacking industry. Perhaps the foremost of these innovations was refrigeration—and specifically, the introduction of the refrigerated railroad car in 1867. Within a few years, long-distance rail shipments of refrigerated dressed beef were commonplace, pioneered by major meatpacking companies such as Swift, Hammond, Armour, and Nelson Morris, which could shoulder the high capital costs associated with industrial slaughterhouses and fleets of refrigerator railcars.

The Morrill Act of 1862

In the 1850s, a wide variety of voices—congressmen, agricultural societies, farming periodicals, and others—called for the federal government to take a more active role as an advocate of vocational training for farmers and mechanics. This campaign, which stemmed from a universal recognition of the importance of agriculture and industrial development to America's socioeconomic growth, ultimately resulted in the 1862 Morrill Land-Grant Act.

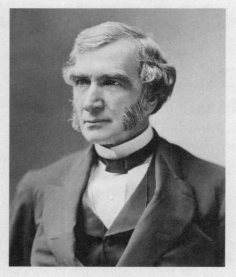

Vermont Senator Justin S. Morrill championed the Morrill Land-Grant Act of 1862, which paved the way for the creation of numerous land-grant colleges across the United States. (Library of Congress)

The leading champion of this effort—and the namesake of the legislation that paved the way for the establishment of a plethora of agricultural and technical colleges across the country—was Republican senator Justin S. Morrill of Vermont. In 1856, Morrill responded to state petitions for federal land that could be used for educational purposes by introducing a congressional resolution to explore the possibility of establishing agricultural schools similar in many respects to the military schools at Annapolis and West Point. When this resolution failed to get any traction in Washington, Morrill followed up with another bill that expressly called for public lands to be donated to the states so that the latter could establish vocational colleges.

Morrill's proposal was opposed by a variety of constituencies, worried that it would unduly reward eastern states and hinder settlement in the West. Nonetheless, it managed to pass both houses of Congress, only to be struck down by a stroke of President James Buchanan's veto pen. Buchanan argued that Morrill's bill was unconstitutional and that such a "giveaway" of federal land would deprive the federal government of a potential revenue source.

Undaunted, Morrill introduced yet another land-grant bill in December 1861. Supporters coaxed the bill through both houses of Congress, their efforts given further urgency by the fear that because of the Homestead Act of 1862, large blocks of unclaimed federal land in the West would soon be unavailable. President Abraham Lincoln signed the bill into law on July 2, 1862.

Under the terms of the act, the federal government was authorized to give a state 30,000 acres of public land for each U.S. senator and member of Congress representing it in Washington. This land was distributed for the express purpose of establishing agricultural colleges. Those states without public lands were issued scrip for the equivalent amount of land; they could sell these "scrip-acres" to help support these colleges. All told, eleven states received nearly 1.8 million acres of land, and public land states later admitted into the Union received similar grants. Twenty-seven other states, meanwhile, received almost 8 million scrip-acres, which enabled well-established, heavily populated states in the East to claim large lots of land in the Great Lakes region and the prairie states.

On March 2, 1887, Congress passed the Hatch Act, which authorized the creation of agricultural experimental stations in every state, and in August 1890, Congress approved a second Morrill Act. This legislation mandated Congress to make regular appropriations to support land-grant colleges with curricula oriented toward agricultural and mechanical (A&M) fields. It also provided funds to black colleges for agricultural education and permitted the states to establish separate land-grant colleges for African Americans. Today, numerous major universities across the country, including Michigan State University, the University of Illinois, Texas A&M, and the University of California, can trace their history back to Morrill's original 1862 legislation. It is for this reason that Justin Morrill is still known today as the father of America's agricultural colleges.

Source

Nevins, Allan. 1962. *The Origins of the Land-Grant Colleges and State Universities: A Brief Account of the Morrill Act of 1862 and Its Results.* Washington, DC: Civil War Centennial Commission.

The major meatpackers embraced the shipment of dressed beef rather than live animals because it was much less expensive and because it enabled them to squeeze greater profits out of animal by-products. Local butchers and slaughterhouses, though, immediately recognized that the growing trade in dressed beef posed a significant danger to their economic future. They reacted with a cacophony of warnings about the alleged health risks of eating refrigerated beef and calls for federal intervention. Their actions temporarily slowed the trend toward increased consumption of western beef. Eventually, however, the effectiveness of this rhetoric faded, and by the end of the nineteenth century, dressed beef from the western rangelands was generally accepted as a perfectly acceptable alternative to locally raised and butchered beef. By the early 1900s, the major Chicago-based meatpackers had driven many smaller regional packers out of business; established dominating presences in western meatpacking cities such as Omaha, Kansas City, and Fort Worth; and taken control of about 80 percent of the national meatpacking trade.

In the early twentieth century, the industry—by now one of the most economically important in the entire country—became more sophisticated in some respects. For example, the so-called beef trust (the nation's leading meatpackers, who often engaged in cooperative, monopolistic practices) worked with ranchers to introduce and nurture improved breeds of cattle that would yield a better quality of beef. During that period, English white-faced Hereford and Scottish Black Angus breeds became common on American ranches.

But even as the beef trust recorded tremendous profits, the industry became soiled with severe public relations problems. In 1905, author Upton Sinclair published *The Jungle,* a work of fiction that nonetheless provided American readers with an all-too-realistic portrait of the appalling working conditions in Chicago slaughterhouses. Sinclair's tale of carnage, disease, and dehumanizing toil prompted widespread public revulsion and calls for reform. The U.S. Congress responded with the comprehensive Meat Inspection Act and the Pure Food and Drug Act.

Cattle Ranching in the West

The economically powerful meatpacking industry owed its affluence to the explosion of cattle-ranching activity that took place in the

American West in the second half of the nineteenth century. The commercial raising of cattle in America actually dated back to the early 1700s, when Spanish colonists maintained cattle herds along the Gulf of Mexico and the shores of the southern Mississippi River and assorted tributaries. This economic activity continued into the early nineteenth century.

But the American beef industry did not become a major commercial enterprise until the mid-nineteenth century, when western cattlemen began using the Iron Horse to make inroads into lucrative eastern markets. The first type of cattle to be shipped in this way in any significant number was the Texas longhorn. Ranchers and meatpackers alike often complained that longhorns carried a relatively small amount of beef on them, considering their overall stature. But the longhorns were a hardy breed, able to sustain themselves on prairie grasses without additional feeding expenditures and resistant to Texas fever, a deadly tick-borne virus common during that era.

The exporting of cattle from the Texas plains began in the 1840s and 1850s, when some intrepid cattlemen drove herds to Memphis and New Orleans. But it did not become a major commercial enterprise until the post–Civil War era.

> The golden age of the range cattle industry was the period from 1869—the date of the completion of the Union Pacific—to the middle of the 1880s. These dozen or fifteen years were a period of prosperity. The prosperity varied from year to year, depending on the price of beef in the eastern markets, the weather on the Plains, and other factors. In the early 1880s the profits of cattlemen were likely to be 20 to 30 percent on the capital investment. (Merk 1978)

The proliferating railroads and cattle trails gradually established during those years connected the ranches to the vast cornfields of the upper Midwest. The corn crops became the raw material for the development of the "feeder market"—beef fattened on corn a few months before they were sent to slaughter. Other cattle, meanwhile, were targeted for fattening on the nutritious tall grass of the northern plains. This type of cattle came to be known as stockers, and they proved nearly as profitable to the cattleman as the feeders (Merk 1978). For example, cattlemen such as J. W. Iliff, who sold beef to mining and timber towns in Colorado and Wyoming, made tremendous fortunes selling grass-fed cattle.

It was in Texas, though, that the beef industry first became a major force. Cattlemen there were blessed with state land policies that gave them significant competitive advantages over similar outfits in other states. Texas had never ceded its public lands to the federal government; instead, its lawmakers—many of them with ranching interests of their own—had thrown open these lands for grazing at virtually no expense for state ranching outfits. This largesse was further enhanced by the availability of vast tracts of cheap land that had long been owned by Mexican families.

This fertile business environment enabled some of the giants of the nineteenth-century western beef trade to emerge—men such as Richard King, whose million-acre ranch had as many as 100,000 head roaming across its length at one time; Jesse Chisholm, who established the famous Chisholm Cattle Trail, extending from Texas all the way to Abilene, Kansas; and the formidable duo of Charles Goodnight and Oliver Loving. All of these ranch operations and countless smaller ones were reliant, to one degree or another, on the open range that prevailed on federal public lands. Under the open-range system, ranchers could graze their herds on federal lands without paying even nominal grazing fees. Instead, a hierarchical program was maintained in which range rights were allocated on a first come, first served basis. Some of the larger outfits appropriated several hundred thousand acres for their herds.

The lucrative financial stakes involved in raising cattle, which were valuable not only for the beef they carried but also for their hides, inevitably attracted the attention of investors. "By the 1880s, western cattle had become creatures of the world capitalist market," wrote one scholar. "The greed of investors became as essential to the propagation of cattle as grass on the western plains. Western banks, particularly those in Denver and Kansas City, had financed much of the early cattle industry at rates of interest ranging from 10 percent to 25 percent, but now eastern and European investors, who commanded much more abundant and cheaper capital, took over the industry" (White 1994).

Closing of the Range

Many western ranchers specialized in the so-called long drive, in which they herded their cattle by trail and railroad car to the slaughterhouses of Chicago and Kansas City. The first of these long drives was carried out in the years immediately after the end of the Civil War, and by 1870, nearly half a million head of cattle were being exported from Texas on an annual basis via this route to the slaughterhouses of America's beef trust. By the late 1870s, though, the first cracks in this method appeared. Overgrazing of the grasslands along the cattle trails became a growing problem, as did proliferating homesteading claims along the way. Indeed, pioneer farmers sensibly gravitated toward the most fertile and water-accessible areas of the range, which forced increasingly frustrated cattlemen to turn to inferior, semiarid rangelands. Moreover, northern cattlemen, with their steadily growing and robust herds, did not want the competition from down south.

This combination of factors put more and more pressure on lawmakers on the central plains to curb the disruptive drives. By the early 1880s, a number of Great Plains states had passed quarantine laws forbidding Texas cattle from being driven or shipped across their borders. These measures were driven in part by genuine concerns that southern cattle could carry herd-destroying Texas fever, but they also were rooted in the ruthless desire of northern interests to knock their Texas competitors down. These factors, coupled with a succession of harsh winters, had taken a terrible toll on the long drive specifically and the open-range cattle industry in general by the late 1880s (Merk 1978). The 1886–1887 winter was particularly brutal in this regard. Snow built up so high on ranches and public lands on the northern plains that the region lost fully half of its cattle to starvation and exposure, according to some estimates.

As the acreage of rangelands available for cattle began to dwindle, ranching interests engaged in increasingly frantic efforts to protect themselves. Many ranching outfits built fences around "their" range rights on public lands, and others became sophisticated purchasers of water rights and adjacent land. That they obtained title to these territories, whether by legitimate or underhanded means, showed that the ranchers understood that in the semiarid West, water was key to the survival of any agricultural enterprise. Ranchers utilized all sorts of strategies to augment their holdings in this regard. Some recruited cowboys in their employ to file false homestead or preemption paperwork for acreage, which the ranching company would then use. Others made cynical but effective use of federal land-distribution mechanisms, such as the Timber Culture Act of 1873 and the Desert

Land Act of 1877: cattlemen routinely purchased land in the name of their ranch hands and converted it to rangeland for their herds, paying only minimal heed to the land improvement stipulations contained in the 1873 and 1877 acts (Skaggs 1986).

Northern cattlemen reaped increasing profits during this period. Buoyed by their growing understanding of animal husbandry (they became adept at providing winter feed and shelter to bolster the animals for calving season, for example), by the superior meat carried by their breeds, and by their relative proximity to major railroads and fast-growing population centers, these cattlemen became important economic forces in their communities. In the meantime, cattlemen in Texas and other parts of the West abandoned longhorns in favor of Herefords and other breeds that carried higher concentrations of beef. All of these ranching interests found a ready market for their refrigerated beef in the population centers of the East. Indeed, beef became the dietary centerpiece of the middle and upper classes, which in turn encouraged further investment in the industry. As a result, the number of cattle maintained by the industry jumped from approximately 24 million head in 1870 to about 68 million head by the turn of the twentieth century.

But cattle ranching remained a hard and unforgiving business. The growth of the railroad and the advent of refrigeration enabled cattlemen to stay afloat and in some cases to achieve significant levels of prosperity. But competing claims on quality rangeland sparked anger and, in some cases, violence. This was especially true in the late nineteenth century, when sheep-raising outfits proliferated in the West.

Some westerners raised both sheep and cattle on their holdings, but they were a minority. In most regions, cattlemen and sheepmen were clear competitors for the finite natural resources—water and land—necessary to nurture their herds. This tension was further exacerbated by the fact that most ranch owners and cowboys were of Anglo-American descent, whereas many sheep owners and sheep workers were Mexican Americans, Scotsmen, or individuals of other ethnic descent. But despite their inferior social status and their limited access to the halls of political power—which big ranchers had long enjoyed—the sheepmen made steady inroads across the West. In New Mexico alone, the number of sheep rose to an estimated 5 million by the late 1880s, and by the beginning of the twentieth century, sheep outnumbered cattle eight to one on the Columbia plateau (Skaggs 1986; White 1994).

The sheep industry constituted a second major consumer and de-spoiler of land and water resources, and not surprisingly, it proved to be a heavy blow to the western environment.

> When sheep battled cattle for the land, the fight was between two in-dustrial animals—animals whose very bodies, whose genetic makeup, humans had altered through selective breeding to fit their needs and whose every part humans processed into a product. Reshaped, these animals, in turn, reshaped the land. The results of their relentless over-grazing differed from place to place, but everywhere they opened up the land to invasion by other exotic species, everywhere they changed the composition of plant communities, and virtually everywhere they brought increased erosion. (White 1994)

Dark Days for Western Farmers

America entered the last two decades of the nineteenth century in a state of barely suppressed excitement about its agricultural prospects. After all, midcentury expansion into the Great Lakes region and the Ohio and Mississippi valleys had paid enormous dividends, both for millions of pioneer families and for the maturing nation's socioeco-nomic growth. Pioneers lured to the Great Plains during the 1860s, 1870s, and early 1880s by confident promises from railroad agents and government officials that "rain would follow the plow" could not be blamed for assuming that their ambition and hard work would translate into rewarding livelihoods for themselves.

Certainly, the early 1880s got off to an auspicious start, as several consecutive years of above-average rainfall assuaged lingering con-cerns that the western plains would prove too arid for successful farming. This cycle, combined with "dry-farming" methods, in which half of a farmer's land was left fallow each year to accumulate moisture and nutrients, burnished the confidence of many home-steading families that they could build lives for themselves under the big sky of the plains.

As more and more land was converted to agricultural use and as new railroad arteries proliferated across the American landscape, the United States experienced a massive increase in its levels of crop pro-duction. From 1870 to 1900, the total number of farms rooted in the

American landscape jumped from 2.7 million to 5.7 million, and the amount of farm acreage underwent a parallel increase, expanding from a shade over 400 million acres to more than 840 million acres. This expansion in land under cultivation and the arrival of mechanization drove big increases in crop yields. Wheat production jumped from 250 million to 600 million bushels during the last three decades of the nineteenth century, and corn production rose from 1.1 million to 2.7 million bushels. Cotton production more than doubled during that time as well, rising to 10.1 million bales annually by the turn of the twentieth century.

But this explosion in yield volume occurred at the same time that other nations were experiencing similar upward trends in the production of many of the same crops. Consequently, there was a glut in many staple crops on the world market, which in turn drove farm prices down. This negative development was further exacerbated by recurring quarantines against American meat—pork in particular—during the 1880s.

Eastern farmers were rocked but, for the most part, not undone by this turbulent environment. Many farmers in New England and other regions farther south along the Atlantic seaboard who were blessed with good soil simply got out of the grain-growing business and diverted their resources to fruit growing, dairying, and other types of "high farming." It should be noted, though, that their brethren without the soil resources and capital necessary to make this switch to dairy farming or fruit orchards were often forced to abandon their farms altogether. The cotton-dependent South suffered as well. Overproduction of cotton both in the United States and around the world produced a terrible sag in cotton prices during the 1880s and 1890s. As usual, large plantation owners were better positioned to absorb these financial blows than the small landholders, tenant farmers, and sharecroppers who depended on the fiber for their livelihoods. In the Midwest, meanwhile, abundant harvests and gradually coalescing political power (manifested most visibly in the emergence of the Grange Movement) enabled many farmers to weather the economic storms of the era.

In the West, however, the repercussions were far more universally negative. Great Plains farmers in Colorado, Nebraska, Kansas, and South Dakota experienced a succession of crop failures as a result of drought conditions. Somewhere between a third to a half of the farms in these regions were destroyed as a result, and thousands of other luckless farmers were plunged deeply into debt. By the end of the 1880s, droves of despondent and penniless farming families were fleeing the central plains. Some of them stayed in the West, scrabbling together meager livelihoods by hooking up with regional mining, timber, and other extractive industries. Others retreated to the East, where industrializing metropolises were eager to welcome new workers. Still others ventured farther west to the Pacific Northwest, where reliably high annual rainfall made farming seem like a less cruel and capricious enterprise (Merk 1978).

The Twentieth-Century Farmer

The grim economic fallout of worldwide agricultural overproduction, the drought years on the Great Plains, and the increasing industrialization of the expanding American empire all acted to moderate the country's reliance on agriculture as the social and economic wellspring of its existence. To be sure, the American farmer remained an integral part of the nation's cultural and economic fabric. Farmers and ranchers and their employees continued to be formidable forces in most states, especially in the West. The Grange Movement, for example, was instrumental in the elevation of the U.S. Department of Agriculture to cabinet-level status in 1889 and in the expansion of mail delivery to the rural countryside by 1896. Still, from the beginning to the end of the nineteenth century, the total percentage of Americans who made their homes on farms and ranches declined roughly from 90 percent to 41 percent.

Speaking in general terms, the economic picture for American farms was a mixed bag in the first few decades of the twentieth century. The number of people living and working primarily on farms continued to decline, to about a quarter of the national population by 1930. Equally important, the number of farmers who owned their own farms shriveled significantly during that period. Across America, the number of farm owners dropped by nearly 500,000 between 1910 and 1930, whereas the number of tenant farmers and sharecroppers—farmers who lived on and worked land owned by others—jumped by about 300,000 during that same span of time. This trend was particularly acute in two regions of the country. The first of these regions was the land where cotton was king—the Deep South. There, tenant farmers and sharecroppers outnumbered farm owners by more than a million. The other region in which this trend was most evident encompassed California and the Pacific Northwest. In this area, migrant workers and other landless workers accounted for almost half of the region's total farm population (Watkins 1999).

But even though these demographic trends were disquieting, those farmers who managed to remain solvent during the lean years of the 1880s found the early twentieth century to be a rewarding time. Steadily rising demand for agricultural goods among the rapidly growing American population produced a significant boost in overall farm income. In addition, farmers of the early twentieth century became even more adept at pooling their resources for the collective good. Farmers' cooperatives proliferated during that time, aided in no small measure by antitrust exemptions handed down by the federal authorities. Finally, farmers were able to improve their yields via an increasingly sophisticated use of new plant varieties, chemical fertilizers, and the mechanization of planting and harvesting tasks.

Indeed, mechanization ushered in the era of the "corporate farm." One 1934 government survey, entitled *Farming Hazards in the Drought Area,* quantified the impact of industrialization on American farms in stark terms. It found that a single farmer using a horse or mule was cultivating an average of 211 acres of cropland on an annual basis, whereas farmers equipped with a tractor were working an average of 529 acres each. Since increasingly sophisticated farm machinery could handle large tracts of farmland, it was inevitable that the average size of the American farm would undergo major growth. Indeed, the average American farm jumped in size from 139 acres in 1910 to 157 acres by 1930 (Watkins 1999).

In addition, the public reputation of the American farmer as an emblem of the nation's moral and economic core remained intact. But this reassuring image cloaked some troubling areas of erosion:

> For more than a century and a half, the farmer—or, more accurately, the *idea* of the farmer—had lain at the mythic heart of America's view of itself, and the small family farm had been perceived as the ideal social unit for the preservation of democratic ideals, explained one historian. For most Americans, that fond vision still obscured the fact that by the 1930s, economic imperatives and an often overweening ambition had made many farmers as vulnerable to the gyrations of the market as the most rawly unschooled urban speculator. (Watkins 1999)

Indeed, the growth of the American farm of the 1910s and 1920s—the expansion in cultivated land held by single landowners, the investment in tractors and combines and other machinery, and the attendant surge in production—made the American farmer more economically vulnerable than ever before. This was especially true after April 1917, when the U.S. government implemented one of its key measures to get the country on a war footing—the establishment of the Food Administration for War. This department set artificially high price supports for agricultural activity, which in turn convinced countless farmers to borrow money to invest in operations and take advantage of the spectacular business environment.

During the 1920s, however, the farming boom eased and then came to an end. With the removal of price supports after World War I, farming operations suddenly found themselves awash in debt but unable to demand the high prices on which they had become dependent. This changing dynamic actually prompted many farmers to borrow even more money in the mistaken belief that if they could become even more productive and generate even greater volumes of wheat, corn, and other crops, they would be able to reverse their increasingly precarious economic situation. By 1930, the debt load of America's agricultural sector had reached $9.6 billion. The entire federal debt, by contrast, was only $16.5 billion (Watkins 1999).

The agriculture industry, then, was in an extremely vulnerable position when the Great Depression rolled over the nation in 1929. The Depression devastated farmers, ranchers, and associated communities all across the country, and when presidential candidate Franklin D. Roosevelt promised government intervention and assistance for the agricultural sector, these people lined up behind the New York governor by the thousands. On taking office on March 3, 1933, Roosevelt quickly moved to implement his New Deal economic recovery strategy.

There were several pillars on which Roosevelt's New Deal rested, including programs of direct federal relief, economic regulation, and job creation. Among these initiatives were major banking reforms; the passage of the 1935 Wagner Act, giving labor unions the right to organize and engage in collective bargaining; and the 1933 creation of the Civilian Conservation Corps and the Tennessee Valley Authority and the 1935 creation of the Works Progress Administration, which put millions of young men to work on conservation and infrastructure development projects. The New Deal legislation that most directly tar-

geted the beleaguered American farmer was the Agricultural Adjustment Act of 1933. This legislation sought to reduce financially devastating crop surpluses, which were depressing prices for crops, by paying millions of farmers to reduce their production of important crops
such as wheat, cotton, corn, and rice. All told, the program removed
an estimated 9.6 million acres of wheat land and 10.3 million acres of
cotton land from cultivation. One year after its inception, the Agricultural Adjustment Act was expanded to include rye, flax, barley,
peanuts, sugarcane, and tobacco (Watkins 1999).

This state of affairs seemed surreal to many farmers, though they
nonetheless seized on the program. It also was harshly criticized by
New Deal opponents, and in 1936, the Supreme Court declared the
Agricultural Adjustment Act unconstitutional in *United States v.
Butler et al.,* ruling that it infringed on states' rights. The Roosevelt
administration absorbed this news with equanimity, then simply set
about following the same basic procedures in new legislation such as
the Soil Conservation and Domestic Allotment Acts. Then, in 1938,
a second Agricultural Adjustment Act was passed for the purpose of
stabilizing farm income via the creation and maintenance of the "ever
normal granary." Under this scheme, the government loaned money
to farmers and kept their surplus crops in flush times; the government received loan payments in times when the law of supply and
demand placed farmers in a position to command top dollar for their
crops. Other New Deal legislation attacked problems of soil and water conservation, insured crops against weather-related losses, and
ushered in rural electrification. The Farm Credit Administration,
meanwhile, became the dominant lender in agriculture, holding 40
percent of the nation's farm-mortgage indebtedness by 1937 (Danbom 1995).

These New Deal programs became even more important during
the mid-1930s, when dust storms ravaged millions of acres of farmland in Oklahoma, Texas, Kansas, and the Dakotas: "Everywhere in
the agricultural checkerboard of the heartland, crops not already
eaten by grasshoppers shriveled under the withering blight of the
sun, and livestock grew skeletal and frantic with thirst and hunger"
(Watkins 1999). The Dust Bowl storms, the product of drought and
years of intensive cultivation of wheat and cotton that had made the
topsoil vulnerable to erosion, sent the populations of some of these
primarily rural states plummeting. Nearly a million people fled the
Great Plains states during the first of the 1930s, and another 2.5

million left after 1935. Oklahoma was the hardest hit, as an estimated 440,000 residents abandoned the state during the Dust Bowl years—approximately 18.4 percent of its 1930 population. Many of these ecological refugees fled to California, which did not welcome the "Okies" with open arms. The net loss in Kansas was about 227,000 residents (Worster 1979).

Without Roosevelt's New Deal initiatives, the Great Depression and the Dust Bowl would have wreaked much greater damage on the American agricultural industries. Indeed, the raft of programs implemented by the administration in its first years helped raise net farm income across the United States by 50 percent between 1932 and 1935. Nonetheless, approximately 750,000 landowners lost their farms, their homes, and all their savings through foreclosures and bankruptcies. Farming income would not return to its pre-Depression levels until 1941, when the nation once again found itself in a war economy (Horwitz 1980).

Sources

Atack, Jeremy, and Fred Bateman. 1993. "Was There Ever an 'Agrarian Democracy' in America? The American Middle West in 1860." In *Outstanding in His Field: Perspectives on American Agriculture in Honor of Wayne D. Rasmussen,* edited by Frederick V. Carstensen, Morton Rothstein, and Joseph Swanson. Ames: Iowa State University Press.

Bogue, Allan G. 1963. *From Prairie to Corn Belt: Farming on the Illinois and Iowa Prairies in the Nineteenth Century.* Chicago: University of Chicago Press.

Cronon, William. 1991. *Nature's Metropolis: Chicago and the Great West.* New York: W. W. Norton.

Danbom, David B. 1995. *Born in the Country: A History of Rural America.* Baltimore, MD: Johns Hopkins University Press.

Davies, Ralph. 1973. *The Rise of the Atlantic Economies.* Ithaca, NY: Cornell University Press.

Ebeling, Walter. 1979. *The Fruited Plain: The Story of American Agriculture.* Berkeley: University of California Press.

Horwitz, Elinor Lander. 1980. *On the Land: American Agriculture from Past to Present.* New York: Atheneum.

Hurt, R. Douglas. 1991. *Agricultural Technology in the Twentieth Century.* Manhattan, KS: Sunflower University Press.

Isern, Thomas D. 1990. *Bull Threshers and Bindelstiffs: Harvesting and Threshing on the North American Plains.* Lawrence: University Press of Kansas.

Jefferson, Thomas. *Notes on the State of Virginia.* Philadelphia: Printed for Mathew Carey, November 12, 1794.

Jordan, Terry G. 1981. *Trails to Texas: Southern Roots of Western Cattle Ranching.* Lincoln: University of Nebraska Press.

McDonald, Forrest. 1984. *The Great Depression: America, 1929–1941.* New York: Times Books.

Merk, Frederick. 1978. *History of the Westward Movement.* New York: Alfred A. Knopf.

Myres, Sandra L. 1982. *Westering Women and the Frontier Experience, 1800–1915.* Albuquerque: University of New Mexico Press.

Schlebecker, John T. 1975. *Whereby We Thrive: A History of American Farming, 1607–1972.* Ames: Iowa State University Press.

Skaggs, Jimmy M. 1986. *Prime Cut: Livestock Raising and Meatpacking in the United States, 1607–1983.* College Station: Texas A&M University Press.

Walsh, Margaret. 1982. *The Rise of the Midwestern Meat Packing Industry.* Lexington: University of Kentucky Press.

Watkins, T. H. 1999. *The Hungry Years: A Narrative History of the Great Depression in America.* New York: Henry Holt.

White, Richard. 1994. "Animals and Enterprise." In *The Oxford History of the American West,* edited by Clyde A. Milner II, Carol A. O'Connor, and Martha A. Sandweiss. New York: Oxford University Press.

Worster, Donald. 1979. *Dust Bowl: The Southern Plains in the 1930s.* New York: Oxford University Press.

———. 1987. *The Texas Longhorn: Relic of the Past, Asset for the Future.* College Station: Texas A&M University Press.

Yeager, Mary. 1981. *Competition and Regulation: The Development of Oligopoly in the Meat Packing Industry.* Greenwich, CT: Jai Press.

Innovations and Inventions

Jacob Jones

Agriculture was America's first industry: in fact, well into the nineteenth century, the value of the nation's agricultural production exceeded the output of its factories. Moreover, many of the other industries, from textiles to meatpacking, relied on agriculture for their raw materials, and the export value of the country's farm goods regularly exceeded that of manufactures even up to the turn of the twentieth century (*Report of the Industrial Commission* 1901). Additionally, without the prospect of an increasing demand for agricultural goods and thus the necessity of moving those goods from farm to market (domestic and overseas), many a nineteenth-century transportation system would have failed of completion from a lack of investor interest.

Equally as important perhaps, agriculture—or, more properly, the "agrarian ideal"—was an integral part of national self-definition in the United States throughout the nineteenth century. Indeed, many of the nation's Founding Fathers styled themselves "gentleman farmers," and the most famous of this group—including Thomas Jefferson, Benjamin Franklin, George Washington, and James Madison—hoped that the new nation would remain a largely agrarian republic for the foreseeable future, thus avoiding what they saw as the pathological social consequences of rapid industrialization in late eighteenth-century Britain. "While we have land to labor then," Jefferson famously declared in his 1794 book, *Notes on the State of Virginia,* "let our workshops remain in Europe" (Jefferson 1794).

This painting, touting America's agrarian origins, shows George Washington standing among African American field workers. (Library of Congress)

Yet the type of agriculture the Founders had in mind for the young republic differed significantly from actual farming practices in post-Revolutionary America. Wide availability of inexpensive land on the eastern seaboard (once taken from its Indian occupants) had encouraged wasteful farming practices since the beginning of European settlement, and by 1800, evidence of that neglect could be found throughout the former thirteen colonies of British America. Eroded hillsides in Virginia, soils leached of their nutrients in New England, and everywhere the diminution or destruction of once-mighty forests told an all-too-familiar tale of squandered resources. Agricultural "improvement" advocates such as Jefferson, Madison, and Washington criticized their compatriots for such abuse and recommended that farmers rebuild their soils utilizing more modern methods of husbandry. But many farmers wondered why they should invest in the maintenance of soil fertility using "intensive" methods—for example, by contour plowing, crop rotation with nitrogen-fixing legumes, or better manuring—when it was just as easy and often cheaper to abandon an overworked farm and move west to start again on fresh land using traditional "extensive" farming practices.

In fact, many Americans did just that, beginning a wave of migration westward that did not abate until the early twentieth century (the number of farms in America doubled between 1870 and 1900, for instance) (Danbom 1995). But migrant farmers found out rather quickly that they could not always transfer their customary agricultural practices to new climes, particularly when trying to secure a living from the tall-grass prairies of the Midwest or the semiarid flatlands of the far west. Environmental conditions were radically different than in the East, and there was often an acute shortage of labor in the new sections of the country. These difficulties, however, also encouraged development of innovative solutions, both technological—new reapers, mowers, steel plows, windmills, and barbed wire (among many others)—as well as biological—better cattle, sheep, and horse breeds, for example, in addition to new crop varieties suitable for the range of western climatic zones.

Meanwhile, throughout the nineteenth century, both eastern and western farmers had to contend with the rapid growth of a national and international market economy linked together by an ever-expanding array of transportation systems, including canals, steamboats, and of course railroads. Once canal and rail links joined the East Coast with the Midwest (by midcentury), for instance, eastern grain farmers found themselves in competition with, say, Illinois or Wisconsin wheat growers. These in turn (along with American meatpackers) had to contend in the lucrative European market with exports from Russia, Argentina, and Australia, which arrived as well via cheaper rail and steam transport. Daunted by the competition and resulting low commodity prices, thousands of the nation's farmers (and especially their children) in the last half of the century simply abandoned agriculture for work in the booming industrial and commercial cities. Others, however, trying to maintain profitability by reducing production costs, invested yet more capital in new equipment, and the remaining farmers in the East and on the outskirts of urban areas turned increasingly to dairy and truck farming rather than growing grain for the market.

All of this innovation, coupled with increased national and global demand for American foodstuffs, yielded a brief period of relative prosperity in national agriculture during the first decades of the twentieth century, an era since referred to as the golden age of American farming (Danbom 1995). As had happened so often before, however, good times soon gave way to a new round of heavy competition (globally and nationally) and low prices, resulting inevitably in another wave of migration from the countryside, accompanied by innovation, capital investment, and expansion on the part of those who stayed behind. Even vastly increased government involvement in U.S. agriculture during the twentieth century did not entirely break this cycle, with the result that fewer Americans farm now than ever before and farm operations have becoming increasingly capital-intensive and specialized.

Eli Whitney's Cotton Gin and the Antebellum South

One of the first turns in the intensification cycle—and arguably the most important agricultural invention/innovation of the eighteenth century—came with the invention of the crank-turned, toothed cotton gin (short for engine) by Eli Whitney in 1793. Not surprisingly, given Jefferson's importance to early national agriculture in all of its forms, the soon-to-be president played a role in this agricultural "revolution" as well, albeit in his secondary capacity as a reviewer of patent applications while secretary of state. On November 6, 1793, Secretary Jefferson officially acknowledged Whitney's patent application, promising that the actual patent for the new machine would be forthcoming as soon as the young inventor deposited the required model of his device at the federal government offices then in Philadelphia. In March of the next year, Whitney took the model to Philadelphia himself and forthwith received the patent granting him exclusive rights of production on his design for the next fourteen years (Federico 1960).

Early the previous year, Whitney, just a few months out of Yale, had sailed south from New York to take a temporary Carolina teach-

Eli Whitney, inventor of
the revolutionary cotton
gin. (Library of
Congress)

ing position in order to finance his planned legal studies. En route to
his Savannah debarkation point, he happened to meet the widow of
Revolutionary War hero Gen. Nathaniel Greene, and she invited the
young man to stop for a while at her Georgia plantation home before
taking up his duties. He agreed, and when his teaching appointment
fell through, he stayed on as a guest of Mrs. Greene. As local cotton
planters were regular visitors to the household as well, Whitney
quickly learned from their conversations that one of the primary
roadblocks to the expansion of the region's cotton industry was the
lack of an efficient means of cleaning seed out of upland, "green
seed," short-staple" varieties (staple, or "lint," refers to the cotton
fiber itself). Though long-staple Sea Island cotton (so named because
it was largely grown on islands off the coast of Georgia and the Carolinas) brought good prices from British textile millers, its geographic range was limited. Meanwhile, the roller gins used to separate
the looser black seed from Sea Island cotton did not work with the

more tenacious seeds of the short-staple type, though the latter would grow just about anywhere in the southern Piedmont. As a result of this bottleneck, millions of pounds of short-staple cotton failed to make it to a very willing market (the British textile industry was clamoring for more cotton). As Whitney noted in a 1793 letter to his father, the planters congregating at Mrs. Greene's "all agreed that if a machine could be invented which would clean the cotton with expedition, it would be a great thing both to the Country and the inventor" (Gray 1933).

Intrigued by the mechanical problem—he had been an inveterate tinkerer since childhood (Cooper 2003)—and no doubt by the potential for profit, Whitney took over a work space on the Greene farm and began developing the prototype of a cotton gin, based on a design he apparently already had in his head. In less than two weeks, he had a small machine ready that "required the labor [of but] one man to turn it, [yet] will clean ten times as much cotton as he [could employing] any other way before known" (Hammond 1897). Whitney was not the only inventor working feverishly on the cotton-ginning problem (as he would soon find out), but unlike the majority of his competitors, who tried to adapt the roller method to short-staple ginning, Whitney "invented a new principle . . . for removing the seeds . . . A cylinder filled with wire teeth set in annular rows. As the cylinder was turned, the teeth drew the cotton into a breastwork of transverse grooves through which the lint passed, but not the seed" (Aiken 1973).

A brush inside the boxlike contraption then removed the lint from the cylinder and deposited it in a pile ready for collection. Gravity, meanwhile, allowed the seeds to drop to the bottom of the device, where they, too, could be collected and either pressed to extract their oil (though the cottonseed business did not develop in earnest until after the Civil War) or saved to plant next year's crop.

Excited by the prospect of his invention and with financial help from his new partner, Phineas Miller (Mrs. Greene's plantation manager), Whitney immediately "returned to the Northward for the purpose of having a machine made on a large scale and obtaining a patent for the invinction [*sic*]" (Hammond 1897). After his meeting with Jefferson, Whitney set up shop back in New Haven, "employed several workmen in making machines," and planned on a return to Georgia, where he and Miller intended to buy up much of the upland cotton crop, gin it themselves, and reap the profits. These latter Whitney expected to be large. "It is generally said by those who know anything about it," he wrote to his father in September of 1793, "that I shall make a Fortune by it [the gin]. I am now so sure of success," he added, "that ten thousand dollars, if I saw the money counted out to me, would not tempt me to give up my right and relinquish the object" (quoted in Hammond 1897).

Whitney's projections were not a complete fantasy. For instance, within two years of the arrival of the first gins in Natchez, Mississippi, in 1795, cotton output in the area (later considered the very capital of "King Cotton's" realm) increased from less than 40,000 pounds a year to over 1 million pounds (Wayne 1990). National production soared as well, from 3,000 bales in 1790 to 73,000 in 1800, after which the cotton crop almost doubled in size every decade until the outbreak of the Civil War. Over that same antebellum period, cotton exports financed the young nation's economic expansion (including industrial), kept British (as well as New England) textile mills humming, enriched innumerable merchants and financiers, and directly or indirectly provided employment for millions on both sides of the Atlantic (Hughes 1987).

Yet all of this expansion came with a terrible human cost, for in the end, "world cotton textile development and the expansion of American slave agriculture went hand in hand" (Hughes 1987). True, free white farmers in the South grew a significant amount of cotton without the direct utilization of slave labor. But increasingly during the antebellum era, large plantation enterprises—commanding the labor of dozens and sometimes hundreds of enslaved human beings—became the primary centers of cotton production across the South. In the Natchez "district" (an area comprising five Mississippi counties and three Louisiana parishes), for example, a region responsible for almost 10 percent of the nation's cotton output in 1860, "the number of district landowners holding fifty or more slaves was well over six hundred" in that last year before the war (Wayne 1990). Not surprisingly, one of the largest slave markets in the antebellum South was located on the outskirts of Natchez, just a short carriage drive from the elegant homes of the city's cotton elite (the same homes that annually attract thousands of tourists to the area even now).

Of course, neither Whitney nor his gin can be held solely responsible for the expansion of the "cotton kingdom," for its attendant slave regime in antebellum America, or for the bloody Civil War that followed. Even on purely technological grounds, such an indictment would be difficult to sustain, for much to Whitney's chagrin, his imagined gin "monopoly" was rather quickly superseded by illegal copies of his own device and by a competing "saw gin" (where a toothed saw separated the cotton seeds from the fiber rather than Whitney's "spiked cylinder"). In much-enlarged form (some gin "stands" were as long as 18 feet, as wide as 6, and armed with sixty saws), this machine became the standard across the antebellum South (Aiken 1973). Whitney argued vociferously that the saw gin was, in fact, not a new invention at all but merely a minor variation on his basic ginning principle (he developed a saw gin of his own as well), and he finally won a judgment to that effect in federal court in 1807. By then, however, it made little economic sense for him to continue pursuing the matter. He had, moreover, already sold his patent rights in South Carolina and other southern states for much less than the hundreds of thousands of dollars he had expected to gain from his invention. Embittered by the experience—he took to calling his seemingly innumerable opponents rogues, children, and infernal rascals— Whitney nonetheless persevered by starting a second career as one of the nation's pioneers in the production of interchangeable parts utilizing machine tool manufacturing methods at his gun armory in New Haven. He died in 1825 a wealthy and internationally famous inventor and industrialist.

Go West (and North) Young Man (and Woman)

In the first two decades of the nineteenth century, hundreds of thousands of migrants, both voluntary and compelled (coffles of chained slaves were often seen marching south from Virginia in those years), expanded the borders of the cotton kingdom steadily to the Southwest, a human exodus propelled at least in part by the success of Whitney's gin. By 1840, in fact, more than 2.5 million Americans lived in the prime cotton lands between the western border of Georgia and the Mississippi River, eight times the population of the region in 1800 (Hughes 1987). Just two decades later, King Cotton's realm was pushing into the middle of Texas, and the population of the south-central area of the country had doubled yet again.

Over this same period, however, the trans-Appalachian north (from Ohio to Kansas and from North Dakota to the Ohio River) saw an even larger increase in population but with a critical difference from the pattern of southern migration. With the exception of Missouri, this new region lacked that most "peculiar" of southern institutions: slavery. The Northwest Territory Ordinance of 1787 had outlawed the institution from the state of Ohio up to the banks of the Mississippi, and the Missouri Compromise of 1820 extended the boundary of "free" northern territory all the way to the far western edge of the nation.

That this vast new area—soon to become the breadbasket of the nation and indeed much of the world—was based on "free labor" had immense significance for agricultural innovation. Since colonial times, North America had been land rich and labor poor, meaning that transplanted Anglo-Europeans could—in the aggregate—expect to earn more there than they did at home. This traditional labor shortage was only magnified by the exodus westward in the nineteenth century. In some regions of the eastern United States, labor shortages became significant because of the drain of workers to the West. In the West, meanwhile, most newcomers were intent on tending their own crops and livestock—not hiring themselves out to other farmers. Add to this the necessity on the part of migrating farmers to adapt to new conditions in the western territories—in particular, the challenge of the prairies—and you had a situation ripe for technological and agricultural inventiveness.

Northern migrants had never encountered anything quite like the tall-grass prairies of the Midwest, and for much of the first half of the century, they opted to settle on the wooded verge of these verdant oceans instead of venturing out onto such a forbidding and unfamiliar landscape. Yet farmers learned early on that the prairies were extremely fertile (despite the contemporary theory that only former woodlands made good farmland), for occasionally, one of them would slice through the thick mat of prairie grass with an ax and drop in some corn or wheat seed, only to see the plants shoot up out of the deep loam over the course of the season. But when they tried to cut through the never-before-farmed grasslands with their iron-shod wooden plows, the prairies simply cast the implements aside. Big breaking plows, sometimes pulled by ten or more oxen, could cut through the tangled roots, but renting the services of one of these teams was more than ordinary western farmers could afford. Only with the widespread dissemination of the steel plow in the 1840s and after (the most famous of which was invented by an Illinois blacksmith named John Deere between 1837 and 1838) did prairie farming

A Colorado farmer uses a John Deere steel plow to break soil for planting. (Library of Congress)

become a practical possibility for the typical western pioneer. Indeed, once connected to eastern and foreign markets by a new network of canals, steamboats, and finally railroads, the former tall-grass prairies became the prime wheat-growing region of the nation.

In the process, however, another problem arose: how to harvest, thresh, and store thousands and later millions of acres of ripening wheat before heavy rain and/or hailstorms flattened the crop or the grain rotted in the fields. Traditional wheat-harvesting methods—cutting the stalks with a long-bladed grain scythe (with or without an attached cradle), raking and bundling the sheaves, then carrying the bundles to a barnyard where the precious grains were flailed or trod out of their encasement—were notoriously labor intensive. Cooperative harvesting provided one solution. An antebellum midwestern farmer's wheat yield, however, likely represented his only chance for significant cash income during the year, and thus, when an entire neighborhood's crop matured at almost the same moment, each individual farmer understandably felt a greater urgency about his own

fields than those of the neighbors. Farmers could, of course, hire laborers to aid with the harvest, and most did so. But since the neighbors were also bidding for the same scarce labor, the price of those
harvest hands could rise appreciably, cutting severely into potential
profits (Olmstead 1975).

Enter the mechanical reaper, what historian Wayne Rasmussen
once described as "probably the most significant single invention introduced into farming between 1830 and 1860" (Rasmussen 1977).
Perhaps *inventions* might have been a more appropriate word because, as with most problems open to technological solutions, the
harvesting bottleneck in wheat (though the same problem arose with
other small grains and hay mowing as well) drew the attention of a
host of mechanics and would-be inventors, much as the cotton-
ginning obstacle had done in the previous generation. Thus, even
though Cyrus McCormick and his Virginia reaper dominated the industry by the Civil War, his path to that perch was by no means easy,
and in fact, the McCormick Company had to contend with serious
competition for market dominance all the way up until it became
part of the giant International Harvester Company in 1902.

Cyrus McCormick and the Realm of the Reaper Kings

By all accounts, however, even determined opposition did not deter
Cyrus McCormick—quite the contrary. Indeed, almost every rival in
the reaper industry could expect to be sued by McCormick at one
time or another (usually for patent infringement), and Cyrus was
such a stubborn man that he continued a lawsuit against a passenger
railroad for twenty years because he believed a clerk had overcharged
him on a baggage fee. But to succeed in the early reaper industry
seemed to require such combativeness. In the first place, the stakes
were very high, as demand kept pace with the rapid expansion of the
westward agricultural frontier throughout the nineteenth century.
Over 3 million new farms were established in the country in the last
three decades of the century alone, and a large percentage of these
would require reliable reapers and mowers (Danbom 1995). Yet it
seemed, at times, that success or failure in this business sector hinged
less on the quality of the product than on the aggression with which
it was promoted. Only those who combined both—like Mc-
Cormick—could hope to win the prize of market dominance.

Cyrus McCormick
revolutionized American
agriculture through his
invention and
manufacture of the
mechanical reaper.
(Library of Congress)

In any event, Cyrus (like Eli Whitney) had displayed inventive prowess at a young age, perhaps not surprising given that his father, Robert, also had the bug. In fact, the elder McCormick had been trying to invent a horse-drawn reaper for years before his son took up the task and came up with a workable machine in 1831 (James 1931). It is important to note, however, that the 1831 McCormick reaper was not the first in the United States, as over twenty reaping machines of various types had already appeared in America by that date, along with a few dozen others in Europe (James 1931). But the McCormick apparatus combined all of the elements of the earlier devices—reciprocating knives (with guards) and a cutter bar against which the grain stalks were pushed for severing; dividers to separate the stalks as they entered the cutter; "a platform on which the grain fell after being sliced"; a "gear wheel" that, when pulled along the ground by horses or other draft animals, gave the apparatus its motive power—along with the novelty of a large reel (looking something like a smaller version of a steamboat paddle wheel) that rotated over and down against the crop to push it into the cutting mechanism

(Fite 1966). Despite the fact that reapers allowed farmers to cut almost four times as much grain in one day as they could by hand, with lower labor costs and less grain waste as well (Gates 1960), the McCormicks found few customers for the ungainly looking contraption among their neighbors in the Shenandoah Valley, where the farmsteads were generally on the smallish side and often sloped and rocky to boot. Thus, Cyrus set the reaper aside for several years while the family engaged in other business pursuits (an iron foundry, selling plows and hemp breaks), almost all of which met with failure. Only when faced with the challenge of Obed Hussey's competing reaper—Hussey, wrote Craig Canine, was "the first person to make, patent [1833], and sell a reaping machine in the United States"—did Cyrus actually patent his own (1834) device. And it was later still before he set about actively promoting and improving what he called his Virginia reaper (Gates 1960).

Even then, the story was not one of quick success, for Hussey proved a stubborn rival, and several other entrants into the field offered reapers with components as good as or even superior to McCormick's original machine. The Atkins reaper, for example, included a "self-raking device" (which alone "freed the labor of one man," according to historian Paul Gates) that was originally absent from the Virginia reaper, and the Manny reaper had "stronger and more effective cutter bars" that "were better for mowing grass," an important consideration for cash-strapped farmers who could not generally afford both a reaper and a mower (Gates 1960). But, as Gates noted, "the keen competition was helpful for stimulating improvements on all the machines," and the McCormicks in particular (Cyrus's brothers were very active in the firm) worked steadily on the improvement of their machine in the immediate antebellum decades. They added the elements from their competitors noted earlier (though the self-raking device would not be ready until the 1860s), as well as a raker's seat and better weight balance to compensate for the tendency of the machine to pull, or "draft," to one side (Gates 1960; Olmstead 1975).

Yet McCormick's ultimate success rested as much on his abilities as a businessman as it did on the technical capacities of his product. For example, after a tour of the then "new" midwestern farming regions in 1844, Cyrus decided to establish the company's main production facility in Chicago, hardly an obvious choice at the time given that the muddy city on the banks of Lake Michigan still lacked railroad, canal, and telegraph connections with the rest of the country. Within a year of his arrival in 1847, however, the city would acquire all three, and McCormick's modern, steam-powered South Side factory was well poised to cash in on the boom in commercial agriculture that thereafter swept over the region to the west and north of the Windy City (Cronon 1991).

But a better location did not solve McCormick's biggest challenge—getting hesitant farmers to pay over $100 for a newfangled machine that they had managed to do without for years. In fact, farmers had been doing without it for millennia: with the notable exception of the grain cradle (which gained widespread popularity in late eighteenth-century America), the basic tools used throughout the western world to harvest wheat in the early 1800s—namely, the sickle and/or scythe, the rake, the flail, and the winnowing basket or screen—would have been familiar to a farmer from ancient Rome, Greece, or even Egypt.

To convince farmers they needed a labor-saving machine such as a reaper, McCormick used prodigious amounts of advertising, particularly in the expanding agricultural press. These ads frequently included testimonials from satisfied customers, as well as illustrations showing how the machines worked (Cronon 1991).

Nothing, however, helped convince a skeptical customer more than actually seeing a reaper in operation, and so McCormick made sure that his annual models made the rounds of all the state and county fairs, where they were often pitted in competitions—"field trials"—with rival makes. The spectacle of watching contestants feverishly drive their horses and machines thrilled rural audiences (in a nineteenth-century version of the tractor pull, reapers were even, on occasion, lashed together and pulled in opposite directions to see which models held together the longest under the strain). And such events encouraged sales, at least when the Virginia reaper emerged victorious (a loss to the Manny reaper in one such contest prompted an angry Cyrus to sue his adversary). In fact, McCormick's most famous field trial, which pitted the Virginia reaper against the Hussey machine and a British challenger—all participants in the Great Exhibition at the Crystal Palace in London, one of the first and most important world industrial fairs—resulted not just in a clear victory for McCormick and the award of the Council Medal (the highest honor bestowed at the exhibition) but also invaluable press coverage. And that, in turn, helped open European markets over the subsequent decades (Carstensen 1996; Cronon 1991).

All of this exposure undoubtedly raised the public profile of McCormick and his reaper. But it was probably the much more prosaic provisions of credit sales, local agents, and service after the sale—in addition to regular design improvements—that eventually won for McCormick the title of "reaper king." For example, since local dealers sold the Virginia reaper on commission, they had a vested interest in promoting the McCormick product, and Cyrus offered his representatives other incentives as well, including exclusive sales territories and aggressive advertising support (Cronon 1991). Area farmers, moreover, could rely on the local agents to have display models available, to aid in the initial setup after purchase, and for repair and parts replacement after the sale (like a modern auto company, McCormick kept many model years' worth of prefabricated replacement parts in inventory). Finally, local agents helped negotiate credit sales on an installment plan for those farmers who could not come up with the $115 to $125 in cash for a new machine.

Utilizing all of these marketing tools, plus the addition of the self-raking device and other design improvements (an automatic binder would come later), secured for McCormick and his company a significant (though not majority) share of the ever-widening national and eventually international market for "harvesting machines." Population growth in the United States and Europe, especially in urban areas, coupled with the extension of rail lines into the wheat-growing districts of the upper Midwest, also boosted demand for reapers, particularly when combined with the rapid rise in the price of wheat brought on by the disruption in Russian exports caused by the Crimean War (1854–1855).

By the late 1850s, McCormick was selling over 4,000 machines a year, and sales increased even more with the onset of the American Civil War. The war not only enlarged the demand for food grains (and their price) but also removed many thousands of male harvest workers from the field, compelling those who stayed behind on the farm—often the women of the family—to find a technological fix for all of that lost labor (Cronon 1991). McCormick's version of the self-raking reaper, introduced in 1863, fit that bill well, though stiff competition continued to dent potential sales. Nonetheless, even though wartime constraints on materials and transportation (not to mention the increased scarcity and cost of factory labor) made normal production runs difficult, company sales still rose 25 percent from 1859 to 1864, and "in 1863 for the first time the cash income of the McCormicks exceeded one million dollars a year" (Lerner 1956). Postwar migration out onto the gently rolling prairies of the Great Plains—land ideal for wheat growing and reapers—further enlarged the market for the McCormick Harvesting Machine Company and further enriched the McCormick clan. By that time, however, Cyrus Sr. had, in effect, surrendered day-to-day management of the company to his brothers (he died in 1884) and his wife, Nettie, who resurrected the company after the disastrous Chicago Fire of 1871 (Carstensen 1996).

"Butcher for the World"

The rest of Chicago also rose out of the ashes of that 1871 inferno to become an industrial and agricultural metropolis, as proclaimed most famously in the city's literary signature piece, the Carl Sandburg poem "Chicago." Sandburg's verses, besides celebrating the continued dynamism of the still-booming metropolis—"Shoveling, Wrecking, Planning, Building, Breaking, Rebuilding"—explicitly acknowledged in the first stanza the importance of agricultural processing and transport to the city's success:

> HOG butcher for the World
> Tool Maker, Stacker of Wheat,
> Player with Railroads and the Nation's Freight Handler;
> Stormy, husky, brawling,
> City of the Big Shoulders. (Sandburg 1916)

In fact, Chicago had already served as the nation's chief "hog butcher" and "stacker of wheat" for over half a century before Sandburg wrote those lines (Cronon 1991). Its combination of canal and railroad links, along with direct access to Great Lakes shipping, made the city an early and natural entrepôt for the agricultural commerce of the northwestern frontier regions. In the decades after McCormick's arrival, however, that base expanded exponentially, creating a "Nature's Metropolis," in historian William Cronon's formulation—a city that received, processed, and transported the agricultural bounty of almost the entire American West, while returning to those same western customers a torrent of manufactured goods from the nation's factories, many now located in Chicago itself. Seemingly endless carloads of western wheat filled the towering elevators of the city each year, and the reapers to cut that grain, the barbed wire to enclose fields and livestock, innumerable household goods, timber to build the houses, and even the houses themselves (Sears, a Chicago-based company, and other mail-order merchants sold house "kits" ready for assembly) returned along the same rail lines to the cities, towns, hamlets, and individual farms connected by these steel arteries to the pumping mechanical heart of the Second City (the "first" city being New York) on Lake Michigan.

But the story of Chicago's role in U.S. and, indeed, world agriculture would be incomplete without a discussion of the city's famous meatpacking industry. As the first line of Sandburg's poem suggested (in capital letters no less), Chicago meatpackers made their reputation processing hogs, taking the title of "Porkopolis" from rival Cincinnati in 1862 (Cronon 1991). Swine had been the favored livestock of midwestern farmers since the earliest years of settlement. Among other advantages, pigs required very little upkeep (in the frontier period, they were often set loose to forage in the woods), and they were highly portable. That mobility proved particularly important in the antebellum decades, when the region's dearth of good roads made it an expensive proposition to haul bulky products such as corn or hay to distant markets without incurring more in costs than the freight was worth. Hogs, by contrast, could be fattened on corn ("for what is a hog," one contemporary asked facetiously, "but fifteen or twenty bushels of corn on four legs"), then driven under their own power to market, where they generally fetched higher prices than the amount of grain they consumed (Cronon 1991).

River cities such as Cincinnati were the most likely destinations for midwestern hog drovers in the precanal, prerailroad days because much of the demand for dressed pork (slaughtered and packed as opposed to "live" stock) came from the plantation South, where it was a staple of the slave diet. Many of the "disassembly" and packing techniques later employed in Chicago were actually developed in the huge packing houses of Cincinnati, which processed over 300,000 hogs a year in the 1850s (Cronon 1991). Cincinnati also had the advantage of regular steamboat links with New Orleans and other southern river ports, not to mention excellent canal and river connections with its own agricultural hinterland. Of course, many midwestern farmers simply bypassed the middleman and floated their own pigs to the southern market on keelboats or even homemade rafts. Indiana and Illinois farm boy Abraham Lincoln made this trek twice, but he was only one among thousands to tie up each year at Natchez, St. Francisville, New Orleans, or one of many plantation wharves along the way, ready to sell their salt or smoke-cured hams and barrels of lard to the highest bidder (Cronon 1991).

As happened with many other products, however, the advent of the railroad era began to redirect the meat trade to transportation hubs such as Chicago, a trend accelerated by the loss of the southern market during the Civil War. Indeed, Chicago pork packers benefited mightily from accelerated wartime demand for meat, in particular to feed the Union army. Hog receipts in Chicago amounted to 392,864 animals in 1860, reaching a peak of almost 2 million by war's end, and the number of pigs actually processed and packed in Chicago rose from 150,000 to 970,000 over the same period, the latter figure close to a quarter of all the pork packed in the entire western region of the United States (Hill 1923). The growth trend continued after the war, and by the early 1870s, Chicago companies were packing over 1 million hogs every year (Cronon 1991).

Taking advantage of their experience and of the city's position as terminus for several western railroads, Chicago meatpackers soon captured the lion's share of the rapidly expanding market for western beef cattle as well. Thus, when pioneering cattle men such J. G. McCoy and Charles Goodnight arrived at the railheads of Wichita, Abilene, or Dodge City, Kansas, in the late 1860s and early 1870s—having driven their huge herds of semiwild steers (including the famous longhorns) from as far as the Nueces River valley of Texas—the trains those animals trundled into more often than not headed off to Chicago, specifically to the vast Union Stock Yards on the city's South Side, which had opened on Christmas Day in 1865 (Webb 1981; Cronon 1991).

They did not as yet, however, go into the Chicago abattoir itself in any great numbers at this early stage in the industry. "As late as 1871," historian William Cronon indicated, "less than 4 percent of the cattle that arrived in Chicago were packed there" (Cronon 1991). Instead, western steers were transshipped in livestock cars from

A bird's-eye view of the great Union Stock Yards of Chicago, ca. 1878. (Library of Congress)

Chicago to East Coast wholesalers, where they would be slaughtered and sold as fresh meat to retail butchers in urban areas throughout the Northeast. Consumers, it seems, might have gotten used to dressed pork by the 1870s, but they still wanted their beef freshly butchered. In fact, it would be at least another decade before Chicago meatpackers managed to convince eastern customers that precut meat—even though it might have been in cold storage for a week or more—was just as fresh and tasty as newly butchered beef.

Despite consumer doubts, several enterprising Chicago packers, including George H. Hammond (who located his operations just across the state line from Chicago in the town that now bears his name, Hammond, Indiana), Gustavus F. Swift, Philip Armour, and Nelson Morris—later termed the Big Four, saw an opportunity in developing a dressed-beef business similar to the successful dressed-pork industry. After all, they argued, it was wasteful to transship live western cattle from Chicago to the East because one had to pay to transport the whole animal when only a portion of the beast actually made it to the butcher's counter. "The shipper," one contemporary commentator explained, "must not only pay freight on good butchers' meat, but also on blood and bones, horns and hoofs and all manner of offal; he must hire men to care for them, and buy hay and grain to feed them" (quoted in Hill 1923). Moreover, the animals themselves often suffered from the journey, and many died en route (Kujovich 1970). It would be better to butcher, process, and package the beef in Chicago, then ship the finished products to market, thereby saving unnecessary freight charges on the unused portions of an animal. Hammond made the first significant effort in this dressed-beef trade in 1868 when he sent an 8-ton shipment to Boston, using a sort of "icebox on wheels" originally designed for "fruit shipments" (Cronon 1991). "By 1873," Cronon added, Hammond "was doing a million dollars worth of business annually" packing dressed beef in the Chicago area and transporting it to his native New England for sale.

The rest of the Big Four soon followed suit, but their efforts were fraught with difficulties. Customers initially shied away from prepackaged beef, and the Big Four also encountered serious resistance from those interests invested in the existing livestock trade. For instance, both the wholesale livestock dealers and the eastern butchers they served, as well as the big eastbound trunk railroads, had capital tied up in warehouse facilities, holding pens, intermediate feeding stations, and specialized railcars, which would all come to naught if the dressed-beef trade seriously eroded their market share in the East. These interests, moreover, were in a position to keep freight rates high enough for dressed beef that the Big Four would have to struggle to profit from their innovations (Kujovich 1970).

But Swift, Armour, Hammond, and Morris were not to be deterred so easily. In fact, one of their original reasons for venturing into the dressed-beef trade in Chicago was to eliminate several layers of middlemen and reap the profits thereby (Cronon 1991). Thus, if they had to develop a separate delivery network to reach the eastern markets with their novel products, then so be it.

The Refrigerated Railroad Car

Chicago, it should be added, had always had an additional advantage over rival packing cities such as Cincinnati, for, as anyone who has spent a winter season in or near the Windy City knows, it can get extremely cold on the shores of Lake Michigan. Though uncomfortable for human residents, the frigid air provided just the right environment for meatpacking, which was an exclusively cold-weather trade until packers began harvesting ice from ponds and rivers and storing it for use in chilling meat during the warmer months. Taking advantage of the cold weather, Gustavus Swift made his first dressed-beef shipments eastward from Chicago in 1877 by placing the meat in regular freight cars and sending them off in midwinter with the doors open so the cold air would flow continually across the carcasses. Needless to say, such an arrangement did not offer a practical, long-term business solution (due to the dirt and detritus blowing in, the lack of security, and so forth).

The earliest refrigerated railcars did not offer much improvement. Hammond's pioneering dressed-beef shipments, for instance, involved packing a freight car with ice and keeping the meat in direct contact with the blocks, which had the unfortunate side effect of discoloring the beef and actually speeding up spoilage (Hill 1923; Cronon 1991). Chicago packers next tried hanging the meat in the interior of the railcars, but the swinging slabs of beef destabilized the trains while rounding curves, resulting in a number of wrecks (Hill 1923; Cronon 1991). Thus, not until Swift hired the Michigan Car Company of Detroit to build ten specialized refrigerator cars with an improved design (developed by engineer Andrew J. Chase) did the dressed-beef industry pick up steam (Kujovich 1970). The Chase/Swift car incorporated a vented ice and brine compartment at either end, with a large packing space in the middle utilizing rails for suspending the carcasses and storage areas underneath for all manner of dressed-beef and pork products; the whole car was packed closely to prevent shifting during transport, yet with enough space to allow the chilled air to flow over all of the materials (Cronon 1991). Because of constant melting, ice still had to be replenished on the eastbound trip. But even after making an investment in intermediate stations along the route, as well as cooling warehouses at both Chicago and destination points such as Boston and New York, there were still savings to be had—and profits made—in the competition with traditional livestock shippers.

Before that profit could be fully realized, however, Swift and the other members of the Big Four had to find a way to bypass those same livestock shippers and their railroad allies. The major railroads,

A refrigerated railroad car from the fleet of Chicago meatpacking titan
Armour and Company. (Library of Congress)

in fact, not only refused to build the new refrigerator cars, but under
pressure from livestock shippers and wholesalers, they even adjusted
freight rates for dressed-beef upward to negate the competitive advantage the Big Four had over live-animal shipments (Kujovich
1970). Swift managed to find a struggling railroad—the Grand Trunk
Line (which ran through Canada and then connected with Boston via
the Vermont Central)—that would carry refrigerator cars out of
Chicago in defiance of the other roads. The Grand Trunk needed the
business and carried little in the way of livestock, but it also did not
have the capital or the willingness to build refrigerator cars.

Railroads in general were averse to building specialized fleets of
cars because they worried that a huge initial investment (as they had
made with livestock cars, for example) might become worthless if the
next turn of the business cycle—such as the emergence of the
dressed-meat industry and its refrigerator cars—left them with an
obsolescent technology. Better then, so cautious rail managers argued, to build multipurpose gondolas, hoppers, and flatcars that
could be used for all manner of freight. But these kinds of cars were
not the most efficient means of transporting either dressed-beef and
dressed-pork or bulk commodities such as petroleum and chemicals.

Thus, like other late nineteenth-century giants, Standard Oil, Swift, and Armour were forced to develop their own fleets, which all three companies proceeded to do, reaping some unexpected rewards in the process (O'Connell 1970). For once these goliaths had developed markets for their products and the cars to carry those products to the markets, then the railroads were in a much weaker bargaining position in regard to rates (though they continued to make trouble on this score). Despite the initial expense, then, the new fleets of refrigerator cars developed by Swift and Armour gave these corporations even more tools with which to control prices and increase profits.

Lowering costs as a percentage of revenue (for example, by developing markets for meat by-products and cheaper cuts such as bologna) and using vertical integration (the major packers secured dedicated ice supply operations and built their own eastern distribution and sales network) allowed the Big Four, by the 1880s, to significantly undercut their fresh meat competitors on the retail price of beef in the East Coast market (Cronon 1991). Of course, Armour and Swift both offered high-end cuts and corn-fed beef, but they understood that it was good business to offer attractively packaged meats for the economy market as well. Though the eight cents per pound charged for fresh beef in, say, a Boston butchery in 1885 versus the five or six cents for dressed-beef at a shop down the street might not seem like such a large differential, the savings added up for a working-class family that might very well be living on less than a dollar a day in late nineteenth-century America.

Since those cost savings would not have been possible without the dressed-meat industry and it, in turn, would not have developed without the refrigerated railcar, this innovation belongs with Whitney's gin and McCormick's reaper as a transformative technology in American agriculture. "The invention of the refrigerator car," one historian declared, "revolutionized the entire industry and made it possible to place in the world's markets fresh dressed meats prepared at points thousands of miles distant" (Hill 1923). In the process, "Chicago became the meat packing center of the world," and the Chicago industry was ruled by the Big Four. Even the meatpacking scandals and antimonopoly sentiment of the Progressive Reform Era—magnified as they were by the popularity of novelist Upton Sinclair's scathing critique of the Chicago industry in *The Jungle* (1906)—did not dislodge Armour, Swift, and later entrant Cudahy from their dominant position in the dressed-meat industry.

By the 1930s, however, the Chicago meatpacking industry was in steep decline, and by the 1960s, the "major packers" such as Armour and Swift had abandoned the Windy City (Cronon 1991). What happened? The expanded use of trucks certainly played a role in weakening Chicago's dominance, as such a mobile transportation medium partially negated one of the important competitive factors in the city's favor, its rail connections. But even before the advent of the trucking industry—which, after all, could be utilized by Armour and Swift as well—Chicago packers had begun decamping from the city, ironically pursuing some of the same business logic that created the Chicago industry in the first place. Thus, if it had originally been more cost efficient and thus more profitable to pack dressed meat in Chicago rather than shipping the entire animal to the East Coast to be butchered there, then why ship the steer from the western range country in the first place? Why not develop packing plants even closer to the supplier in places such as Kansas City, Omaha, or Wichita instead? This is, in fact, what Swift and others began doing even before the turn of the twentieth century (Cronon 1991).

The move westward also impacted the refrigerated railcar, for, besides servicing these new packing facilities in the Great Plains, the Armour and Swift companies found they could utilize their cold-storage fleets for all manner of other shipping, including transporting fresh fruits and vegetables from the "harvest empire" of California to markets all over the country (via Chicago, of course). In fact, Swift's refrigerator car line eventually came to be called the California Fruit Transportation Company, and Armour's became the Continental Fruit Express (O'Connell 1970).

Some California fruit had been marketed in the East before the advent of refrigerated cars, and 300 tons went eastward during the first season after the driving of the golden spike in Utah (1869) opened transcontinental rail service. By the turn of the twentieth century, however, the volume of produce heading east from the rich fields of the harvest empire had increased exponentially, with California producing over 20 percent of the nation's fruit in 1899, including almost 90 percent of the nation's citrus harvest. Without the advent of cheaper refrigerator car service to eastern markets, this growth would have been impossible, as transportation costs were a key factor in determining profit or loss for all manner of "exports" from the West Coast, in particular, of course, perishable commodities.

The "Search for Genes"

Equally important to California's success and indeed to the global ascendancy of U.S. agriculture throughout the twentieth century was the country's massive investment in agricultural research and innovation (both technological and biological), in particular the introduction and domestic development of foreign plant species (either as new crops or as genetic material to "improve" existing crops) by the U.S. Department of Agriculture (USDA) and its Office of Seed and Plant Introduction (SPI). According to a 1937 history of the SPI, "practically all" of the "seventy-eight principal field, fruit and nut, and truck crops" grown in the United States that year "had their beginning in this country in small quantities of seed or propagating material obtained in plant explorations of the Department, by trained specialists searching the four corners of the earth" (Jones 2004). Incorporated in those figures were commodities such as soybeans, durum wheats, and Acala cotton that had been almost unknown as commercial crops in the United States at the turn of the twentieth century.

The SPI's primary task was, in fact, to offset a peculiarity of North American agriculture. Nature did not bless the geographic area now comprising Canada and the United States with many marketable crops (in the modern context), sunflowers and cranberries being the chief exceptions. Even corn, a Native American staple, likely originated south of the Rio Grande. Of course, Anglo-European immigrants brought with them to North America a full panoply of traditional European grains, fruits, and livestock (as well as South American natives such as potatoes), most of which thrived in the temperate regions of the eastern United States. But when U.S. farmers moved out onto the short-grass prairies of the Great Plains in the mid-nineteenth century and especially when they ventured into the arid regions of the Southwest and Southern California a few decades later, they found that yields for their traditional crops declined precipitously (or harvests failed completely) in the extreme temperatures (from the over 100-degree heat of the Southwest to the subzero winters of the Great Plains) and the spotty or almost nonexistent rainfall of these western areas.

Only by introducing new crops from similar regions in other parts of the world—for example, durum wheats from the cold steppes of Russia and the Ukraine—or hardier varieties of traditional crops could U.S. farmers hope to thrive in these harsh environments. Much of that introduction was undertaken by private groups in the nineteenth century, among them the Russian Mennonites who brought their own hard-winter wheats with them to the Great Plains (Klose 1950). Such a piecemeal approach, however, could not address the monumental difficulties confronted by new western farmers, particularly when the country as a whole began to worry that with the close of the frontier in the 1890s, the "world's breadbasket" might actually have to look abroad for some of its food supply in future decades. Moreover, the traditional agricultural species themselves, both scientists and farmers agreed, needed to be supplemented by entirely new crop regimes for the near-desert regions of the Southwest or the semitropical climes of south Florida, not to mention the large swaths of tropical territory—the Philippines, Puerto Rico, Hawaii, and the Panama Canal Zone—brought under national control through imperial expansion at the turn of the twentieth century.

Organized between 1897 and 1898, the SPI endeavored to satisfy all of these demands, and in large part, it succeeded. That 1937 list, for example, included several fruit varieties—avocados, figs, dates, and citrus—secured through SPI efforts (though private concerns played a significant role as well). Thus, Wilson Popenoe, the SPI's principal avocado explorer, spent over five years (from 1916 to 1921) combing—by muleback, horseback, and on foot—the prime avocado regions of Central and South America as well as the Caribbean to secure germplasm (the parts of a plant—seeds, scions, cuttings—from which the organism could be fully reproduced) of all the best avocado varieties; they would be used by scientists and growers in the United States, mainly in California and a handful of other southwestern states, as well as in Florida (where the Caribbean types thrived). In 1934, California avocado growers acknowledged that the USDA and the SPI were "largely responsible for the development of the avocado industry in this country," an industry that covered over "10,000 acres in California" alone (in 1931) and accounted for over a million dollars of revenue by the latter part of the decade (Rosengarten 1991; Jones 2004). Meanwhile, nurturing the country's date industry required a similar investment and commitment on the part of the SPI, which sent several major explorations to secure the best date "suckers" (a duplicate of the "mother" tree that sprouts at the base) from local growers in oases dotted all over North Africa, the Near East, and the Middle East.

Some of these plant introductions followed a straight path from their place of origin directly into the crop mix of American farmers, spending only a brief period of propagation, observation, and/or quarantine at one of the SPI's six plant introduction gardens—"Ellis Islands," in office terminology—spaced around the country. Consequently, the durum wheats collected by agronomist Mark Carleton at the SPI's behest were already transforming grain growing in western Minnesota and the Dakotas less than five years after he gathered them on the steppes of Russia (Isern 2000). Not long thereafter, several of the thousands of SPI soybean "accessions" (the formal name for varieties secured by the office) were making their way into the crop schedules of farmers in the upper Midwest (particularly Illinois), where they would become the foundation of an entirely new crop industry by World War II (Hymowitz and Bernard 1991). Meanwhile, those California navel oranges rocking their way across the plains by the millions each year traced their genetic roots directly to one tree in Bahia, Brazil, parts of which had been sent to the USDA in 1873 and then transferred to an interested grower in Southern California (Klose 1950; Sackman 1995).

More commonly, however, plant introductions had to undergo years of propagation, testing, and crossbreeding before they entered into commercial agriculture. In fact, after the turn of the century, the search for plants increasingly became more of a search for specific, genetically encoded traits—resistance to drought or particular insects, early ripening, better color, and so on—that could subsequently be bred into existing grain or fruit crops to offset the attacks of pests and diseases; extend the growing range of valuable crops such as wheat, cotton, and soybeans; or even improve the marketability of a particular fruit, such as the navel orange or the Chinese persimmon. This "search for genes," which often meant the worldwide collection of a wide array of both cultivated varieties and their wild relatives, was predicated on the assumption that the needed characteristics could be successfully isolated and transferred into existing varieties (Kloppenburg 1988).

Though the human-manipulated breeding of plants and livestock had been a staple of settled agriculture since the ancient era, it was not until the emergence of modern genetics and especially the "rediscovery" of Mendelian laws of inheritance around 1900 that scientists began to exert control over the process. It would take several decades more before commercial agriculture began to reap the benefits of that scientific work, for example, with the arrival of high-yielding "hybrid" corn in the 1920s (Rosenberg 1976; Danbom 1995; Fitzgerald 1990). Thereafter, as the genetic revolution spread into almost every corner of national and eventually global agriculture, the demand for genes to "feed the machine" grew as well, making the work of plant explorers more important than ever (Danbom 1995; Kloppenburg 1988).

Yet the adoption of these "modern" crops came accompanied with—in fact, almost necessitated—a whole host of other innovations; herbicides and pesticides to protect valuable monocrop systems (large geographic areas planted to only one plant variety) from natural threats; and a range of specialized equipment to plant, irrigate, cultivate, harvest, store, and transport the increased bounty. All of these inputs consumed vast amounts of money and energy (particularly petroleum), making the modernization of farming in the twentieth century an expensive, often environmentally destructive, and therefore extremely controversial transition (Kloppenburg 1988). International debates over gene-manipulated agriculture (GMA) at the turn of the twenty-first century suggested the controversy would not end soon. But whatever direction national and global agriculture takes in the new millennium, innovation and invention will undoubtedly still be driving the process.

Sources

Aiken, Charles S. 1973. "The Evolution of Cotton Ginning in the Southeastern United States." *Geographical Review* 63, no. 2 (April): 196–224.

Benedict, Murray R. 1953. *Farm Policies of the United States, 1790–1950: A Study of Their Origins and Development.* New York: Twentieth Century Fund.

Carstensen, Fred V. 1996. "Review of Esko Heikkonen, *Reaping the Bounty: McCormick Harvesting Machine Company Turns Abroad, 1878–1902.*" *Business History Review* 70, no. 3 (Autumn): 412–414.

Casson, Herbert Newton. 1909. *Cyrus Hall McCormick: His Life and Work.* Chicago: A. C. McClurg.

Cooper, Carolyn C. 2003. "Myth, Rumor, and History: The Yankee Whittling Boy as Hero and Villain." *Technology and Culture* 44, no. 1 (January): 82–96.

Cronon, William. 1991. *Nature's Metropolis: Chicago and the Great West.* New York: W. W. Norton.

Danbom, David B. 1995. *Born in the Country: A History of Rural America.* Baltimore, MD: Johns Hopkins University Press.

Danhof, Clarence H. 1969. *Changes in Agriculture in the Northern United States, 1820–1870.* Cambridge, MA: Harvard University Press.

Federico, P. J. 1960. "Records of Eli Whitney's Cotton Gin Patent." *Technology and Culture* 1, no. 2 (Spring): 168–176.

Fite, Gilbert C. 1966. *The Farmers' Frontier: 1865–1900.* New York: Holt, Rinehart and Winston.

Fitzgerald, Deborah. 1990. *The Business of Breeding: Hybrid Corn in Illinois, 1890–1940.* Ithaca, NY: Cornell University Press.

———. 2003. *Every Farm a Factory: The Industrial Ideal in American Agriculture.* New Haven, CT: Yale University Press.

Gates, Paul W. 1960. *The Farmer's Age: Agriculture, 1815–1860.* Vol. 3 of *The Economic History of the United States.* New York: Holt, Rinehart and Winston.

Gray, L. C. 1933. *History of Agriculture in the Southern United States.* Vol. 2. Washington, DC: Carnegie Institution of Washington.

Hammond, M. C. 1897. "Correspondence of Eli Whitney Relative to the Invention of the Cotton Gin." *American Historical Review* 3, no. 1 (October): 90–127.

Hill, Howard Copeland. 1923. "The Development of Chicago as a Center of the Meat Packing Industry." *Mississippi Valley Historical Review* 10, no. 3 (December): 253–273.

Hughes, Jonathan. 1987. *American Economic History.* 2nd ed. Glenview, IL: Scott, Foresman.

Hutchinson, William T. 1930. *Cyrus Hall McCormick: Seed-Time, 1809–1856.* New York: Century.

———. 1935. *Cyrus Hall McCormick: Harvest, 1856–1884.* New York: D. Appleton-Century.

Hymowitz, Theodore, and R. L. Bernard. 1991. "Origin of the Soybean and Germplasm Introduction and Development in North America." In *Use of Plant Introductions in Cultivar Development, Part I.* Crop Science Society of American Special Publication, no. 17. Madison, WI: CSSA.

Isern, Thomas. 2000. "Wheat Explorer the World Over: Mark Carleton of Kansas." *Kansas History* 23 (Spring–Summer): 12–25.

James, James Alton. 1931. "Review of William T. Hutchinson, *Cyrus Hall McCormick: Seed-Time, 1809–1856.*" *Mississippi Valley Historical Review* 17, no. 4 (March): 630–631.

Jefferson, Thomas. *Notes on the State of Virginia.* Philadelphia: Printed for Mathew Carey, November 12, 1794.

Jones, Jeffrey Jacob. 2004. "The World Was Our Garden: U.S. Plant Introduction, Empire, and Industrial Agri(culture), 1898–1948." Ph.D. diss., Purdue University.

Kloppenburg, Jack Ralph, Jr. 1988. *First the Seed: The Political Economy of Plant Biotechnology, 1492–2000.* Cambridge: Cambridge University Press.

Klose, Nelson. 1950. *America's Crop Heritage: The History of Foreign Plant Introduction by the Federal Government.* Ames: Iowa State College Press.

Kujovich, Mary Yeagar. 1970. "The Refrigerator Car and the Growth of the American Dressed Beef Industry." *Business History Review* 44, no. 4 (Winter): 460–482.

Lerner, Eugene M. 1956. "Investment Uncertainty during the Civil War—A Note on the McCormick Brothers." *Journal of Economic History* 16, no. 1 (March): 34–40.

McGreen, Constance. 1956. *Eli Whitney and the Birth of American Technology.* Boston: Little, Brown.

Mirsky, Jeannette, and Allan Nevins. 1952. *The World of Eli Whitney.* New York: Macmillan.

Mitman, Carl W. "Eli Whitney, 1765–1825." *Dictionary of American Biography.* American Council of Learned Societies, 1928–1936.

O'Connell, William E., Jr. 1970. "The Development of the Private Railroad Freight Car, 1830–1966." *Business History Review* 44, no. 2 (Summer): 190–209.

Olmstead, Alan L. 1975. "The Mechanization of Reaping and Mowing in American Agriculture, 1833–1870." *Journal of Economic History* 35, no. 2 (June): 327–352.

Page, Brian, and Richard Walker. 1991. "From Settlement to Fordism: The Agro-Industrial Revolution in the American Midwest." *Economic Geography* 67, no. 4 (October): 281–315.

Rasmussen, Wayne D. 1977. "The Mechanization of American Agriculture." In *Agricultural Literature: Proud Heritage—Future Promise, a Bicentennial Symposium, September 24–26, 1975,* edited by Alan Fusonie and Leila Moran. Washington, DC: Associates of the National Agricultural Library and Graduate School Press, U.S. Department of Agriculture.

Report of the Industrial Commission on Agriculture and Agricultural Labor. 1901. Vol. 10. Washington, DC: Government Printing Office.

Rogin, Leo. 1931. *The Introduction of Farm Machinery in Relation to the Productivity of Labor in the Agriculture of the United States during the Nineteenth Century.* Berkeley: University of California Press.

Rosenberg, Charles E. 1976. *No Other Gods: On Science and American Social Thought.* Baltimore, MD: Johns Hopkins University Press.

Rosenberg, Nathan. 1972. *Technology and American Economic Growth.* New York: Harper and Row.

Rosengarten, Frederic, Jr. 1991. *Wilson Popenoe: Agricultural Explorer, Educator, and Friend of Latin America.* Lawaii, Kauai, HI: National Tropical Botanical Garden.

Sackman, Douglas Cazaux. 1995. "By Their Fruits Ye Shall Know Them: 'Nature Cross Culture by Hybridization' and the California Citrus Industry, 1893–1939." *California History* 74 (Spring): 83–99.

Sandburg, Carl. 1916. *Chicago Poems.* New York: Henry Holt.

Scarborough, William K. 1994. "The Cotton Gin and Its Bittersweet Harvest." *Journal of American History* 81, no. 3 (December): 1238–1243.

Shalhope, Robert E. 1988. "Agriculture." In *Thomas Jefferson: A Reference Biography,* edited by Merrill D. Peterson. New York: Charles Scribner's Sons.

Skaggs, Jimmy M. 1986. *Prime Cut: Livestock Raising and Meatpacking in the United States, 1607–1983.* College Station: Texas A&M University Press.

Wayne, Michael. 1990. *The Reshaping of Plantation Society: The Natchez District, 1860–80.* Urbana: University of Illinois Press.

Webb, Walter Prescott. 1981 [1931]. *The Great Plains.* Lincoln: University of Nebraska Press.

White, John H., Jr. 1990. "Riding in Style: Palace Cars for the Cattle Trade." *Technology and Culture* 31, no. 2 (April): 265–270.

Major Entrepreneurs and Companies

Leigh Kimmel

In the early years of the Industrial Revolution in America, improvements in technology were slow and incremental. From hoe to scratch plow to moldboard plow, from wooden plowshare to iron to self-scouring steel, the changes unfolded over the space of decades. Farmers continued to live by the biblical injunction to eat by the sweat of one's brow, for the work of cultivating the soil required enormous muscular effort from human and beast alike. These limitations imposed seemingly intractable limits on a farmer's productivity. But in the nineteenth and early twentieth centuries, a host of entrepreneurs and inventors changed the landscape of American farming forever, introducing new machines, processes, and business models that lifted the United States to a place of worldwide agricultural hegemony.

From Horses to Horsepower

The invention of the steam engine created a new and vastly superior power source for farmers. The steam engine was utilized for transportation, mining, and other industrial applications, and it was only a matter of time before enterprising inventors would consider the possibility of applying this technology to America's farmlands.

However, major problems remained to be solved before a practical agricultural engine could be produced. Early steam engines were heavy behemoths that required the constant attention of a skilled operator. Due to the low quality of materials and machining in that period, the engines were prone to boiler explosions, which killed and maimed. Furthermore, they were expensive, in a time when most farmers possessed limited capital to invest in cutting-edge technology that had yet to prove itself.

One of the first agricultural processes to undergo mechanization was threshing, the process of separating wheat or other cereal grains from their stalks and associated structures. The first mechanical threshing machines replaced millennia-old techniques of beating with flails and treading by oxen, but they still depended on animal power for their operation. The two most common means of transferring the motion of the horses' legs to the working parts of the threshing machine were the treadmill, in which the horses walked on a moving belt, and the sweep, which resembled a carousel in which the horses walked around in a circle. Both of these methods required reliable horses with a steady pace, since any change in the speed of their walk would result in poor threshing efficiency and lost grain.

Because threshing machines were so expensive, very few farmers could purchase them on their own. Most had to pool their resources with a number of their neighbors and purchase a single thresher that would be owned and operated cooperatively. Since it was necessary to move the shared threshing machine from farm to farm, a stationary steam engine set on a foundation, such as those used in operating mine pumps, would not be suitable, and the sheer size and weight of the steam engine made the use of horses for locomotion impractical. In recognition of these factors, the first steam traction engines were fitted with wooden wheels not dissimilar to those on horse-drawn wagons, but even the strongest wood splintered and broke under the weight. This situation forced manufacturers to switch to steel wheels with broad rims that would be less likely to tear ruts in roads or the soft surfaces of barnyards and threshing fields.

When discussing the use of powered machinery in agriculture, particularly in the steam era, it is important to distinguish between traction engines and actual tractors. Although the traction engine was able to move under its own power and often towed a burden, such as a threshing machine or a wagon being transported on the road, it was not suitable for use in the field. Rather, its primary function was as a

Innovations such as this J. I. Case steam-powered threshing machine rapidly changed the character of American farming. (Library of Congress)

transportable power source for stationary tasks such as threshing. The ability to do field work was the mark of the true tractor. However, to complicate the distinction, many companies of the nineteenth century produced both steam traction engines and true steam tractors. In some cases, the distinction was further blurred when farmers adapted smaller steam traction engines to pull plows or used the larger tractors as stationary power sources between field work seasons.

Many of the first companies to build steam traction engines for agricultural use, such as Rumely and J. I. Case, were established manufacturers of other kinds of implements, such as threshing machines. They often saw steam engines as a complementary line of products relative to their existing offerings. Other early traction engine manufacturers, such as Allis-Chalmers, were industrial equipment manufacturers who were already producing steam engines for industrial applications and saw agricultural steam traction as a potentially lucrative new market.

However, steam had major limitations for agricultural applications. Building up a sufficient head of steam to do useful work required time, and during the warm-up period, the person tending the steam engine was not available for other farm chores. And operating a steam engine generally required at least two people, one to drive and one to stoke the fire. All these operating costs, in addition to the large initial outlay for the machine itself, meant that a steam traction engine could be economical only on the largest of operations.

As a result, by the turn of the twentieth century, there was intense interest in developing internal combustion engines for the agricultural market. Internal combustion might make it possible to develop a machine that could be operated by a single person, as well as a lighter, more responsive engine that would be suitable for a variety of applications. Developing a practical internal combustion engine for a tractor was a daunting task, however. Internal combustion required a much higher quality of materials and finer machining tolerances to operate. In addition, the structure of the tractor had to be redesigned. In steam traction engines, the boiler had served as the primary structural element, providing a stable anchor for the rest of the machine's parts. As a result, it was not possible to simply substitute an internal combustion engine for the steam engine. A few early experimenters tried various bolted frames, but these proved unsatisfactory under the operating conditions of field work; often, they literally shook themselves apart. Only when designers turned to steel frames with members running the length of the tractor in place of the steam engine's boiler were they able to produce a machine that would stand up to field work.

Tractor Makers Transform the American Farm

The first decade of the twentieth century was a period of enormous turmoil in the emerging tractor industry. Hundreds of companies formed, produced a few tractors, and disappeared. Many promoters made wild, unsubstantiated claims about the capabilities of their machines. Farmers who purchased those tractors were quickly disappointed, and their negative experiences led many to vow their eternal opposition to the new machines and renewed allegiance to the unglamorous but dependable and familiar beast of burden.

One of the worst offenders in terms of a shoddy product that gave early tractors a bad reputation was D. M. Hartsough's Bull tractor.

Marketed as a small tractor for the small farm, it seemed to be a godsend for farmers who had no use for the 10-ton behemoths other tractor manufacturers were producing. When it was first released in 1913, it sold so well that the manufacturer could not keep up with orders. However, the Bull (sometimes called the Little Bull) was grossly underpowered, with only 5 horsepower at the drawbar, and it had difficulty pulling even a small plow. Worse, its peculiar design, with a single driving wheel directly behind the steering wheel and a smaller outrigger wheel for balance, left the Bull dangerously prone to tipping over, particularly when working a hillside with the driving wheel downslope. Furthermore, the entire gear train was exposed to the elements, which not only gave the tractor a rickety, unfinished look but also made it vulnerable to very rapid wear on the gears and bearings. Under normal usage, most of the models expired after a few months. Within two years, word had gotten around about these issues, and Bull went out of business.

However, not all tractor manufacturers were shysters interested only in milking the farmer for a quick buck. The Rumely Company of LaPorte, Indiana, long known for its high-quality threshing machines and traction engines, recognized that internal combustion was the way of the future. It set out to build a machine that would offer farmers a powerful, reliable, and economical piece of equipment. Because gasoline was still an expensive by-product of the refining process at that time, Rumely settled on kerosene as a fuel. Although kerosene was common and inexpensive, it was more difficult to burn. It required much higher temperatures to vaporize and had a nasty habit of leaking around gaskets to invade the crankcase and dilute the engine oil. Rumely engineers tackled the problem by abandoning any idea of adapting an existing engine. Instead, they designed their engine from the ground up to burn kerosene. Rather than using water or air as a coolant, they used oil, which permitted the engine to reach far higher temperatures and better vaporize the fuel. Rumely consultant John A. Secor designed a special carburetor that mixed water into the kerosene when the engine grew hot, reducing the problem of preignition in a spark engine.

The result of all this careful work was the Rumely OilPull, one of the best of the heavyweight tractors. This handsome machine was painted a dark olive green with brilliant yellow detailing, including pinstriping along its flywheel. Unlike other manufacturers, Rumely eschewed extravagant claims about horsepower, even though the power of its engines compared favorably with most tractors being produced by competitors. The only guarantee that Rumely made about the OilPull was that it had the capacity to burn kerosene at all loads—a promise that was printed under its name on the huge, boxy radiator.

With the success of the original OilPull, Rumely broadened its line to include several models, ranging from the giant Model E, rated at 30 drawbar horsepower and 60 on the belt, to the much smaller W series. However, Rumely stuck too long with the fruits of past success, instead of continuing to innovate. By the Great Depression, the OilPull was clearly outdated, and Allis-Chalmers bought the company primarily to obtain its extensive network of dealerships. The OilPull was discontinued, and the Rumely name was retired. Yet the Rumely OilPull would live on in fond memory, and some survivors have been lovingly restored for display on the antique tractor circuit.

Allis-Chalmers, meanwhile, developed its own innovative line of tractors. One particularly interesting one was the Model 6-12, which had its drive wheels in the front and pivoted in the center, rather like a modern center-articulated four-wheel-drive tractor. Although it was financially successful, its design did not become an industry standard, and it soon disappeared from the market. Center articulation would be redeveloped independently after World War II by several companies, including Wagner, Steiger, and Versatile.

Other Notable Tractor Manufacturers

In 1896, Charles Hart and Charles Parr, both students at the University of Wisconsin, collaborated on a thesis on internal combustion engines. They subsequently decided to put their work into practice, and in 1901, they organized the Hart-Parr Tractor Company, which produced its first gas traction engine the following year. In 1903, Hart and Parr rolled out their first production units. These models were massive in size, similar to the giant steam traction engines that were still chuffing about the rural landscape. Although its governor and ignition elements were mechanically crude, the engine's simple design also made it very reliable. This engine became the foundation of two more sophisticated models. These models marked a shift away from the crude open look sported by the steam traction engines toward a sleeker appearance in which the engine was surrounded by a

A North Dakota farmer hauling grain, using a Hart-Parr tractor, ca. 1911. (F. A. Pazandak Photograph Collection, NDIRS-NDSU, Fargo)

sheet-metal fairing. The company also discarded the term *gas traction engine* as being too cumbersome, describing its offerings instead by the more concise sobriquet of *tractor.*

By 1920, Hart-Parr had merged with three other tractor companies to form the Oliver Corporation. Hart-Parr's big tractors had become outdated, largely because they could not be used for row-crop production. The new Oliver tractor was the company's first row-crop tractor, and it enabled the new corporation to survive and thrive in the next several decades. Oliver's green-and-white paint scheme became a familiar sight on the rural landscape.

Caterpillar was another notable early tractor maker. Today, the Caterpillar name is generally thought of primarily in terms of industrial crawlers such as bulldozers. But its founders were actually interested in developing tracked crawlers for agricultural work as well as for construction and other industrial applications. Caterpillar founders Daniel Best and Ben Holt developed a continuous-track system that reduced soil compaction in soft ground, enabling farmers to work in conditions that were impossible with standard wheeled tractors. In a time when gearing was often tricky, they found that driving each side's tracks separately enabled an operator to steer without a differential. The operator simply stopped one side's tracks while keeping the other side's operating, leading the tractor to turn in the direction of the stopped track. Although they originally started working in California, Best and Holt soon moved to Peoria, Illinois, where they established Caterpillar's corporate headquarters as well as manufacturing plants. They also adopted a distinctive yellow paint scheme, which adorned all of Caterpillar's products, both for agricultural and industrial applications. The success of Caterpillar's crawler tractors prompted other companies to conduct experiments in the field of crawlers. Cletrac was one of the best known and longest lasting, but it eventually was bought out by Oliver, which continued its line of crawlers for a while.

Another early line of tractors was produced by Massey-Harris, a Canadian-based firm that had been formed by the 1891 consolidation of operations maintained by business rivals Daniel Massey and Alanson Harris. Massey-Harris sold some tractors across the border into Wisconsin and the other northern-tier states, but it remained primarily a Canadian company until after World War II, when it underwent a reorganization and consolidation with Henry Ferguson's tractor company to become the Massey-Ferguson Company. From that point forward, the reconstituted company had a much stronger presence in the rural landscape of the United States.

The Minneapolis-Moline Tractor Company owed its existence to the Minneapolis Steel and Machinery Company's decision to enter the tractor business on a contract basis. After developing experience in the business in this way, Minneapolis Steel and Machinery produced its own tractor in 1910 under the name Twin City Oil Tractor. The company's earliest tractors were of the heavyweight style, except for the 1917 Model 16-30, a little machine that looked more like an automobile than a farm tractor. Built low to the ground, it sported a sleek sheet-metal body that was in marked contrast to the open styles then common among tractor manufacturers. Its unusual design failed to make inroads with the tractor-buying public, however, and it was soon abandoned.

In 1919, Minneapolis-Moline unveiled another tractor that featured enclosed gearing to protect it from field dust. This tractor should have been potent competition for popular small tractors such as the Fordson, but it was not priced competitively. However, it was a rock-solid machine, and as a result, it remained in production for the next fifteen years.

In 1929, Minneapolis Steel and Machinery joined forces with Minneapolis Threshing Machine Company and Moline Plow Company to form Minneapolis-Moline. This new venture produced a number of innovative tractors, including models outfitted with rubber tires at a time when most tractor companies were still using lugged steel wheels. It also shifted from the old gray color scheme to a rich yellow one known as Prairie Gold.

One of the most innovative tractors produced by Minneapolis-Moline was the UDLX Comfortractor, which was marketed as the tractor for a family that could not afford both a tractor and an automobile. This odd tractor design featured an assortment of "carlike" features, including a sporty exterior with full fenders and an enclosed cab with a space in the back where the rest of the family could ride. According to the company's promotional material, the Comfortractor would enable a farmer to work the fields in comfort all week long and then take the family to church or the store on Sunday in the same vehicle. However, in a time when farming was still regarded as hard, sweaty work, such luxury was automatically suspect. Many farmers were concerned that their neighbors would think less of them for employing a "sissy" tractor with an enclosed cab. And even if they were not concerned about the opinions of others, many farmers balked at the hefty price tag attached to the UDLX, particularly in a time where the lean years of the Depression were still a painful memory. In the end, only 150 of the vehicles were sold, mostly during World War I when farmers were desperate for any tractor they could get. Because so few were sold and because most farmers got rid of them as soon as new tractors became readily available after the war, UDLXs have become valued collectors' items on the old-tractor circuit. However, the ideas that the designers of the UDLX espoused would ultimately have their day, as concepts of ergonomics and occupational health began to penetrate the farming community, making the "executive-style" enclosed cabs of the later large tractors more socially acceptable.

Minor players in the tractor business included Cockshutt and White, both primarily Canadian companies. Although these firms sold some tractors across the border into the United States, they never had a major presence on the rural landscape in America. In the consolidations that followed World War II, they were both bought out by other companies and reduced to "badge lines," whereby the parent company maintained the characteristic color scheme and insignia of the old brand in order to cash in on customer loyalties.

A Tractor for the Rest of Us

However successful the handsome Rumely OilPull and the other behemoths of the opening decades of the twentieth century might have been, they all had one problem. They were simply too big for all but the largest of farms. Their clumsy steering systems could require as much as an acre just to turn at the end of a row. Although this was not a problem on some of the new giant wheat farms of the Great Plains, it was an insurmountable barrier to their adoption on the smaller farms in the East.

As time passed, however, innovative designs made tractors much more suitable for farmers with smaller landholdings. Henry Ford is best known for his automobiles (particularly the Model T, which put the automobile in reach of the masses), but he also introduced important changes in tractor manufacturing. Born and raised on a farm, he developed a bone-deep dislike for the heavy work that went into farming. His fierce antipathy for farm labor first fueled his determination to find success as an automobile manufacturer and then fed his interest in developing small, practical tractors. His farm background gave him a particular understanding of just what a small farmer needed in a tractor.

Ford recognized early on that the tractor market was wide open. Although the number of tractors in use on American farms had jumped from 1,000 to about 25,000 in the five years between 1910 and 1915, there were still a hundred farmers using draft animals for every farmer using mechanized power. If Ford wanted to completely transform the rural landscape, he needed to be able to manufacture small, inexpensive tractors in the same way he did his Model T—in enormous numbers so that the small profit realized on each unit would add up to a cumulative bonanza (Leffingwell 2000).

Even as early as 1907, Ford had explored the possibility of adapting his car-making capacity to tractor manufacturing. His automobile plow, while primitive and rickety, proved to him that it was possible to apply lessons learned from the automobile business to the development of a practical, efficient, inexpensive tractor for small landholders.

While Ford was perfecting his tractor designs, he lost the right to use his own name on a tractor. In 1915, a Minneapolis, Minnesota, firm, eager to cash in on Ford's enviable reputation in rural communities, hired an unrelated man by the name of P. B. Ford solely to stamp the Ford name on an ill-conceived tractor model it was pitching. This creation was designed to drive with its front wheels and steer with a tiny rear wheel, but it could not possibly function when pulling any kind of load. The rickety device led directly to the establishment of the Nebraska Tractor Test Law, after a Nebraska legislator purchased one to use on his own farm only to have it fail catastrophically on the way home from the dealership. From that point forward, all tractors to be sold in Nebraska had to be tested by the state, and companies could only make those claims that had been substantiated in the official tests.

Unable to apply his own name to a tractor and faced with reluctance from the stockholders in his automobile company, Ford and his son Edsel pooled their own money to create a new company, Ford and Son. The tractor model itself was known as the Fordson, and it was originally produced in Great Britain as a response to the labor shortage created by World War I. In 1917, Ford brought his tractor home, just in time for America's entry into the war. Farmers welcomed this substitute for suddenly scarce able-bodied young men, and nearly 30,000 were sold in 1918. By adapting the mass-production methods he had mastered in the assembly lines of his Model T, Ford was able to keep up with demand quite handily, even while making constant improvements in the tractor's design. For instance, the initial drive system was so powerful that it was prone to tipping backward if the implement it was towing encountered an obstruction; Ford and his designers addressed this flaw by adding long fenders that would catch it before it flipped and crushed its operator.

Ford would continue to be involved in tractor manufacturing as well as the automobile business until his death in 1947. And tractors would continue to be made under the Ford name until the great agricultural consolidations of the 1970s and 1980s, during which time the Ford tractor line was subsumed into the New Holland line of farm machinery.

The success of the Fordson was a powerful wake-up call for established agricultural companies. Giant tractors might be welcome for a few specialized, power-intensive applications such as threshing and sod busting, but the real market lay in small, maneuverable machines that even small farmers could afford. Such farmers could not make a major capital outlay to buy a machine only suitable for plowing and still retain horses for row-crop cultivation; tractors had to become capable of working between the rows of growing crops. Simply downsizing existing medium-range tractors was not sufficient.

The International Harvester Company (IHC) was one of the first to respond to the shifting agricultural landscape, rolling out the Farmall tractor in 1924. IHC had a long pedigree in farm machinery, having been produced from the merger of the company Cyrus McCormick had created to manufacture his mechanical reapers before the Civil War. In fact, several versions of the Farmall carried the McCormick name rather than the International Harvester name. The arrival of the Farmall marked the first significant threat to the Fordson's status as the undisputed king of American tractors. A spirited "tractor war" ensued during the second half of the 1920s. The competition ultimately led Ford to cease tractor production at his massive River Rouge factory in Detroit; instead, he gave the River Rouge plant entirely over to automobile manufacture and moved all agricultural manufacturing operations overseas to his factory in county Cork, Ireland.

IHC had just established a position of preeminence in the marketplace when new competitors emerged. These included Case, an old name in the steam traction engine and big-tractor market that rolled out the Model CC in 1930. John Deere, the eponymous corporation originally founded by the inventor of the Prairie Queen self-scouring steel plow, came out with their Johnny Popper around the same time. This small tractor was named for the "pop-pop" sound made by its two-cylinder engine as it fired on every other stroke of the four-stroke Otto cycle.

The 1930s were also shadowed by the Dust Bowl and the Great Depression, which made it difficult for farmers to make major capital outlays such as purchases of new farm equipment. Trapped between sinking grain prices and high interest on loans they had taken out during the boom times of the twenties, many farmers went out of business altogether. In turn, many manufacturers of farm equipment also were forced to close their doors, for lack of customers. During the White House years of Franklin D. Roosevelt, various programs to stabilize and rebuild the agricultural economy were introduced. These measures helped, but it was really only World War II that turned around the dire financial situation of farmers. With large numbers of workers being diverted to the war effort—both directly as soldiers and indirectly in industries producing airplanes, tanks, clothing, and other equipment—farming became yet another essential home-front occupation.

A New Age of Fertilizers and Pesticides

Although the application of steam and internal combustion power to farming was the most obvious change wrought on agriculture by the Industrial Revolution, developments in other areas of farming were profoundly influential as well. By the last decades of the nineteenth century, scientists were making a rapid succession of discoveries about chemical processes and how they related to living things. The development of the industrial research laboratory—in which the scientific method was systematically applied to practical problems with an eye toward producing a marketable product—made possible the vast expansion of the range of products a chemical company could offer.

Among these chemicals were artificial fertilizers to increase crop yields and various herbicides and insecticides for controlling pests that have been the bane of farmers since time immemorial. One of the foremost companies to enter the agrochemical business was Monsanto, founded by **John F. Queeny,** a midwestern businessman with a peculiar vision of the future. Born in Chicago on August 17, 1859, he was the eldest of the five children of John and Sarah (Flaherty) Queeny, Irish immigrants from county Galway. When he was young, his father enjoyed modest success as a businessman, owning several buildings that he rented out, as well as working as a carpenter. As a result, John was able to attend school for six years.

All that changed in 1871 with the Great Chicago Fire, which wiped out his family's entire holdings. Facing these suddenly straitened circumstances, John Queeny left school in order to obtain employment. After several months of wandering the burned-out streets of Chicago, he finally secured a job as an office boy for Tolman and King, a druggist. With diligent application to his duties, he soon rose to the position of delivery boy. From there, he worked his way up through successively more responsible positions in a number of drug companies until he became sales manager for Merck and Company in 1894.

Queeny's career path put him in contact with an industry that dealt with industrial organic chemistry. At the same time, he made an important personal contact in the person of his wife, Olga Mendez Monsanto, a Spanish immigrant with an astonishingly aristocratic background. By 1899, Queeny was in St. Louis working for Meyer Brothers, but he also was thinking of starting his own business. His first attempt, a sulfur refinery, proved a disaster, burning to the ground while still uninsured and losing him his entire $6,000 investment (a substantial sum at the time). However, he was not the sort of man to allow one failure to define his life—and he had access to additional start-up capital from his wealthy wife.

In 1901, Queeny launched the Monsanto Chemical Works, whose primary product was an artificial sweetener known as saccharine. It has been speculated that he used his wife's maiden name for his company in part because of the financial aid she provided him but also for more pragmatic reasons. Queeny was still employed by Meyer Brothers when he opened Monsanto's doors, and he had actually obtained the formula and manufacturing techniques for saccharine from his employer. To have used his own name for the new company almost certainly would have drawn unwelcome scrutiny to his activities.

In any case, the Monsanto company soon proved a success, and before long, it was able to expand beyond its initial offerings to produce a wide variety of pharmaceutical chemicals. During that time, Queeny successfully battled the Dye Trust, a group of organic chemical manufacturers who sought to shut out upstarts by reducing the price of the chemicals those companies were producing until the smaller rivals could no longer compete.

World War I, however, led to a significant change in the way nitrogen compounds were produced. Previously, most of those compounds were derived from manure—in particular, the vast supplies of bird dung that were found in South America. In addition to being used as fertilizer, they were vital components in the manufacture of explosives. When the Royal Navy assumed dominion over the seas during World War I, it was able to prevent Germany from importing South American bird dung. As a consequence, German leaders came to the realization that they might lose the war simply because they could not manufacture enough bullets for their military.

Enter Fritz Haber, a German organic chemist who discovered industrial processes to transform gaseous nitrogen into useful compounds for explosives. Since Germany was at war at the time, the first practical purpose to which the Haber Process was put was the production of explosives. However, after the war was concluded, chemists discovered that these nitrogen compounds formed a wonderful sort of "artificial manure." The artificial nitrogen compound had several advantages over natural manure. It lacked the unpleasant odor of the real thing. It did not attract flies and other noxious insects. It contained none of the weed seeds that often survived intact after passing through an animal's digestive system. Finally, it was easier to handle and could be made to a predictable strength, so a farmer could know exactly how much was being applied, rather than applying natural manure that could vary greatly in potency depending on the health and diet of the animals generating the manure.

Monsanto already had an established practice of obtaining chemical techniques from Germany and adapting them to American manufacture. Moving from pharmaceuticals to the production of nitrogen for fertilizer was not that huge of a step, and soon Monsanto was one of the principal producers of nitrogen fertilizer.

John F. Queeny retired as head of Monsanto in 1928, succeeded by his son Edgar. Suffering from cancer of the tongue, he left for England to acquire another company and run it for two years. In 1931, he returned to St. Louis, ravaged by his illness and so weak he could barely function. He died on March 19, 1933, just as events in Nazi Germany were moving the country and the world as a whole on a track that would lead to a second world war. During the war itself, the Monsanto company played an important role in keeping America's war machine functioning. In addition to the obvious contributions of nitrogen-based ordnance and of pharmaceuticals to treat the wounded, it also produced fertilizers that enabled American farmers to maintain their yields and keep the armed forces fed even in the face of critical labor shortages.

Another major chemical company that had a substantial role in the agrochemical business was Dow, founded in 1897 by Herbert Dow. The founder got his start with a method to extract bromine from salt by using electricity, and his firm soon expanded into numerous other lines of chemicals, including fertilizers, herbicides, and other agrochemicals. DuPont was yet another prominent agrochemical manufacturer in the early years. Originally founded in 1802 by French immigrants to make gunpowder for the U.S. military, it—like Dow—used its success in agrochemicals as a launching pad to become one of America's leading chemical companies in the early twenty-first century.

Butcher to the World

The Industrial Revolution also transformed the system by which food moved from farm to consumer, in two major ways. The first transformation was brought about by the railroads, which made it possible to transport livestock and other foodstuffs over long distances and in high volume at prices that were economical for the ordinary consumer. Suddenly, it became possible to feed a large population with food generated hundreds of miles away. Indirectly, that transformation was driven by the development of the very industrial technology base that made those railroads possible. The modern factory system of manufacture, employing thousands of people per enterprise, led to the development of far larger urban populations than had ever been seen before. Only by drawing on a much larger area of agricultural lands could such huge cities be fed.

The second transformation resulted from a commercial restructuring that separated producer from consumer with a thick layer of middlemen. No longer did farmers cart their produce into the city market and sell directly to the housewives who would convert that produce into meals. Instead, farmers sold their crops to large companies that processed and packaged foods for end distribution.

One of the pioneers of this transformation was the Jacob Dold Packing Company, formed by a German immigrant who settled in Buffalo, New York. Although he started with a rather typical butcher shop of his time, Dold gradually developed a large slaughterhouse operation that sold to multiple butcher shops. Other companies of the period that expanded beyond the single small butcher shop included Cordukes, Sinclair, and Kingan, all founded by Irish immigrants, and the American meat market operator John Plankington.

However, one of the first of the true meatpacking giants was the company created by **Philip D. Armour.** Armour was born on May 16, 1832, in a Scottish-Irish Presbyterian family on a farm near Stockbridge, New York. Twenty years later, he decided to seek his fortune in the California gold rush. Setting out on foot in the company of three other men, he was the only one to make it to the West Coast. However, by the time he arrived in California, all of the most promising land had been claimed, and he realized that trying to strike a rich node for himself was a risky gamble. Instead, he developed a scheme to dig ditches to run the sluices of men who had located good

Philip Armour, pioneer of
the American meatpacking
industry. (Circer, Hayward,
ed., *Dictionary of American
Portraits*, 1967)

gold beds but lacked adequate water. After a brief period of doing the work on a day labor basis, he soon set up a contract system and hired other men to do the actual work of digging. Within five years, he had accumulated a substantial sum, sufficient to return to New York with the intention of becoming a merchant.

On the way back east, Armour stopped in Milwaukee, Wisconsin, where he met John Plankington and became a junior partner in his meatpacking business. Both were ambitious men, and they steadily expanded their business until they had developed a complex of slaughterhouses covering 9 acres and capable of handling as many as 7,000 hogs per day. In addition, they established branch slaughter-houses in Chicago and Kansas City, the latter devoted entirely to beef packing. Armour concentrated on the merchandising side of the business. Paying careful attention to the development of military contracts during the Civil War, he was able to both garner capital for the further expansion of the business and amass a sizable personal fortune.

By the close of the Civil War, Armour had also established a Chicago-based grain commission business, in partnership with his

Men work side by side on the hog-scraping rail in Armour's meat-packing plant in Chicago, ca. 1909. (Library of Congress)

brothers. A short time later, he decided that it was time for Armour and Company to expand into the Chicago meatpacking business. In 1865, the Armour brothers established the Union Stock Yards and began slaughtering hogs under that name. By 1868, they had expanded their operation to handle cattle and sheep as well, and they were developing means to ship meat and meat products from the slaughterhouses to rapidly growing industrial cities all over the eastern part of the United States.

These efforts had potentially enormous commercial potential. Traditional methods of preserving meat for storage and shipping had included drying and salting, but they were both susceptible to spoilage. The nearly inedible salt beef that formed a substantial portion of the nineteenth-century soldier's and sailor's diet was the source of an entire genre of morbid jokes and anecdotes. Canning, the method by which meat and other products could be sealed into metal or glass containers at high heat and stored indefinitely at room temperature, was just being developed in the second half of the nineteenth century, and it was not without problems. The heat involved in the process often induced undesirable changes in the flavor and consistency of foods, and there were several incidences of disastrous heavy-metal poisoning as a result of some of the substances used in the containers and their seals.

In northern climates, it was common for hunters and farmers to take advantage of winter's cold to preserve carcasses that could not be consumed immediately. People who wished to take advantage of winter's chill year-round developed icehouses, in which blocks of ice cut from northern lakes were stored in bulk. Properly handled, an icehouse full of blocks could last throughout the summer and well into the fall, providing a steady supply of ice that could be used to chill food. In cities, one could receive twice-weekly deliveries of ice from an iceman, who had an established route. One of the most common uses of ice by the second half of the nineteenth century was in the icebox, a precursor of the refrigerator; essentially, it was an insulated box in which one could put perishable foods alongside a block of ice.

However, this natural means of refrigeration had several drawbacks. There was no way to precisely control the temperature of an icebox. As the ice melted, it was necessary to empty the meltwater from the drip pan and add fresh ice. Finally, the supply of ice was heavily dependent on the weather. An unusually warm winter would mean that lakes would not freeze well enough for ice blocks to be harvested. An unusually hot summer could overheat the icehouses, leading to premature melting of the stored ice.

These shortcomings prompted Armour and other meatpackers to take great interest in scientific developments in artificial refrigeration systems. They recognized that if efficient refrigeration systems could be developed in railcars and households, the market for their perishable beef and pork products would see an exponential increase. The earliest refrigeration systems were huge and suitable only for very large installations, such as refrigerated warehouses. However, with the development of better refrigerant chemicals, it became possible to steadily reduce the size of the machinery to the point that refrigerators could become household appliances and could be mounted on

The New Cool Way

The greatest beneficiaries of refrigeration technology were the cattlemen and meatpackers of the West. However, the benefits of this method of food transportation also became obvious to other agricultural products industries, particularly the fruit and vegetable industry. Suddenly able to transport fresh fruits and vegetables far from their original growing areas, the companies were in a position to tap into much larger markets and thus grow very wealthy.

Unlike the situation with row crops, in which the principal producer was the yeoman farmer and family, ownership in the fruit and vegetable industry tended to be concentrated in the hands of a very few wealthy and powerful individuals. The labor in this industry sector was generally done by impoverished and powerless migrant workers. As a result of this often gross disparity of power, many of the great fruit and vegetable companies began to see themselves as above the law—or even to see themselves *as* the law in the communities in which they operated.

This was especially true with growers of tropical fruits such as pineapples and bananas, which were grown outside the United States

railroad cars to keep foods fresh while they were being shipped from coast to coast. (Refrigeration technology also fed directly into the development of air-conditioning, the branch of engineering that deals with the regulation of humidity and temperature in areas where human activity is present.)

Armour steadily expanded his holdings throughout the second half of the nineteenth century, bringing his brothers and other relatives into his expanding empire in various ways. He even established a bank in Kansas City—Armour Brothers' Bank—under the management of his brother Andrew Watson Armour. By the time Philip D. Armour died in January 1901, his sons and nephews were well trained to take over the complex of companies that he had founded.

The Swift Meatpacking Empire

The major rival to Armour for much of the second half of the nineteenth century was the Swift Company, founded by **Gustavus** and then transported to markets in America in refrigerated ships. Hawaii became the fiftieth state in the Union as the direct result of events set in motion by the Dole Pineapple Company. Unhappy that the indigenous monarchy was interfering with their ability to make unrestrained profits, the American executives of Dole engineered a coup d'état that overthrew the queen and established a republic, with the head of Dole's Hawaii branch as its president. The newly installed president subsequently petitioned the United States to grant Hawaii territorial status. When this petition was granted, Dole and other fruit-growing companies incorporated in the United States were able to operate more freely, enjoying the protections of U.S. laws that strongly favored management.

Source

Anderson, Oscar Edward. 1972. *Refrigeration in America: A History of New Technology and Its Impact.* Port Washington, NY: Kennicat Press.

Franklin Swift. Born on June 24, 1839, Swift was the progeny of English stock who had settled on Cape Cod, Massachusetts, to make a living as farmers. At the tender age of fourteen, he struck out for himself to become an apprentice to the local butcher.

Using every possible opportunity to earn extra money, Swift bought off the remainder of his apprenticeship at the end of a mere four years. (At the time, an apprentice generally signed a contract promising seven years of service in return for being taught the skills of a trade during that period. However, apprentices could often fulfill their contractual obligations early by paying a sum representing the value of the lost years of labor.)

Free of his apprenticeship, Swift soon set up his own butcher shop in Cape Cod. The business prospered, but as time passed, he took increasing note of the problems the local farmers had in selling their stock. Realizing that there was a strong market in Boston, he became involved in the transportation of cattle and hogs to the markets there. This venture proved so lucrative that his butcher shop business became a mere sideline to his work as a cattle dealer. So successful was

Meatpacker Gustavus Swift revolutionized the industry with his embrace of refrigerated transportation and assembly line production techniques. (Library of Congress)

his business that he decided to leave Cape Cod and move to Lancaster, 40 miles north of Boston, in order to be closer to his principal market. Soon, he was handling livestock all over New England, bringing the animals to the Brighton, Massachusetts, stockyards for slaughter. In 1872, he formed a partnership with Henry Hathaway, known locally as a seller of dressed meat. Swift specialized in purchasing livestock, leaving the butchering end of the process to his partner, and he soon expanded into upstate New York, where he sought out new sources of meat for a hungry city.

This expansion led him to turn his attention to Chicago, which was rapidly becoming the Midwest's center of slaughterhouse operations. He bought out Billy Moore's packinghouse and set himself up in direct competition with Armour. He specialized in preparing meat for the eastern markets and became very successful at it. Although Swift was not the inventor of the refrigerated railroad car, he made extensive use of it and was able to greatly expand his dressed-beef business as a result of its skillful application. His meatpacking empire soon made "Swift" a household name.

Other Leading Meatpackers

The third of the great Chicago meatpacking companies of the late nineteenth century was founded by Nelson Morris, an immigrant from Germany's Black Forest area. Morris opened his first packing-house in 1859, specializing in slaughtering cattle. By the time of his death in 1907, his slaughterhouses and meatpacking plant covered 30 acres and handled thousands of cattle, hogs, and sheep on a daily basis. In addition, his company had satellite plants in several other cities and was doing $100 million in business per year.

Although Chicago was generally considered the heart of the meatpacking industry, a strong satellite meatpacking industry was developing in the West, where America's largest cattle herds roamed. In 1887, Michael Cudahy, an Irishman, founded the Cudahy Packing Company in Omaha, Nebraska. Initially, it was a partnership with Philip D. Armour, but within a few years, Cudahy bought out Armour's share in exchange for selling his share of Armour's business in Chicago. He was able to rapidly expand his business, since his only competition came from two rather small packinghouses that sold primarily to the British export market.

Wilson and Company was founded by Thomas E. Wilson after he left his position with Morris and Company. He had been eased out of the presidency of the latter because the elder Nelson Morris wanted his sons to be able to take over the company, and they were getting to be of an age to take on such responsible positions. Wilson took the knowledge and skills that had made him a success as an employee and used them to found his own business. He was particularly skilled at appropriating operations and business strategies that worked for rival companies, as well as identifying locales that were underserved by other meatpacking companies.

Sources

Aldrich, Lisa J. 2002. *Cyrus McCormick and the Mechanical Reaper.* Greensboro, NC: Morgan-Reynolds.

Anderson, Oscar Edward. 1972. *Refrigeration in America: A History of New Technology and Its Impact.* Port Washington, NY: Kennicat Press.

Bak, Richard. 2003. *Henry and Edsel: The Creation of the Ford Empire.* Hoboken, NJ: John Wiley and Sons.

Blandford, Percy W. 1976. *Old Farm Tools and Machinery: An Illustrated History.* Fort Lauderdale, FL: Gale.

Brinkley, Douglas. 2003. *Wheels for the World: Henry Ford, His Company and a Century of Progress.* New York: Viking.

Clemen, Rudolf Alexander. 1923. *The American Livestock and Meat Industry.* New York: Ronald Press.

Dregni, Michael, ed. 1998. *This Old Tractor: A Treasury of Vintage Tractors and Family Farm Memories.* Stillwater, MN: Town Square Books.

Ertl, P. W. 2001. *The American Tractor: A Century of Legendary Machines.* Osceola, WI: MBI Publishing.

Fetherston, David. 1996. *Farm Tractor Advertising in America, 1900–1960.* Osceola, WI: Motorbooks.

Forrestal, Dan J. 1977. *Faith, Hope and $5,000: The Story of Monsanto.* New York: Simon and Schuster.

Gray, R. B. 1975. *The Agricultural Tractor, 1855–1950.* Saint Joseph, MI: American Society of Agricultural Engineers.

Green, Constance. 1956. *Eli Whitney and the Birth of American Technology.* New York: HarperCollins.

Leffingwell, Randy. 2000. *Farm Tractor Milestones.* Osceola, WI: MBI Publishing.

Swift, Louis F. 1927. *The Yankee of the Yards: The Biography of Gustavus Franklin Swift.* Chicago: Shaw.

Swinford, Norm. 2000. *A Century of Ford and New Holland Farm Equipment.* Saint Joseph, MI: American Society of Agricultural Engineers.

Wendel, Charles H. 1988. *The Allis-Chalmers Story.* Sarasota, FL: Crestline Publishing.

Whitehead, Don. 1968. *The Dow Story: The History of the Dow Chemical Company.* New York: McGraw-Hill.

Lives of the Workforce

Laurie Collier Hillstrom

The daily lives of Americans who supported themselves and their families in the fields of farming, ranching, and meat-packing from the colonial era to the early twentieth century could hardly have been more different from one another. American farming was overwhelmingly a family enterprise, an endeavor in which every able-bodied family member contributed as much as possible in accordance with their background and abilities. The ranch hand's life was a similarly hard one, marked by long days of strenuous labor in weather that was often inclement, but in contrast to the farmer's, the life of the cowboy was marked by long periods of solitude. And unlike most Americans who tended crops for a living, employees in the ranching business did not own the land on which they toiled. Thus, they were much more nomadic than American farmers, who more often than not became the sturdy foundation of the thousands of communities that sprouted up across the continent during the nation's inexorable westward expansion. The immigrants who toiled in the slaughterhouses of Cincinnati, Chicago, and Kansas City, meanwhile, struggled in an environment that was both dispiriting and dangerous. To many of these poor workers, even the worst deprivations endured by pioneer farmers cut by the icy winds of the Great Plains and dusty cowboys riding across the baking surface of the Texas panhandle would have been preferable to the drumbeat of blood and slaughter they endured on a daily basis.

The American Farming Family

For much of its history, the dominant entity driving the American agriculture industry has been the family. Family farms formed the backbone of the economy of colonial New England, and as the nation expanded steadily southward and westward, farming families led the way. Indeed, the owner-operated family farm is accurately regarded as the cornerstone of early American society, which was, of course, dependent on agriculture for most of its early economic growth.

But the nuclear family unit of agrarian America was also the primary fountainhead for the dissemination of social values; the passing down of basic reading, writing, and arithmetic skills; the handing down of practical skill sets (which were of premium value in early America, where independence and self-sufficiency were the ultimate goals of most settlers); and the defense of the health and welfare of children. In short, the early American farming family was both a social and an educational institution.

This state of affairs endured long after American farming had strayed beyond the rolling hills of New England to the humid shores of the Gulf Coast, the rich soil of the Great Lakes region, and the wind-swept terrain of the Great Plains. As one historian wrote:

> Rural people brought to new areas strong families, a durable sense of community, and a tradition of neighborliness reinforced by kinship ties. Also buttressing the rural community were churches and schools, institutions that moved with settlers and imparted a sense of familiarity and stability in newly settled areas. . . . The foundation of rural America was the nuclear family. It was the key institution in other rural societies as well, of course, but the American practice of family settlement on individual farmsteads seemed to give it a special centrality here. (Danbom 1995)

The division of labor on American family farms was (and is) largely the same, irrespective of time period and geographic region, with gender playing a determinative role in work assignments. Historians note that early nineteenth-century farming ventures in the Ohio River valley, antebellum plantation operations in the Deep South, wheat-growing farms of the Dakotas, and California orchard outfits at the beginning of the twentieth century all followed patriarchal models of governance.

In all of these cases, the male landowner (or lessee) was understood to be the primary decisionmaker about land acquisitions and divestments, purchases of equipment, crop and livestock selection, prioritization of field work, and allocation of family labor resources (whether offspring, hired hands, or seasonal workers). Women on the farm—usually wives but occasionally sisters, mothers, aunts, or other members of the extended family—often had a voice in these matters, but the ultimate authority and responsibility for these decisions was known to rest with the adult male landowner in the household. Similarly, adult males typically spoke for the family when interacting with the larger community on local economic or political issues.

Male members of the farming family also assumed primary responsibility for the myriad outdoor tasks associated with maintaining a successful agricultural operation. These chores included tending existing fields; clearing land for new cultivation; caring for draft animals; repairing fences and buildings; and hunting, fishing, and trapping for supplementary food and income. Sons typically began helping out in the fields and the barn around age five or so, and by twelve, they were expected to put in the same day's work as their fathers. Not surprisingly, the labor benefits of having strapping young men proved to be a powerful incentive for farming couples to raise large families. After all, these offspring not only attended to the countless tasks associated with running a farm but also typically received no compensation but room and board, which increased net earnings at harvesttime.

The American men who oversaw family farms of the eighteenth and nineteenth centuries were a hardy breed. But scholars assert that few of them could have been successful over the long term were it not for their partnerships with women. Rural women understood that they lived in a patriarchal world in which their economic subordination to men was codified by inheritance statutes, property laws, and other legal strictures. But many pioneer husbands recognized that their spouses' contributions to the success of the family enterprise were essential, and these men certainly considered their wives' perspectives when assessing operational choices on the farm or commenting on community issues (Myres 1982).

The litany of responsibilities shouldered by women (and girls) on American family farms is a formidable one, especially since virtually all of the tasks were meant to either increase the family's economic self-sufficiency or ensure the health and well-being of family members and regular hired hands—who, after all, comprised the farm's workforce. Responsible for the nutritional sustenance of the family, farmwives and their daughters typically milked cows; churned butter; made cheese; collected syrup; made cider; kneaded dough for bread making; collected eggs; slaughtered the occasional barnyard animal; and planted, tended, picked, and prepared fruit and vegetables from large gardens adjacent to the farmhouse. They not only produced or collected all these goods, they also cooked them for consumption, usually over open hearths that were in such constant use that farmhouse interiors became virtual sweatboxes.

When they were not growing, collecting, or preparing food, farmwives turned to cleaning chores. These tasks included sweeping and dusting; washing and drying laundry by hand; making soap over hot fires; and creating new garments, blankets, and other woven goods for family members on balky spinning wheels. In addition, they were often called out to labor in the fields during harvesttime and other periods of intensive work. All of these chores would have been exhausting in their own right. But farmwives were also charged with the daily care and supervision of the family's young children. It is little wonder, then, that an administrator for the U.S. Department of Agriculture in 1862 felt obliged to comment that "a farmer's wife, as a general rule, is a laboring drudge. . . . It is safe to say, that on three farms out of four the wife works harder, endures more, than any other on the place" (Myres 1982).

The lot of the average farmer's wife improved somewhat during the course of the nineteenth century, as the twin forces of mechanization and commercialization took some responsibilities out of her hands. For example, the advent of commercial butter, cheese, soap, and textile making led many farming families with disposable income to simply buy these items rather than produce them at home. But even in these cases, it seemed that the void created by the outsourcing of those tasks to commercial enterprises was quickly filled by a host of other duties.

Children comprised the last major component of the family farm workforce. In the majority of cases, adolescent and young adult family members were an invaluable—and ubiquitous—asset for farming families. One demographic analysis for the years from 1800 to 1840,

Children comprised an essential labor force for countless pioneer families in the American West. (Library of Congess)

for example, indicated that children constituted at least half of the household in 72 percent of northern frontier households and 83 percent of those on the southern frontier (Bogue 1994). These youths led envious existences in some ways. The sense of belonging and shared responsibility for family success was palpable in many respects, and their daily work side by side with father, mother, brother, and sister instilled in many of them a deep appreciation for family ties and a strong allegiance to the land on which they were raised. Yet, as one historian noted,

> the romantic popular image of barefoot boys and apple-cheeked girls frolicking through meadows has little relation to reality. While there were some farmers—substantial southern planters, for example—who indulged their children, and while there was a good deal of affection between parents and children everywhere, farm children usually functioned as an economic resource. . . . Nineteenth-century farm life did not put a premium on childhood. (Danbom 1995)

"Farmers Are Very Much Dispirited"

In the Reconstruction era, many southerners predicted that an industrialized and economically vibrant "New South" was imminent. As time passed, however, it became clear that socioeconomic and racial stratification remained a major problem. Indeed, sharecroppers, tenant farmers, mill workers, and miners were all left behind by the new southern economy. In one representative report filed by a frustrated staffer with the North Carolina Bureau of Labor Statistics, complaints from tenant farmers and sharecroppers about depressed crop prices, predatory lending practices by landowners, and neglected school systems reached epidemic proportions by the late 1880s. Following is an excerpt from that report:

> Time was in this vicinity nearly every farmer not only supported himself and family from the products of the farm, but had something to spare as well. That time has passed away, I fear, forever. Then very little cotton was raised, and the farmers looked well to grain crops, horses, cattle, hogs and sheep. There was not much opulence, but much of substantial independence. Now, instead of being a year before, they are a year,

The American Farmhand

The small family farmer also relied on laborers to help clear fields, plant and harvest crops, tend to horses and other livestock, and take care of other duties on the property. This supplementary labor resource was especially important in the colonial era. In the eighteenth and early nineteenth centuries, these workers were typically young men from the community, the sons of area blacksmiths, shopkeepers, or even other farmers. In general, hired hands received a modest wage (which disciplined young men hoarded so as to eventually acquire their own land) and room and board, and in many cases, they became de facto members of the families they worked for, taking meals with them and participating in birthday celebrations and other signal family events. They also learned the many tricks of the trade of independent farming at the feet of their mentors. In return, these young men lent their vitality and strength to the arduous business of farming.

at least, behind, and, toil as they may, too many of them at the close of the year, when the books are opened, find the balance-sheet against them, "though every nerve was strained." The mortgage system, which hangs like a pall of death over many an honest, hard-working man, will ruin any business interest in this country. No farmer can borrow money, or buy on crop-time, at an advance of from thirty to fifty per cent. No farmer can farm successfully without some money; the present rates offered him amounts to prohibition. I cannot, in the brief space allowed, recount many of the ills now affecting us, or make any suggestion in palliation of them. To be brief, farmers are very much dispirited at the outlook, while they have worked harder for the last two years than at any time within my knowledge.

Source

Escott, Paul D., and David R. Goldfield. 1990. *Major Problems in the History of the American South.* Vol. 2, *The New South.* Lexington, MA: D. C. Heath.

The other type of farm laborer common in colonial America was the indentured servant, usually a European of English, Scottish, Irish, or German descent. In some respects, the indentured servant's circumstances were little different from those of the black slaves who labored for white masters in the American South until the end of the Civil War in 1865. For example, indentured servants received no wages for their long hours of labor, and the happiness or misery of their daily existence was predicated to a large extent on whether fate cast them into the circle of a humane master or under the shadow of a capricious, mean-spirited one.

Still, in most—though certainly not all—cases, the indentured servant entered into bondage of free will, and even the most miserable servant could count the days until purgatory would come to an end (some vagrants and convicted criminals were involuntarily drafted into the indentured servant system). One of the central elements of the indentured servant system, which coalesced into being as a method for poor immigrants to pay their passage to the New World, was that terms of service were limited to a given period of time, usually three, five, or seven years. After the agreed-on time period expired, the indentured servant could go wherever he or she wished, with all debts associated with his or her passage to the colonies and subsequent settlement wiped clean. The slaves who had been spirited away from their ancestral homes in Africa and deposited in the South's cotton and tobacco fields had no such end date of servitude to look forward to.

Seasonal Fluctuations in Farmwork

The daily rhythms of work on the American farm were always dictated by the seasons. Springtime was devoted to planting and calving (on dairy farms), summertime to cultivation, and autumn to harvesting and storage of crops and butchering of hogs and cattle selected for consumption, either on the farm itself or in distant towns and cities. Of course, regional variations in farming influenced seasonal activities as well. For example, in the southern states, cotton picking extended into December in many regions, and in the northern states and western territories, where sheep raising was concentrated, time needed to be set aside in the spring for the all-important task of shearing.

Wintertime, meanwhile, was the season of comparative rest for farmers. During those cold, dark months, farming families all across the United States enjoyed a measure of respite from the hustle and bustle of the other seasons. Some chores, such as harness repair, trap line runs, and livestock maintenance, still had to be addressed in those months. But opportunities for pleasure reading, quiet nights of conversation by the hearth, and visiting with neighbors were definitely more plentiful in December and January than they were in April or October. Of course, these relaxing evenings were generally only within the grasp of those farmers who were on sound financial footing. Farmers in less advantageous economic circumstances often sought out work as carpenters, loggers, or packers during the winter months to supplement their income.

The seasons even exerted a significant influence on the scope and character of community events in farming areas. Some treasured holidays, such as Christmas and the Fourth of July, were celebrated regardless of their placement in the calendar year, and life events that

An 1858 cornhusking party in New England. (Library of Congress)

called for community gatherings, such as weddings, baptisms, and funerals, took place throughout the year.

But many other social occasions were closely linked to the farm's seasonal work cycles, and they often had a strong utilitarian component to them. Harvest gatherings, barn raisings, husking bees, and other events closely tied to farmwork gave American farming families the opportunity to effectively combine business and pleasure. During these gatherings, men, women, and children who went days or weeks without seeing anyone outside the family circle were able to luxuriate in hours of interaction with other community members while simultaneously seeing to the construction of a much-needed barn or the preservation of goods for the long winter ahead.

Gazing Westward

Farming families comprised the core of America's great nineteenth-century migration westward into frontier lands. Indeed, pioneer farmers sounded the most resonant calls to undecided brethren back east. Their encouraging reports, replete with assurances that the same rules of farming that brought success in the East or Europe applied on the western frontier, lured ever greater waves of hardy souls into the untamed West: "Always and everywhere that, and that alone, was the unquestionable magnet—The evidence that success with soil could be won on terms of farm or plantation life as the prospective emigrants knew it; that known reactions to soil and to weather would be experienced; that wood with which they were used to working lay ready at hand; that all the old tricks of the trade would work in the new land" (Hulbert 1933).

Most pioneer farming families set out for the new promised land in early spring, both to avoid the heart of winter and to give themselves enough time to establish basic shelter, clear fields, and plant crops once they reached their destination. Then, after that first harvest, farmers would set about the laborious process of building more enduring farmhouses and barns and attacking the thick forests surrounding them in order to increase the extent of their acreage available for cultivation.

Early pioneers confronted an array of daunting challenges, from the inaccessibility of quality medical care to violence at the hands of Native American tribes that were greatly alarmed by the whites' growing incursions into their traditional territories. Weather was also less predictable, especially for those pioneer families that settled on the Great Plains and other points beyond the Mississippi.

> It was soon powerfully apparent to any newcomer that western weather was . . . on a grander scale. There were greater seasonal extremes of heat and cold, and far more violent changes, sometimes in a matter of hours, accompanied by spectacular thunderstorms, cloudbursts, hail, blizzards, or, most awesome of all, tornadoes. These extremes of weather, punctuating the seasons with memorable episodes, might well strike those who experienced them as marking an important difference between East and West, but it was the more general patterns of the seasons, weather over the longer term . . . that were critical to the success of an agricultural people, and here experiences in the West were strongly reassuring. (Meinig 1993)

From the mid-nineteenth century forward and especially in the post–Civil War era, the conversion of the West into America's agricultural heartland was greatly aided by mechanization and the introduction of new tools for planting, harvesting, packaging, dairy production, and other farming tasks. These symbols of industrialization—the steam-belching Iron Horses of Jay Gould, Edward Harriman, and other railroad barons, the horse-drawn reaper of Cyrus McCormick, and John Deere's self-scouring steel plow, among others—became emblematic not only of economic development but also of the taming of the prairies, foothills, and mountains of the West.

In addition to providing farmers with new tools for their livelihood, industrialization changed rural life in other ways as well. These changes swept first across the eastern states but were eventually felt across the continent. The advent of steamships and railroads enabled farmers to reach ever more distant markets, and it also brought sensibilities and products generated in urban areas to the hinterlands. For example, expanding transportation networks enabled evolving urban conceptions of child-rearing techniques, political ideas, and fashion to filter into rural communities far more quickly than ever before. And by the late nineteenth century, even farming families in the most remote precincts of Alabama, Idaho, and Oklahoma could purchase a multitude of goods by mail order, including clothing, carpeting and draperies, furniture, toys, decorative art and ornaments, reading materials, musical instruments, barbed wire, farming implements, and plates and serving dishes.

The impact of the Industrial Revolution on American agriculture accelerated at the turn of the twentieth century with the advent of a veritable cornucopia of new chemical fertilizers, herbicides, and insecticides. Together, these advances produced tremendous increases in productivity and crop yields for those farming operations that could afford them. But no single thing had as great an impact on American farming as the internal combustion engine in general and the arrival of gasoline-powered tractors, automobiles, and trucks in the orchards of California, the wheat fields of Minnesota, and the corn rows of Kansas. These vehicles greatly increased the speed at which farmers could complete major seasonal tasks, while simultaneously dramatically lessening reliance on hired hands and opening swaths of new land that had previously been set aside to grow fodder for draft animals.

Many farmers were initially suspicious of the newfangled gasoline-powered tractors that were being marketed to them, partly because of their unhappiness with early steam-powered tractors and partly because they were frankly frightened of the disorienting roar of industrialization that seemed poised to turn their lives upside down. But the obvious utility of the Model T and other early automobiles made farmers more receptive to other motor-powered machines—and the prospect of having a machine undertake various farming tasks that left them bone-weary had an undeniable practical appeal. This latter factor became especially important as tractor manufacturers rolled out a variety of accessory machines that could be utilized with tractors to speed up threshing, seeding, harvesting, and mowing processes. From the 1910s to the eve of World War II, the number of tractors operating on American farmland jumped exponentially, despite the Dust Bowl and Great Depression. From 1915 to 1940, for example, the number of tractors owned by farmers in Kansas grew from 3,000 to more than 95,000.

Mechanization played a pivotal role in ushering in the so-called golden age of American agriculture—roughly the first three decades of the twentieth century. But it also has been cited as the chief culprit in the overproduction and myopic cultivation practices that created conditions for the Dust Bowl of the 1930s. Less visible repercussions for the American farmer included a steady increase in the size of individual farming operations, as small family farmers found themselves at such a competitive disadvantage with wealthier neighbors and emerging corporate farms that they had little choice but to sell to competitors or land developers. So even though agricultural mechanization eased the daily workload of farmers, it also created fertile conditions for the evolution of American farming into "big business." And with this transition, hired hands and migrant workers who had once enjoyed friendly, personalized relations with their employers gradually found that their supervisors no longer knew their names.

White and Black Labor in the Antebellum South

The institution of slavery was the centerpiece of the South's agriculture-based economy in the antebellum era.

> The South's elite and omnipotent planter class had created an airtight argument for slavery, upon which rested the smooth efficiency of their ruling system. Within it the planter assumed total paternalistic responsibility for the health and welfare of his slaves in exchange for their

free labor; he provided shelter, care and protection for a race that in his view was feckless and childlike. Slaves were punished, often severely, for making adult decisions while rewarded for docile, subservient behavior. (Yafa 2005)

As a result of the presence of this "peculiar institution," the fundamental character of daily farmwork in slaveholding states evolved differently than in any other region of the country.

Slaves comprised the single biggest sector of the labor force in the South. In 1860, it was estimated that 4 million people—about one out of eight in the entire United States—were slaves. These slaves were particularly vital to the operations of the region's largest and most powerful cotton, tobacco, and rice plantations. The millions of slaves who toiled on farms and plantations across the American South were responsible for a wide range of tasks. Their most visible work took place in the fields, where they tended cotton, tobacco, and other major crops. Indeed, about three out of four slaves worked primarily as field labor, and the percentage of slaves who spent most of their days out in the field was probably even higher in the Deep South, where labor-intensive cotton production was most heavily concentrated. Field work was arduous for these slaves in every corner of the South, but the treatment of slaves varied significantly, depending on the region and the disposition of overseers and masters. All slaves worked long hours, but some took care of their work at a relatively unhurried pace, whereas others were driven relentlessly. Louisiana sugar planters, for example, were notorious for their harsh treatment of slaves, especially at harvesttime, when many slaves were forced to labor deep into the night for weeks at a time (Kolchin 1993).

Solomon Northrup, a free black living in New York who was kidnapped by slave traders and forced to endure bondage on a Louisiana plantation, wrote a particularly harrowing account of his experiences in the Deep South, called *Twelve Years a Slave* (1853), after gaining his release. His daily regimen, recounted here in part, was by no means unique or unusual in the antebellum South:

The hands are required to be in the cotton field as soon as it is light in the morning, and, with the exception of ten or fifteen minutes, which is given them at noon to swallow their allowance of cold bacon, they are not permitted to be a moment idle until it is too dark to see, and when the moon is full, they often times labor till the middle of the night. They do not dare to stop even at dinner time, nor return to the quarters, however late it be, until the order to halt is given by the driver. . . . Finally, at a late hour, they reach the quarters, sleepy and overcome with the long day's toil. . . . An hour before daylight the horn is blown. Then the slaves arouse, prepare their breakfast, fill a gourd with water, in another deposit their dinner of cold bacon and corn cake, and hurry to the field again. It is an offense invariably followed by a flogging, to be found at the quarters after daybreak. Then the fears and labors of another day begin, and until its close there is no such thing as rest. (Northrup 1970)

In addition to their labor in the fields, slaves were put to work clearing land; erecting and repairing fences; tending livestock; digging ditches; building barns, slaves' quarters, and outbuildings; loading and driving supply wagons and boats; and toiling in mills. Finally, a relatively small percentage of slaves were charged with seeing to the comfort of their masters as cooks, maids, grooms, and gardeners.

Black Farming after the Civil War

Emancipation brought with it some fundamental changes in the way white planters and black laborers interacted, and in the first years of Reconstruction especially, the balance of power—though still uneven—was not as terribly one-sided as it had been prior to the war. Free black farmers now had some room to negotiate with landowners over compensation and cultivation strategies. In addition, the percentage of blacks owning land in the South increased modestly throughout the last three decades of the nineteenth century. And whether they leased land or owned it outright, black farmers during Reconstruction had greater discretion than ever before in terms of deciding how hard and how long they would work on a daily basis. In addition, their newfound freedom gave blacks the option of picking up stakes and relocating elsewhere if they were so inclined.

But the white men who controlled the levers of the South's agriculture-based economy were loath to dismantle the governing principles of the system that had been so lucrative for them in the past. They subsequently moved to institutionalize, both in local and state laws and in community practices, a regional farming system that was reminiscent of slavery in all too many ways. Before long, the

Even after the end of slavery, the South's sharecropping system kept African American farmers at a terrible economic disadvantage. (Library of Congress)

practice of sharecropping dominated southern farming. Under this arrangement, black families leased small plots of land from white landholders in exchange for a percentage of the crop they raised.

Sharecropping enabled African American families to scrape together a meager existence, but the contract was rarely generous enough for them to gather the funds necessary to purchase their own land. Instead, they struggled to exist on credit year after year, and countless farmers fell deeper into debt with each passing harvest. In 1900, for example, black farmers in Georgia had title to only 4 percent of the land in the entire state, even though they constituted half the state's population. One historian summarized the situation as follows:

> Sharecropping was a good choice only in comparison with slavery, or with day or seasonal labor, a status in which many of the former slaves found themselves. While croppers enjoyed a modicum of independence, the law viewed them as laborers without property rights. They could be put off the land at any time. Landlords could cheat them with impunity at the settle in December, when planters informed croppers of profits and losses for the year. . . . Subservience to landlords meant

that croppers did not develop entrepreneurial and managerial skills appropriate to landownership or other business enterprises. And such behaviors as hard work and thrift, which many Americans in a dynamic economy found functional, seemed pointless in the stagnant world of the sharecropper. (Danbom 1995)

White lawmakers and major landholders—who were often one and the same in the Reconstruction era and after—also put the squeeze on African American farmers and field hands in other ways. For example, blacks in the post–Civil War South watched helplessly as many states passed vagrancy, trespassing, and herd laws that dramatically curtailed their access to land on which they had previously relied to fish, hunt, or graze livestock.

Ultimately, sharecropping and other tenant-farming arrangements proved detrimental to all people engaged in southern farming, not just African Americans. The sharecropping system led many white planters to insist that black farmers working their land plant cotton—virtually to the exclusion of other cash crops—for the simple reason that it was the crop that could most easily be sold for cash. This emphasis on cotton production gradually sucked the nutrients out of fields that were used for "King Cotton" year after year, and it also created a glut on the marketplace. In 1866, for instance, cotton grown in the United States was selling for about forty-three cents a pound; in 1894, the fiber was selling for less than five cents a pound. The plummeting value of the crop hit the entire South hard, but as always, poor black and white farmers suffered the most when hard economic times rolled in.

A Migrant Workforce

As in other parts of the country, then, southern farming became increasingly dominated by large commercial operations. Across the nation, some family-owned operations prospered. During the first two decades of the twentieth century, in fact, gross farm income more than doubled, and the value of the average farm more than tripled. This accrual of wealth and financial muscle enabled successful farmers to funnel profits back into their operations. They poured money into tractors, automobiles and trucks, combines and other machinery, additional tracts of land, mountains of fertilizer, purebred livestock, and new barns and silos. They also brought recent urban innovations such as telephone service, indoor plumbing, and electricity into the rural hinterlands.

But for many other people who worked the land for their livelihood, the early twentieth century was not kind. Large-scale agricultural operations crowded out countless small family farms, tenant farmers, and sharecroppers, and many of these people were relegated to the status of hired laborers. Meanwhile, the burgeoning markets for fruits and vegetables—which remained best harvested by hand—increased the demand for cheap seasonal help.

In the West especially, this demand was met by migratory workers who had few other alternatives. During the revolutionary turmoil of the 1910s, huge numbers of Mexicans fled their homeland for the fields and orchards of California, Texas, and points north. But with little education and no money to launch their own business enterprises, entire families were inexorably drawn to seasonal field work. This nomadic life exacerbated their vulnerability to the predations of unscrupulous owners and foremen. Exploitation of migrant farmworkers became epidemic in many regions of the West, and the 1935 National Labor Relations Act offered no respite, for it exclusively excluded farmworkers from its protection.

Cowboys on the Range

One of the enduring icons of American history in general and the settlement of the American West in particular was the cowboy, a figure widely seen as the cornerstone of the beef industry's emergence as a major factor in American commerce—and eating habits—in the second half of the nineteenth century. The mythology surrounding cowboys of the nineteenth century (and later) emphasizes their nomadic independence and impatience with authority, but the reality was less glamorous.

The cowboy's daily life was, in most cases, a dreary existence marked by bad weather, bland and lousy food, hard labor, and long hours of solitude in the saddle, miles from the nearest human voice. And this monotonous and lonely existence was less likely to be punctuated by barn dances and friendly card games than by bone-chilling blizzards, roaring flash floods, skulking cattle thieves, and deadly stampedes. Moreover, the ultimate employer of many a ranch

Stampede: A Cowpuncher's Worst Fear

The life of a cowboy in the nineteenth and early twentieth centuries was a cycle of enduring vicious weather, scraping by on meager pay, putting up with perennial discomfort and broken bones, and wandering nomadically. But of all the unpleasant tasks cowboys faced, few were as frightening as the prospect of bringing a herd of stampeding cattle to heel. In the following interview conducted by Woody Phipps, cowboy Richard Phillips recalls how it felt to deal with stampedes back in his days working in Texas:

> What I'm trying to picture to you is that in them days a man had to be a man every day without no layoffs. Every day! You take in a stampede, now, and I've seen a hundred or more. The boys that are out with a herd must be real good riders willing to take chances with their lives. When a herd starts to running, it goes hell-bent-for-election and will run over anything it can unless it's too big, then the herd will run until it runs up against something it can't run over, then it will split and go around but keep running. That's the way them ornery critters will do every time. Well, when a herd gets to running, it'll run until it runs down or gets so tired it can't run any more. The thing a cowhand has to do is to get that herd to milling, and then they'll run in a circle until they get run down. If they're not put into a mill, they'll run over some bank of a creek, or a cut, or even a canyon if there's one in the way. Then there'll be a lot of beef killed and lost, which can run up into the thousands of dollars.
>
> Now, then, I want you to picture a herd on the stomp and realize that any human or hoss that gets in the way, that the herd will run over them and stomp them into the very ground if it possibly can. Get that picture, then realize that the only possible way to turn a herd into a mill is to get right out in front and beat the lead steer until he starts turning and trying to get away from you. That away, the rest of the herd will follow him, and the herd will then go into a mill. When you get that picture, then you'll see and understand why men had to be he-men in them days.

Source

Lanning, Jim, and Judy Lanning, eds. 1984. *Texas Cowboys: Memories of Early Days.* College Station: Texas A&M University Press.

Cowboys branding cattle, 1891. (Library of Congress)

hand was not a hard-bitten native of Texas or Missouri but coteries of eastern syndicates that accurately saw the American beef industry as one with enormous commercial potential. The mythology surrounding the American cowboy was accurate in one respect, however: he was poorly paid, given the hardships of the job. Most ranching outfits of the nineteenth century only doled out $25 to $40 a month in salary to their hands plus room and board (usually little more than a shack), and those with a large percentage of Mexicans or African Americans on the payroll (one out of every three cowboys in the United States in the late nineteenth century was one or the other) typically paid even less.

The labor force on America's nineteenth-century ranches worked hard year-round, but the busiest seasons on every ranch were spring and fall. In the spring, cowboys were responsible for gathering up all cattle from their grazing pastures and separating them by brand. This was also the prime time of year for castrating young males and branding calves and other unbranded head. Herds were then turned out to fatten up throughout the summer until the fall, when cowboys rounded them up again and selected animals for arduous cattle drives to the slaughterhouse, either directly or via railroad.

Cowboys were a proud and restless breed, though, and when they became fed up with the idiosyncrasies or cheap ways of their employers, they often looked for other employers. This dynamic made high turnover a basic reality on many ranches. But cowboys who felt underpaid and underappreciated usually did not have many options, at least in the ranching industry. When a group of cowboys struck for higher wages in the Texas panhandle in 1883, for example, the Panhandle Cattleman's Association broke their strike with ease. They remained a relatively powerless force, unable to establish any sort of collective identity or organizational unity, long after many other industries that relied on manual labor had been forced to recognize unions and/or make economic and workplace concessions to workers.

Appalling Slaughterhouse Conditions

Another industry in which employees had little leverage was the American meatpacking industry. The daily work regimen in nineteenth-century slaughterhouses and packing plants was oppressive in its toll on both body and spirit. Indeed, these operations, which were concentrated primarily in large midwestern cities, were little more than sweatshops. They utilized poorly educated, job-hungry immigrants who were often unfamiliar with the few legal rights they possessed. As a result, industry leaders and small outfits alike had the necessary leverage to dispense paltry wages, demand long hours of hard labor, and treat workers callously at best and brutally at worst. Indeed, workers routinely toiled under the shadowy threats of capricious wage cuts, production line speedups, debilitating injuries, exposure to disease, and the knowledge that if they protested the conditions under which they labored, they would be fired and blacklisted.

The average workday for slaughterhouse employees was fairly standard, whether they were toiling in a dank Chicago plant or a sweltering Kansas City warehouse. Workers led animals to the pens where they were killed, then dragged them to areas set aside for draining. After the cattle or hogs bled dry, they were skinned and gutted. Carcasses were usually set aside to cool before being butchered—or dressed, as this phase was often called—into smaller cuts. The cuts were then distributed for sale (common with beef) or

A Glimpse into "The Jungle"

In 1906, novelist Upton Sinclair published *The Jungle,* a harrowing account of life and death in the Chicago stockyards as seen through the eyes of a Lithuanian immigrant named Jurgis Rudkus. Sinclair's muckraking work shocked the American public into demanding greater regulatory oversight of the meatpacking industry. Following is an excerpt from the novel:

> There was another interesting set of statistics that a person might have gathered in Packingtown—those of the various afflictions of the workers. When Jurgis had first inspected the packing-plants with Szedvilas, he had marveled while he listened to the tale of all the things that were made out of the carcasses of animals, and of all the lesser industries that were maintained there; now he found that each one of these lesser industries was a separate little inferno, in its way as horrible as the killing-beds, the source and fountain of them all. The workers in each of them had their own peculiar diseases. And the wandering visitor might be skeptical about all the swindles, but he could not be sceptical about these, for the worker bore the evidence of them about on his own person—generally he had only to hold out his hand.
>
> There were the men in the pickle-rooms, for instance, where old Antanas had gotten his death; scarce a one of these that had not some spot of horror on his person. Let a man so much as scrape his finger pushing a truck in the pickle-rooms, and he might have a sore that would put him out of the world; all the joints in his fingers might be eaten by the acid, one by one. Of the butchers and floorsmen, the beef-boners and trimmers, and all those who used knives, you could scarcely find a person who had the use of his thumb; time and time again the base of it had been slashed, till it was a mere lump of flesh against which the man pressed the knife to hold it. The hands of these men would be criss-crossed with cuts, until you could no longer pretend to count them or to trace them. They would have no nails—they had worn them off pulling hides; their knuckles were swollen so that their fingers spread out like a fan. There were men who worked in the cooking-rooms, in the midst of steam and sickening odors, by artificial light; in these rooms the germs of tuberculosis might live for two years, but the supply was renewed every hour. There were the beef-luggers, who carried two-hundred-pound quarters into the refrigerator-cars; a fearful kind of work, that began at four o'clock in the morning, and

THE JUNGLE
BY
UPTON SINCLAIR

DOUBLEDAY, PAGE & Cº
NEW YORK

A poster advertising Upton Sinclair's *The Jungle*, a muckraking novel that uncovered the seamy underside of America's meatpacking industry. (Library of Congress)

that wore out the most powerful men in a few years.

There were those who worked in the chilling-rooms, and whose special disease was rheumatism; the time-limit that a man could work in the chilling-rooms was said to be five years. There were the wool-pluckers, whose hands went to pieces even sooner than the hands of the pickle-men; for the pelts of the sheep had to be painted with acid to loosen the wool, and then the pluckers had to pull out this wool with their bare hands, till the acid had eaten their fingers off. There were those who made the tins for the canned-meat; and their hands, too, were a maze of cuts, and each cut represented a chance for blood-poisoning. Some worked at the stamping-machines, and it was very seldom that one could work long there at the pace that was set, and not give out and forget himself, and have a part of his hand chopped off. There were the "hoisters," as they were called, whose task it was to press the lever which lifted the dead cattle off the floor. They ran along upon a rafter, peering down through the damp and the steam; and as old Durham's architects had not built the killing-room for the convenience of the hoisters, at every few feet they would have to stoop under a beam, say four feet above the one they ran on; which got them into the habit of stooping, so that in a few years they would be walking like chimpanzees. Worst of any, however, were the fertilizer-men, and those who served in the cooking-rooms. These people could not be shown to the visitor,—for the odor of a fertilizer-man would scare any ordinary visitor at a hundred yards, and as for the other men, who worked in tank-rooms full of steam, and in some of which there were open vats near the level of the floor, their peculiar trouble was that they fell into the vats; and when they were fished out, there was never enough of them left to be worth exhibiting,—sometimes they would be overlooked for days, till all but the bones of them had gone out to the world as Durham's Pure Leaf Lard!

Source

Sinclair, Upton. 1906. *The Jungle.* New York: Doubleday, Page and Company.

---

salted, smoked, or pickled preparatory to packing (the standard procedure for pork products). Virtually every step in this process was bloody, exhausting, and dangerous work.

This state of affairs endured for decades, until the reformist mindset of the Progressive Era finally dragged the industry's worst transgressions out into the public spotlight. The pivotal event in this regard was the 1906 publication of Upton Sinclair's novel *The Jungle,* a muckraking work that went into sordid detail about the shocking conditions in America's meatpacking factories. Sinclair's unsparing but accurate description of meatpacking plants as places where beef and pork products were constantly exposed to and contaminated by human blood, feces, rats, cockroaches, and other vermin scandalized the American public, as did his exposure of the deceptive marketing practices employed by the industry to increase its profits. In fact, the uproar that ensued after the publication of Sinclair's book spurred the passage of both the Pure Food and Drug Act and the Federal Meat Inspection Act of 1906.

The Jungle, however, failed to arouse the same level of public indignation regarding the treatment of the laborers who toiled inside the nation's slaughterhouses and packing plants. This deeply disappointed Sinclair, who had written the book specifically to inform America about the plight of the poor immigrants who comprised the industry workforce. "I aimed at the public's heart, and I hit it in the stomach," he reportedly lamented.

Working conditions for laborers in the meatpacking industry did not materially improve until the 1930s, when big trade union organizing drives transformed the business landscape of the United States. After the passage of the National Labor Relations Act in 1935, which gave workers the right to bargain collectively with employers, industry laborers founded the United Packinghouse Workers of America (UPWA). A part of the powerful Congress of Industrial Organizations (CIO), the union became the principal voice of the workers employed by the nation's large beef- and pork-processing firms. It also was an early trailblazer in its emphasis on racial, gender, and ethnic solidarity.

Sources

Bogue, Allan G. 1994. "An Agricultural Empire." In *The Oxford History of the American West*, edited by Clyde A. Milner II, Carol A. O'Connor, and Martha A. Sandweiss. New York: Oxford University Press.

Cooper, William J., Jr., and Thomas E. Terrill. 1991. *The American South: A History.* New York: McGraw-Hill.

Cronon, William. 1991. *Nature's Metropolis: Chicago and the Great West.* New York. W. W. Norton.

Danbom, David B. 1995. *Born in the Country: A History of Rural America.* Baltimore, MD: Johns Hopkins University Press.

Halpern, Rick. 1997. *Down on the Killing Floor: Black and White Workers in Chicago's Packinghouses, 1904–1954.* Champaign: University of Illinois Press.

Horton, James Oliver, and Lois E. Horton. 2004. *Slavery and the Making of America.* New York: Oxford University Press.

Hulbert, Archer Butler. 1933. *Where Rolls the Oregon: Prophet and Pessimist Look Northwest, 1825–1830.* Colorado Springs, CO: Stewart Commission.

Hurt, R. Douglas. 1981. *The Dust Bowl: An Agricultural and Social History.* Chicago: Nelson-Hall.

Jordan, Terry G. 1981. *Trails to Texas: Southern Roots of Western Cattle Ranching.* Lincoln: University of Nebraska Press.

Kolchin, Peter. 1993. *American Slavery, 1619–1877.* New York: Hill and Wang.

Lanning, Jim, and Judy Lanning, eds. 1984. *Texas Cowboys: Memories of Early Days.* College Station: Texas A&M University Press.

Meinig, D. W. 1993. *The Shaping of America.* Vol. 2, *Continental America, 1800–1867.* New Haven, CT: Yale University Press.

Merk, Frederick. 1978. *History of the Westward Movement.* New York: Alfred A. Knopf.

Myres, Sandra L. 1982. *Westering Women and the Frontier Experience, 1800–1915.* Albuquerque: University of New Mexico Press.

Northrup, Solomon. 1970 [1853]. *Twelve Years a Slave.* Reprint ed. New York: Dover Publications.

Schlebecker, John T. 1975. *Whereby We Thrive: A History of American Farming, 1607–1972.* Ames: Iowa State University Press.

Schob, David. 1975. *Hired Hands and Plowboys: Farm Labor in the Midwest, 1815–1860.* Urbana: University of Illinois Press.

Shover, John L. 1976. *First Majority, Last Minority: The Transforming of Rural Life in America.* De Kalb: Northern Illinois University Press.

Skaggs, Jimmy M. 1986. *Prime Cut: Livestock Raising and Meatpacking in the United States, 1607–1983.* College Station: Texas A&M University Press.

Wade, Louise Carroll. 1987. *Chicago's Pride: The Stockyards, Packingtown, and Environs in the Nineteenth Century.* Urbana: University of Illinois Press.

Walsh, Margaret. 1982. *The Rise of the Midwestern Meat Packing Industry.* Lexington: University of Kentucky Press.

Watkins, T. H. 1999. *The Hungry Years: A Narrative History of the Great Depression in America.* New York: Henry Holt.

Yafa, Stephen. 2005. *Big Cotton.* New York: Viking.

Labor Organizations and Reform Movements

Jonathan Rees

I n terms of their impact on labor during the era of industrialization, agriculture and meatpacking were closely related. Put simply, without food to feed the new industrial workforce, none of the other changes associated with industrialization could have occurred. Cheap, abundant food was a prerequisite for giving working-class people the energy they needed to labor in their physically demanding, often-difficult jobs.

Unlike manufacturing industries, in which workers created products themselves, workers in the agriculture and meatpacking industries prepared nature's work for human consumption. In each industry, employers replaced workers with machines to varying degrees and therefore depended on a mixture of skilled and unskilled labor. In agriculture, the labor process had relied on machines since the invention of the cotton gin in 1791, but the degree of industrialization depended heavily on the characteristics of the crop. To this day, many crops have to be picked by hand, whereas the harvesting of many others is largely mechanized. Furthermore, demand for labor in this industry is mostly seasonal and therefore unstable. The only group willing to try to organize agricultural workers during the era of industrialization was the Industrial Workers of the World (IWW). And even if that organization had not been the most radical trade union ever created on American soil, the peculiar characteristics of the agricultural workforce would probably have doomed this quest to failure anyway.

Meatpacking started out as a highly skilled job, but industrialization—specifically, the extensive use of the division of labor—made it easier to dispense with skilled, native-born whites and hire less skilled immigrants or African Americans to perform the increasingly nasty work. The most important factor making this possible was the growing concentration of the industry. The meat trade was originally a local industry, but as transportation improved, packing plants and packing companies grew bigger. Working on a larger scale, companies increasingly replaced the highly skilled employees of old with less skilled workers. However, there were some jobs in a packinghouse that men simply had to do. These skilled positions became the core of the industry's union movement.

Agriculture

Making generalizations about the course of agricultural labor is extremely difficult. American farmers grew countless varieties of crops during the late nineteenth and early twentieth centuries, and what needed to be done to grow and harvest them differed in each case. Furthermore, the industrialization of particular kinds of agriculture was often spread out over time, sometimes before or after the era when the rest of the economy industrialized. In the case of cotton, for example, the cotton gin began the process of mechanized agriculture during the 1790s, but cotton picking itself did not become mechanized until the 1930s and 1940s. It is no coincidence that the latter period was when sharecroppers began to organize.

Also confusing matters is the difference between farmers and farm labor, a distinction that is sometimes difficult to discern a hundred years or more later. Farmers do farmwork, but for the purpose of a historical analysis of labor organizations and labor reform, the employer-employee relationships in farming must be studied in the context of a historical analysis of labor organization and labor reform. Accordingly, the cotton industry—and cotton was the most important crop of the antebellum period—cannot be considered here because most of the farms that grew it were either too small to have employees or else used the labor of slaves, the vast majority of whom obviously did not receive wages. For this same reason, the Grange and Populism, although obviously reform movements, will not be considered in what follows, since these movements were started by small farmers because of their difficult financial circumstances rather than because they worked for someone else as employees.

To find labor organization among farmworkers during the era of industrialization, one has to look west to California. The giant "bonanza" wheat fields there were more mechanized than the smaller farms of the Midwest. Mechanization was a natural reaction to the labor shortage of the 1860s, but it soon helped create a permanent surplus labor force as more and more workers moved west. The agriculture section of this essay will concentrate on large farms, the operations that were most likely to hire labor and utilize machines that significantly affected the nature of the labor process there. Indeed, the larger the farm, the more farmworkers there had to be and the more likely it is that they would have received wages for their work. Many farm machines (such as the steam tractor) were so expensive and required such large economies of scale that only huge farms found them useful.

The record of labor organization in California agriculture is not good. Yet the conditions there were favorable in many ways, as Carey McWilliams wrote in *Factories in the Field:*

> The fact that 250,000 workers, employed in the richest industry in California, have been repeatedly frustrated in their desire to achieve organization is a matter which has long produced discussion among labor's well-wishers and theorizers. The case for organization is indeed remarkably persuasive. Consider some of the favorable elements: a highly industrialized agriculture, thoroughly organized, making huge profits; perishable crops dependent upon transportation (two circumstances that place the industry at the mercy of a strong labor movement); wretched working conditions aggravated by racial discrimination; and, both in the past and present, a strong urban labor movement. (McWilliams 1944)

McWilliams attributed this lack of organization to disinterest on the part of union officials, but even if the labor leaders had had a strong commitment to organizing farm labor, it still would have been an uphill battle. Agricultural labor, unlike the labor of other industries, was largely itinerant because of the seasonal nature of the work. As a result, farmworkers were impoverished and difficult to organize

A seasonal laborer prepares to move on from Napa Valley, California, to the next mine, farm, or lumber camp in his nomadic existence. (Dorothea Lange/Library of Congress)

as they continually traveled between agricultural regions, chasing whatever crop needed labor at a particular time of year.

Industrialization contributed to the itinerant status of farm labor. First, many machines, such as the self-binding reaper (for wheat), eliminated the jobs of some workers. Second, workers displaced from other industries traveled west in large numbers during the depression of 1873, thereby lowering wages and forcing farmworkers to travel longer and work harder to maintain themselves. These itinerant laborers were generally known as bindlemen or bindlestiffs, for the tightly wound blankets that often served as their beds. They would remain a feature of rural American life throughout the era of industrialization.

The Anti-Chinese Movement

It may seem strange to think of the anti-Chinese movement of the 1870s and early 1880s as a reform movement. After all, its sentiments were racist and reactionary. However, the movement itself was in large part inspired by the desire to improve the lot of white farmworkers by making it impossible for Chinese workers to compete with them. The Chinese first arrived in California as part of the gold rush of 1849. Although they faced discrimination and racism, they were not targeted by legislation to block further immigration until the 1870s. Two factors created the anti-Chinese movement. First, when Chinese workers stopped toiling on the transcontinental railroad in 1869, they began to pour into California agriculture. More important, when the depression of 1873 occurred, white workers increasingly came to covet the once-undesirable jobs held by the Chinese. Many racists who had no need for a job in agriculture joined the anti-Chinese immigration movement, and the existence of a coalition between disinterested racists and self-interested white labor ultimately made this movement successful on a national scale.

Large California farmers gladly employed Chinese labor because these immigrants worked hard and asked for less money than their native-born counterparts. Chinese laborers thus progressed from being a hated minority to the primary target of white California workers. In 1876, the *Marin Journal* argued that most Californians believed that

> [the Chinese field hand] is a slave, reduced to the lowest terms of beggarly economy, and is no fit competitor for an American freeman; that he herds in scores, lives in small dens, where a white man and wife can hardly breathe, and has none of the wants of a civilized white man; ... that American men, women, and children cannot be what free people should be, and compete with such degraded creatures in the labor market. (Street 2004)

Never a majority in any section of the industry, the Chinese workers still became a target because of skin color and because they were sometimes hired en masse to replace white labor.

Violence was an important tool of the anti-Chinese movement. Richard Street traced the beginnings of anti-Chinese violence in California agriculture to the murder of a Chinese labor boss at a Santa Clara ranch in 1871. The man who committed the act turned himself in but was never prosecuted. Then, in 1874, anti-Chinese agitators set fire to two barns near Napa City; the idea was to punish farmers who employed Chinese labor rather than the laborers themselves. Ironically, the owner of this property had not yet hired any Chinese workers. From there, however, small incidents of anti-Chinese violence proliferated across the state. The first proposal banning further Chinese immigration came out of hearings held in San Francisco in 1876. Although the testimony in those hearings centered on urban problems allegedly linked to Chinese culture (such as drug addiction), the white supremacist group that orchestrated the hearings, the Order of Caucasians, had, by its members' own admission, been formed in part "to protect white labor" (Street 2004).

As racist labor violence escalated in urban areas, more Chinese workers looked to the fields for a respite. As time passed, the movement of these workers into agriculture gave added economic impetus to anti-Chinese immigration efforts. The most eloquent voice in support of Chinese exclusion was Henry George, who was famous for his 1879 book, *Progress and Poverty,* and as a failed candidate for mayor of New York in 1886. He developed this position as an unsuccessful printer in California during the early 1870s. In a pamphlet entitled "Our Land and Land Values" (which would grow into *Progress and Poverty*), he adopted a virulent racist tone. Much to his credit, though, he eventually changed his stance: by 1880, George was dead-set against letting the racism of the American working class get in the way of the onset of socialism:

> Nor has communism or socialism (understanding by these terms the desire for fundamental social changes) made, up to this time, much progress in California, for the presence of the Chinese has largely engrossed the attention of the laboring classes, offering what has seemed to make a sufficient explanation of the fall of wages and the difficulty of finding employment. . . . With the masses the obvious evils of Chinese competition have excluded all thought of anything else. And in this anti-Chinese feeling there is, of course, nothing that can properly be deemed socialistic or communistic. On the contrary, socialists and communists are more tolerant of the Chinese than any other class of those who feel or are threatened by their competition. (George 1880)

Ironically, by the late 1870s, anti-Chinese immigration advocates began to phrase their arguments as a benefit to Chinese and Ameri-

This 1880 cartoon, which shows Republican and Democratic political leaders nailing a Chinese man to anti-Chinese political planks, shows the universality of anti-Chinese prejudice in the West. (Library of Congress)

can workers alike. As one journalist put it, with little regard to history:

> Coolie labor is worse than African slavery.... For the Southern planter was commonly a gentleman of refinement, intelligence, and humanity, and it was always his intent to look after and care for the health of his slave. The average employer of coolie labor in this state is not a man of education nor of much humanity, nor has he any interest in the health or comfort of the coolie. His sole motive is to obtain the greatest quantity of work at the lowest compensation. If one coolie sickens and dies he can always get another. (quoted in Street 2004)

Nevertheless, the continuing anti-Chinese riots of the late 1870s and early 1880s suggested that most people who shared this opinion could not have cared less about the health of the Chinese worker.

The U.S. Congress passed the Chinese Exclusion Act of 1882, marking the culmination of this reform movement. Its premises were explicitly economic, as is evident from its preface: "Whereas in the opinion of the Government of the United States the coming of Chinese laborers to this country endangers the good order of certain localities within the territory thereof," it began. Chinese immigrants who were not laborers were still technically allowed into the country under the act if they could have their status certified by the Chinese government, but over time, fewer and fewer people could meet this standard, as both skilled and unskilled workers were specifically denied entrance (NARA 1989).

Despite this legislation, Chinese labor did not immediately disappear from the fields. Enough Chinese remained in California agriculture to keep tensions high for a considerable period of time afterward. Indeed, the remaining Chinese workers grew increasingly upset by the conditions they faced in the fields after exclusion. In Napa County and Lake County, California, they organized and therefore managed to raise their wages over one dollar per day for the first time. In 1884, defiant Chinese were fired en masse from a fruit orchard in Los Angeles and replaced with more-pliant Chinese laborers. In 1889, Fresno raisin growers were forced to hire Chinese workers because of a labor shortage, but those workers struck repeatedly during the harvest. In response to this kind of activity, anti-Chinese violence continued, albeit on a smaller scale than in earlier riots, throughout the fields of California.

According to McWilliams, a condition "approximating civil war" broke out in California in 1893, not coincidentally the same year that another depression struck the United States. Chinese workers were driven from the fields, and unemployed whites raided Chinese labor camps and set them aflame. What McWilliams called a union of white farmworkers formed to foment these activities. Large growers who employed Chinese labor to get their crops picked decried such efforts, but this kind of terror—even more than Chinese exclusion—was responsible for eliminating Chinese labor from the agriculture industry. The depression of 1893, which brought desperate white workers into the fields in large numbers, ended Chinese involvement in California agriculture even as it also led to a huge spike in violence (McWilliams 1944).

Japanese Farmworkers Begin to Organize

The first Japanese farmworkers arrived in California in 1890. The growers had invited them, although not specifically to replace the Chinese. Despite their status as migrant workers, the Japanese soon began to form "associations" and "clubs" in order to coordinate where they went to work and when. Like the Chinese before them, the Japanese workers could underbid all competing labor groups. Because of the acute shortage of farm labor in the 1890s, they did not raise the ire of native whites at first. Racial animosity increased as time passed, though, and the Japanese became not only successful farmworkers but also successful farmers. When they acquired land, they created enemies among large growers and other small farmers. The fact that Japanese owners by and large hired Japanese workers almost exclusively probably did not help their popularity.

Farm owners had hoped to achieve a smooth transition between Chinese and Japanese labor, but Japanese farmworkers were not prepared to be a pliant racial minority. Because of their concentration in particular segments of the industry, they were able to use their clout to gain the first collective-bargaining agreements in the history of American agriculture. The 1903 strike of sugar beet workers in Oxnard, California, deserves special attention.

Oxnard was totally dominated by the American Sugar Beet Company: virtually everybody, including the Japanese laborers, worked there in some capacity. The Japanese workers performed the difficult labor necessary to raise a healthy sugar beet crop by hand. In an attempt to hold down labor costs, however, company executives—along with other interested outsiders—created the Western Agricultural Contracting Company (WACC) in 1902. This organization took control of the labor hiring process from Japanese and other independent contractors. Although this approach was initially successful at holding down wages, the second year of operation brought a strike threat, organized by a Japanese labor contractor from San Francisco, Y. Yamaguchi. As Yamaguchi explained in the local paper:

> Many of us have families, were born in this country, and are lawfully seeking to protect the property that we have—our labor. It is just as necessary for the welfare of the valley that we get a decent living wage, as it is that the machines in the great sugar factory be properly oiled—

if the machine stops, the wealth of the valley stops, and likewise if the laborers are not given a decent wage, they too must stop work and the whole people of this country will suffer with them. (quoted in Street 2004)

Although nobody really expected the Japanese workers to carry out this threat, they walked out on February 11, 1903.

Because 200 Mexicans joined the 500 striking Japanese, this dispute has been called the first interracial strike in American labor history. Together, the two groups formed the Japanese-Mexican Labor Association (JMLA), which would lead the effort. The JMLA demanded an end to the WACC monopoly on hiring and a return to previous wage levels. There was violence, and the leaders of the strike were arrested, but in the end, the JMLA included enough of the beet thinners in the area that management had to deal with them. The union won a complete victory.

This strike is also important because of the reaction it prompted from the American Federation of Labor (AFL). Although the AFL had chartered farmworkers' organizations prior to this dispute, this strike was instigated without the formal involvement of established organized labor. After the JMLA won the strike, AFL president Samuel Gompers offered to let the new union have a charter, provided that it denied membership to any Chinese or Japanese worker. The JMLA refused. And without permanent institutional support, the union quickly faded away. Labor contractors returned to their earlier individualistic approach, and the workers still had no one to look out for their interests.

The Japanese success in organizing places such as Oxnard and the Imperial Valley led to the creation of a movement designed to restrict their immigration for the benefit of white labor. A report by California's commissioner of labor, W. V. Stafford, detailing Japanese control of jobs in some counties led to an upsurge in anti-Japanese violence between 1906 and 1907. These attacks culminated in the so-called Gentleman's Agreement of 1907, in which President Theodore Roosevelt terminated further Japanese immigration by executive order. Once again, Japanese tourists and merchants were not restricted; the order was intended to prevent laborers from entering the country, for the benefit of white workingmen. In the wake of the Gentleman's Agreement, growers turned to Hungarians, Italians, and even Sikhs to meet their voracious demand for labor (Street 2004).

The IWW

The Industrial Workers of the World (IWW or "Wobblies") remains perhaps the most radical labor organization ever created on American soil. Although the IWW had no leadership structure and no detailed platform beyond revolution, the federal government still targeted the organization for extinction because it posed a threat to the existing order. Yet the Wobblies made significant contributions to the American labor movement. They pioneered many effective labor tactics, such as the sit-down strike. Theirs was the first labor organization to demonstrate serious concern for non-white workers and among the first to care about workers with very low wages. Therefore, they were a natural fit with West Coast agricultural labor. Even though comparatively few agricultural laborers shared the IWW's radical agenda, the organization's focus on free speech rights in agricultural towns attracted a great deal of attention.

The IWW first moved into California's fields in 1908, creating a local affiliate in the town of Holtville and later others across the Imperial Valley. When the first offices opened, many confused locals tried to pay their water bills at Wobbly meeting halls, thinking the acronym IWW stood for Imperial Valley Water Works. When law enforcement pulled an organizer addressing a crowd off a soapbox in Brawley, enraged workers burned down a packing shed, and the IWW got the blame for that incident. Though the organization had little luck recruiting Japanese labor, the Wobblies made extraordinary efforts to recruit Mexican Americans. As Holtville secretary John R. Boyd explained:

> We are doing our best to get the slaves organized and will get results before too long. There is great field work . . . among the Mexicans. My object in writing this is that we can expect great results from the Mexican workers before long. . . . We held a propaganda meeting in our hall, with about 25 Mexicans present, who listened to fellow worker Berrera and my humble self expound the principles of the one big union. We intend to hold propaganda meetings in Spanish once a week from this time on. (quoted in Street 2004)

Other workers, according to Richard Street in *Beasts of the Field*, considered the IWW's program to be "a colossal waste of energy"

(Street 2004). Although the IWW did have some success in California agriculture, it was often fleeting.

Fresno was the most active center of IWW activity throughout California. In 1909, organizers met with success in organizing Mexican American railroad workers and farmhands. They did this in large part by holding street meetings and relaying their radical message to the masses through soapbox speeches delivered on street corners. When the local sheriff revoked the IWW's permit to hold street meetings, the Wobblies vowed to keep talking. In November 1910, Fresno civic leaders began to enforce the order and simultaneously closed down every IWW meeting hall in the city, then began to arrest Wobbly activists. The IWW counseled passive resistance and continued to offer up arrestees to pack Fresno's jails (Dubofsky 1969).

Like the civil rights movement arrestees of the 1960s, the Wobblies continued their protests in jail. When incarcerated in Fresno's jail, the IWW members would sing and yell and pound on the bars so as to make life difficult for the guards who worked there. When not doing these things, they would transact union business. In response to this activity, the jailers denied the prisoners adequate food, tobacco, and provisions. At one point, firemen turned a hose on imprisoned Wobblies while they were still in their cells. Some union members broke under this kind of pressure, promising to leave town on release, but most stayed put. After six months, the city of Fresno negotiated a truce, releasing all IWW prisoners and guaranteeing their right to speak on Fresno street corners. Yet even though this dispute earned the IWW enormous national publicity, it did not seem to help organizing very much, as activities of the Fresno local disappeared from Wobbly literature after the negotiated settlement.

In 1912, the IWW fought a San Diego ordinance that halted public speaking at a popular speakers' corner for Wobbly and non-Wobbly speakers alike. There was a broad coalition opposed to the ordinance, but city authorities quickly focused on the IWW because of its radical agenda. Since San Diego was cut off from the rest of California's agricultural industry, there were not enough Wobblies from local fields around to pack the jails. Those Wobblies who were jailed often found themselves beaten by vigilantes and then escorted to the county line, where worse treatment was threatened if they dared to return. Such actions could only have been carried out with the cooperation of the local government, and in fact, San Diego leaders readily admitted their involvement in these mob activities.

To make matters worse, San Diego officials called on federal authorities to help them destroy the IWW there. At one point, local prosecutors in San Diego and Los Angeles claimed that an IWW-led revolution against the federal government was imminent. Much to his credit, President William Howard Taft did nothing. Progressive governor Hiram Johnson actually denounced San Diego officials for their stand against free speech, but the local authorities still won: the street corner where Wobblies had been packed off to jail was quiet by the end of the year. Although the IWW gained sympathy from the terrible treatment members received, it did not have the power to change the situation. Ultimately, this dispute was important primarily because it convinced some Wobblies to eschew passive resistance in the future. Others simply quit the movement in frustration.

In 1913, IWW organizers were involved in a struggle against the state's largest employer of agricultural labor, E. C. Durst, who had a giant hops ranch in Wheatland. By that time, the Wobblies had perfected a method for actually organizing agricultural workers rather than simply preserving their rights. IWW organizers would get employed at large ranches and reach bindlestiffs out in the fields. With the help of the IWW, migrant workers presented Durst with a series of demands, including uniform minimum wages, free water in the fields, and better camp conditions. But when Durst called local authorities to break up a mass meeting, the crowd reacted badly as the speaker was pulled off the stage. Four people, including the local district attorney and a sheriff, were killed in the ensuing melee (Dubofsky 1969).

Public officials and local media blamed the IWW members for the violence, even though the strike had begun with minimal involvement from them, and IWW supporters were arrested all over the state, whether they had been in Wheatland or not. Authorities indicted two Wobblies for the murder of the district attorney, despite the fact that both had counseled the crowd to refrain from violence. Between their arrest and subsequent conviction, California newspapers were filled with stories tying the IWW to crop destruction, sabotage, murder, and other violent acts. One might have expected this kind of publicity to hurt their cause, but historian Melvyn Dubofsky has argued that the attraction between the IWW and migrant farmworkers actually increased because of this incident. In 1914, the U.S. Commission on Industrial Relations found there were forty Wobbly locals across California, with about 5,000 members scattered among them (Dubofsky 1969).

In the first seven months after America's entrance into this war for human freedom, enemy agitators in our midst caused 283,402 workers to lose 6,285,519 days of production. Our war industries were heavily handicapped by this unpatriotic strife.

LET US ALL PULL TOGETHER TO WIN THE WAR QUICKLY

This World War I–era poster criticizes labor "agitators" for providing aid and comfort to Germany's kaiser. (Library of Congress)

In 1915, field hands and Wobblies from across the Midwest and the far west met in Kansas City to form a new organization specifically for farmworkers, the Agricultural Workers' Organization (AWO). Its general secretary, Walter Nef, was an excellent organizer who spread IWW agitation to fields across the country. Seeking a ten-hour workday, a minimum wage, overtime pay, and better board, the AWO won many demands for Kansas field hands that year. By September, it had 1,500 members in North Dakota alone, and by the end of the year, it had a total membership of 3,000.

The first California local appeared in December 1915. The AWO entered the wheat fields there the next year, and by year's end, the organization had 30,000 members. The group's success had much to do with timing. In a period when grain orders from war-torn Europe were making many farmers rich, growers had money to improve the lives of their workers and did not want to risk their windfall profits by provoking a strike. Renamed the Agriculture Workers Industrial Union (AWIU), the organization claimed 50,000 members at the height of the war (Dubofsky 1969).

Many of the new recruits were from Oklahoma. Like California, Oklahoma had large bonanza wheat farms during the 1910s. Also like California, the workers there were transitory, moving from field to field during harvesttime. Despite this fundamental problem, the IWW had success in Oklahoma because of an acute shortage of labor and the high price of wheat during the war years (which meant that farmers did not want to risk seeing their crops rot in the fields). The IWW broke an employer-sponsored labor cartel, raised wages, and enlisted thousands of workers in the process.

The Oklahoma campaign marked an important change in the history of IWW job tactics. Like its more conservative counterparts in the American Federation of Labor, Walter Nef's AWO made demands and bargained with employers. Improving the lot of members superseded revolutionary ideology for the first time in Wobbly history. The Oklahoma local was financially stable and brought in more money than any other unit in the entire IWW. Nevertheless, attacks on the patriotism of the IWW during World War I hurt this local, too. For example, mobs attacked Wobblies in three Oklahoma cities during 1918. When faced with this kind of government-sponsored oppression as well as the collapse of agricultural demand at the end of the war, the union largely disappeared with the rest of the IWW (Sellars 1998).

Meatpacking

Unlike agriculture (or most other industries, for that matter), meatpacking depended more on the division of labor than on machines in terms of increasing production during the era of industrialization. As meatpacking firms became concentrated into five huge companies and the scale of production expanded, it became easier to reorganize production so as to render workers' difficult but long-standing skilled jobs obsolete. By the turn of the twentieth century, investigators from the federal Bureau of Corporations marveled at the extent of this process: "In the old-fashioned small slaughterhouses one man, or at most a few men, performed all the tasks from the dealing of the death blow to the final preparation of the carcass for sale. In the largest slaughtering plants of today will be found hundreds, or even thousands, of workmen, each of whom performs a very small, narrowly defined task, in which by innumerable repetitions he becomes an expert" (quoted in Barrett 1987). Yet skilled men remained, and these workers would form the core of the union movement in the meatpacking trade. This part of the essay will first cover labor relations in the large packinghouses and then move on to the unionization of skilled workers in the retail meat trade (that is, butcher shops).

Efforts at unionizing the meatpacking trade began with the growth of the industry in the late 1870s, but workers had little success in these efforts until 1900. (Butchers, who organized into local craft unions, were a notable exception.) Whenever there was trouble in a major packing town, companies would invariably introduce strikebreakers and Pinkerton guards to protect them. Other industries hid their blacklists, but the packers used theirs openly and actually provoked a court decision that said this tactic was legal. In 1896, AFL packinghouse unions only had about 500 dues-paying members (Brody 1964).

The first organizing in Chicago, the center of the industry, began shortly after the Great Railroad Strike of 1877. During the 1880s, some butcher workmen joined the Knights of Labor. Meatpacking workers were also deeply involved in the call for the eight-hour day in 1886, and a strike that year actually won that concession in the Chicago yards. However, later that fall, the city's largest meatpacking companies reintroduced the ten-hour day and withstood a strike called to protest this decision. In 1894, Chicago packers struck in support of Pullman railcar workers, joining the AFL in the process. Alarmed by rioting that accompanied that dispute, the packers used a blacklist to keep the yards in Chicago and elsewhere union free (Barrett 1987).

The Amalgamated Meat Cutters and Butcher Workmen

The Amalgamated Meat Cutters and Butcher Workmen formed on January 26, 1897. The Amalgamated began with twelve preexisting locals that were directly affiliated with the AFL and quickly gained eighteen more. But there were also many locals that went under because of corrupt officers or badly timed strikes. Still, the Amalgamated had firmly established itself across the country by 1900 (Brody 1964).

The Amalgamated went out of its way to bring less skilled workers into the organization. In 1901, President Michael Donnelly declared: "There must be no aristocracy in the labor movement. I have worked at the highest wages paid in the packing plants, but I cannot forget that the man who washed the floor while I worked at the tables is entitled to the same consideration I am. I cannot forget that he is a human being, and that he has a family. It should be our purpose to make the injury of the common laborers the concern of the skilled workman" (Barrett 1987). Although such sentiments were obviously heartfelt, organizing less skilled workers also became necessary in an industry where management consistently employed the division of labor to break down skilled jobs into easier component parts.

Organizing the less skilled required the union to be multiethnic as well as multiracial. The majority of skilled workers in the union's early years were long-standing immigrants of Irish or German stock, rather than the eastern or southern European immigrants whose numbers shot up after 1880 and who were feared by so many native-born Americans during that era. Most of these workers were "knife men." Although they performed the same difficult incision again and again, it was impossible at the time for the task to be done by machine. Hence, they were the best-paid workers in the yards. In Chicago, many knife men owned their own homes in good neighborhoods. These workers clung to the craft traditions of an earlier era and often owned their own tools and cared for them personally.

At the turn of the twentieth century, two-thirds of the industry's workforce consisted of common laborers, and most of these were new immigrants. Like the fictional Jurgis Rudkus of Upton Sinclair's *The Jungle,* many were Lithuanian. There were also many Slovaks and Poles in the industry, especially in Chicago. As these workers were less skilled, they also generally received lower wages than older immigrants and had a harder time getting promoted up the job ladder. Even though the Amalgamated wanted to bring these workers into the union, they organized their locals by department rather than by plant. As a consequence, less skilled immigrants tended to be segregated from skilled, longtime Americans and remain in the same socioeconomic class (Barrett 1987).

Black workers entered the Chicago stockyards in large numbers for the first time during the 1910s. Hobbled by racial discrimination, they were more likely to be stuck in dead-end, less skilled jobs than any European immigrants. By the 1920s, packers consciously decided to replace those immigrants with African American and Mexican American labor. Even though black employment increased during that decade, the conditions the workers faced deteriorated. Unfortunately for the Amalgamated, few African Americans supported the union. Some had gotten their start as strikebreakers. In addition, important institutions in the Chicago black community, such as the Urban League or the Young Men's Christian Association (YMCA), were hostile to the union. Efforts by employers to fan the flames of racial tension in order to keep the union weak only hurt this situation.

Women workers, who had increasingly been undercutting the wages of less skilled men, were also difficult to assimilate. First introduced to the yards during the 1890s, they could be found in nearly every department of a packinghouse by 1920. In that era, as one might expect, they were almost always making the lowest wages of any employee. This situation was related to the fact that they were often the only workers paid by piece rates rather than an hourly wage. Women were also more likely to fall victim to irregular employment than men, and they would be hired and fired more often than their male counterparts. For all these reasons, it seems unwise to attribute sexism as the sole cause of the Amalgamated's decision to group women in separate locals.

Another issue that kept the union from organizing as well as it wanted was the intermittent nature of packinghouse work. Some workers, known as "steady time" men, were guaranteed at least six hours of work each week. Because these positions were prized, they tended to be a source of contention among the men. Getting these positions required speed and efficiency, so there was a constant competition to demonstrate one's worth. This competition made it harder for the union to convince workers that they were all on the same side. Workers who did not have these positions, mostly the less skilled men, were sometimes laid off for seasonal reasons and sometimes because of slack demand for weeks or months at a time. Even on a working day, laborers sometimes had to wait hours before work commenced, and

Workers at a Swift packinghouse produce link sausages under the watchful eye of supervisors, ca. 1900. (Library of Congress)

they were only paid for their time on the job. Such lapses strained the ability of these workers to pay union dues (Barrett 1987).

The union argued that organized workers would be more reliable because the union could prevent trouble on the floor, such as wildcat strikes. In 1901, the first local union council formed in Chicago. This body helped settle jurisdictional disputes and control the militancy of employees throughout the yards. Indeed, large packers, who depended on a reliable supply of labor for operations that capitalized on economies of scale, were friendlier to the union than small packers. The Amalgamated repaid this attitude by only authorizing strikes as defensive measures, such as preventing the dismissal of skilled men with seniority. But the union did not have complete control over all the workers in the yard. In Chicago, for instance, the local labor council was taken over by radicals who resented the union's concessions to large packers (Brody 1964).

In July 1904, the meatpacking workers launched a national strike, even though management had been willing to submit the workers' grievances to binding arbitration. Once the strike began, management held firm because of its resolve to limit labor costs, which had increased noticeably since the union had been established. Firms brought in black strikebreakers. When the strike ended in August, the union had used up its limited bank account, leaving it with only $25,000 on hand, and the AFL refused the Amalgamated's request for a loan. The employees returned to work after a month and a half without achieving a single one of the union's original demands. Furthermore, the managers did not even offer a guarantee that they would continue to bargain collectively with them. Many union men were denied reemployment after the strike ended.

The union suffered steep declines in membership after the 1904 strike. Dissidents attacked the leadership of the Amalgamated for its mistakes during the strike. President Donnelly was barely reelected in 1906 but resigned in 1907, becoming a cigar salesman in Kansas City. The connections between the international union and the local frayed, as the locals increasingly struck out on their own. By 1910, the union had a membership of only a little more than 2,000 and just $850 on hand (Brody 1964).

World War I through 1921

The return of prosperity to the meatpacking industry in 1910 facilitated the resurgence of the union. Between 1910 and 1914, the Amalgamated issued sixty-three new local charters, and membership more than tripled to 6,500 by 1914, which made it possible to hire more full-time organizers. Meanwhile, in 1914, the European demand for meat for World War I coincided with a terrible labor shortage, brought on by the cutoff of immigration from eastern Europe that coincided with that conflict. Minor labor disputes broke out all over the United States that year. In 1916, the American Federation of Labor sent its own organizers into the packinghouses to help line up new members. Despite these positive developments, however, few new workers joined the union until conditions tightened even more after America entered the war in April 1917.

The first strikes during the war years came not from unionized workers but from unskilled workers in South Omaha, Nebraska.

William Z. Foster was a
leading figure in the effort to
unionize the American
meatpacking industry.
(Library of Congress)

Fifty truckers left the plant there on September 1, 1917, and the
walkout grew to include union members a few days later. A federal
mediator arrived and settled the dispute on September 12, with the
plant getting an increase of two and a half cents per hour. To head off
this kind of agitation, the packers offered a series of "voluntary"
wage increases nationwide. They also intensified their welfare programs (which included things such as new pension plans or a new
gymnasium) to make workers happier with their positions. During
the war, the AFL had agreed to a no-strike pledge, so in theory, further strikes would not happen, but the big packing concerns could
not trust the union to keep its workers in line (Brody 1964).

Starting in 1917, the head of the Chicago Federation of Labor
(CFL), John Fitzpatrick, and a former IWW organizer named
William Z. Foster began an organizing campaign in the Chicago
stockyards. Fitzpatrick was an Irish immigrant who got his start
working in the stockyards before becoming a blacksmith. After a
brief stint in the CFL presidency at the turn of the century, he would
again serve in that office from 1906 to 1946. The Chicago campaign
was the first event to bring Foster to public attention. He would go

on to lead the Great Steel Strike of 1919, only to have his former membership in the IWW used by the steel companies as a way to red-bait that effort. Foster joined the American Communist Party in 1921 and was its presidential candidate in 1924, 1928, and 1932 and its chairman after World War II. Fitzpatrick split with Foster in 1923 after the latter's membership in the Communist Party became widely known.

Since Foster's radical ideology had yet to be discovered during the Chicago packinghouse effort (it didn't come out until the Great Steel Strike of 1919), this campaign is the best example available of Foster's organizing skills in action. Founded on July 15, 1917, the Chicago Stockyards Labor Council controlled the effort, which included representatives of every union in the yards. As Foster later explained in his autobiography, "We decided to move towards industrial unionism by setting up an industrial federation and by locking the various component craft unions so firmly together under one Council, one Executive Board, one set of Business Agents, etc., as to create a firm front in the whole of the industry" (Brody 1964). As was the case in South Omaha, the less skilled workers were most interested in the union, and they signed up by the thousands. Many of these individuals were foreign-born Poles and Slavs.

By November 1917, there was considerable pressure coming from the rank and file to strike. Much of this pressure grew out of management's actions. In mid-November, the packers ignored the demands of a multiunion committee for a hearing. They quickly followed that slap with the dismissal of union activists at a number of different companies. Federal intervention got the activists reinstated, but management still refused to talk to union representatives. Because strikes would have hurt the war effort, the AFL had agreed to a no-strike pledge in exchange for binding arbitration. Therefore, the CFL wanted to get the federal government to intervene before a strike was necessary. The mediation between the unions and the management in February 1918 resembled a public trial of labor policies in the stockyards, and the details of working-class life for employees in this industry shocked the public. The following headline provides a sense of the emotional tone of the hearings: "LIFE'S HARD-SHIPS TOLD BY WOMEN OF STOCKYARDS /ONE LIVED IN CHICAGO SIX YEARS, NEVER SAW MOVIE, PARK, NOR LAKE MICHIGAN / SAY ALL ARE UNDERPAID / TESTIFY STRUGGLE FOR MERE EXISTENCE IS HARD" (Brody 1964). As a result of arbitration, wages jumped 42.5 percent.

Furthermore, workers got the basic eight-hour day, overtime, paid lunches, and equal pay for equal work done by men or women (Barrett 1987; Brody 1964).

The workers who benefited the least from this result were the African Americans who had come north in droves to work in dirty jobs such as those of the stockyards. Blacks had been largely identified as a "scab race" by white workers because of their role in breaking earlier strikes. Even though the unions used African American organizers in their campaign, many blacks were simply resistant to joining any union, recognizing that many white workers would not welcome them. Estimates of the number of black workers who joined the union—and therefore benefited most from its efforts— range between one-fourth and one-third, as compared to 95 percent for white workers. One indicator of the racial hostility found inside the plant is that a brutal 1919 race riot in Chicago was centered in communities near Packingtown, the slum neighborhood that housed many of the industry's workers (Barrett 1987).

In 1919, with the war safely over and no government interest in continued peace in the yards, wildcat strikes broke out all over Chicago. But the real showdown between labor and management came in 1921. That year, 45,000 packinghouse workers struck in order to preserve their union against employer attacks. The precipitating event was a regressive wage cut that affected the lowest-paid and most volatile unskilled workers more acutely than anyone else. The union requested arbitration, but management welcomed the strike as a way to remove union workers from its shrinking postwar employment ranks. Besides wage cuts, packers had created an elaborate series of welfare programs and company unions to help win the loyalty of nonunion workers.

Unfortunately, by 1921, the solidarity of the war years had broken down. The engineers' and firemen's unions refused to honor the Amalgamated's strike call. In Chicago, a court injunction issued by Judge Dennis Sullivan prevented picketing. He wrote, "I have come to the conclusion that there are no absolute rights in society today. All rights are relative. . . . As I understand the law in Illinois there is no such thing as 'peaceful picketing'" (quoted in Barrett 1987). Two thousand policemen poured into Packingtown to enforce the order, and bloody riots ensued. Compulsory arbitration laws in Kansas and Colorado prevented strikes in those states from ever getting off the ground. And in St. Paul, Minnesota, the police put down violence associated with the conflict. The large packers had no trouble finding replacement workers. The union was busted until the industrial union movement of the 1930s.

The Meat Cutters

As a group, meat cutters, the people who cut meat for the retail trade, were quite distinct from the people who worked in packinghouses. They were more highly skilled, and they were widely dispersed rather than concentrated in large packing towns. Moreover, they usually worked alongside their employers in small butcher shops. These men sustained the Amalgamated through its worst years, and they often held enormous influence over the local meat trade. For all these reasons, they had far more success than their colleagues in the giant packinghouses.

Before 1900, there were no serious strikes in the retail meat trade. In fact, the meat cutters hardly ever organized because they were incipient capitalists, hoping to be taken into the business by their employers. Local employee associations appeared during that era, but they had little class consciousness. Sometimes they offered petitions, but as these organizations were not trade unions, they did not attempt to bargain collectively with employers. The Knights of Labor attracted a few butchers in the 1880s, but the first sign of real unionism came from ten or twelve butchers' locals directly affiliated with the AFL in the early 1890s. Relations with employers were amicable, but only a couple of these units survived the panic of 1893. Permanent organization came only with the formation of the Amalgamated in 1897; the impetus was the consolidation of the packers around that same time. "The matter of an international organization for our craft had been on my heart a long time," one meat cutter later explained, "for I could see how rapidly was the downward course of all butcher workmen. I was confident that if our craft should ever be recognized other than the tools of a great monopoly it must be by independent organization" (Brody 1964). Although the packinghouse union membership ebbed and flowed, the membership in retail butcher shops, especially in large cities, was comparatively strong and consistent.

The chief concern of early meat cutters' locals was their work schedule. Many meat cutters worked eighty hours per week around the turn of the century. Retail butchers were staunch supporters of early and Sunday closings, and a large number of locals allied with religious conservatives to create blue laws in many states that banned meat sales on Sundays. These unions were also valuable allies in lobbying for meat inspection laws, which kept unscrupulous producers from undercutting their employers' prices. As time passed, locals began to ask for half days during summer months or legal holidays during the year. Wage scales were seldom questioned in collective bargaining. Unlike the situation in the big stockyards, compensation was viewed as a private matter between employer and employee. Only in large cities were wages considered regularly (Brody 1964).

At first, small employers (the corner butcher, in effect) greeted the unions as a way to strengthen loyalty in the workplace. But as the union increasingly got in the way of management prerogatives, even the corner butcher began to object. Many were against early closing legislation, as they often needed all the sales they could get. Others objected to the personalities of the "walking delegates" who appeared regularly in their stores. Union boycotts organized against medium-size shops engendered enormous hostility in some locales.

After the turn of the twentieth century, retail meat dealers in large cities began to organize themselves in response to the union threat. As one New York employer explained in 1904, "We realize that we must meet the force of organized labor. The grocers and butchers must keep up with industrial progress. Unorganized, the time might come when we would find ourselves unable to cope with labor conditions that might arise" (Brody 1964). These efforts relied on cooperation from large packers, who could cut off the meat supply to conciliatory butchers who might otherwise have chosen to deal with the union.

The kosher meat trade, centered in New York City, was distinct enough to merit consideration on its own. First organized in 1909, a New York local covering kosher shops conducted a disastrous strike in 1913 that almost wiped it out. It grew strong again during World War I, and these workers, known as "schochtem," also organized in other cities such as Chicago, Detroit, and Cleveland at that time. Interestingly, these locals were distinct enough (for instance, they had to answer to rabbinical authorities) that they refused to affiliate with the Amalgamated until the late 1920s. Once they finally joined up with the Amalgamated, their common religious ties made them very strong locals.

Conclusion

Labor and reform efforts in agricultural and meatpacking industries had as many differences as similarities. Agricultural workers were almost exclusively rural; packinghouse workers were largely urban. Agricultural workers could not keep a permanent union going; packinghouse workers, despite adversity, could. Large farmers used mechanization to replace as many workers as they could; many aspects of meatpacking were almost impossible to mechanize.

Nevertheless, the similarities were also strong. Both industries required a mix of skilled and unskilled labor. Even though the agricultural industry used mechanization to replace skilled workers whenever it could, it still had an insatiable demand for labor, just as the packers did. Both industries relied on immigrant labor to fill their ranks. Agricultural workers were hampered by the seasonal demand for their labor; packinghouse workers were hired and laid off depending on the fluctuating demand for their product.

When considered together, these two industries suggest that in order to understand the fate of organization and reform efforts, it is necessary to understand the work process. Since these firms were, in essence, processors rather than producers, it was impossible to "make" things more efficiently. Even in agriculture, where machines were used, there were so many parts of the process that remained labor intensive that worker concerns had to be addressed. But ultimately, success at translating that influence into better working conditions depended on factors unique to each industry.

Sources

Barrett, James R. 1987. *Work and Community in the Jungle: Chicago's Packinghouse Workers, 1894–1922.* Urbana: University of Illinois Press.

Brody, David. 1964. *The Butcher Workmen: A Study of Unionization.* Cambridge, MA: Harvard University Press.

Dubofsky, Melvyn. 1969. *We Shall Be All.* New York: Quadrangle.

George, Henry. 1880. "The Kearny Agitation in California." Available on-line at www.sfmuseum.org/hist9/hgeorge3.html.

McWilliams, Carey. 1944. *Factories in the Field.* Boston: Little, Brown.

National Archives and Records Administration (NARA). 1989. *Teaching with Documents: Using Primary Sources from the National Archives.* Washington,

DC: National Archives and Records Administration. Available on-line at www.ourdocuments.gov/doc.php?flash=true&doc=47.

Sellars, Nigel Anthony. 1998. *Oil, Wheat, and Wobblies: The Industrial Workers of the World in Oklahoma, 1905–1930*. Norman: University of Oklahoma Press.

Street, Richard Steven. 2004. *Beasts of the Field: A Narrative History of California Farmworkers, 1769–1913*. Stanford, CA: Stanford University Press.

Environmental Impact

Kevin Hillstrom
Laurie Collier Hillstrom

O f all the major economic activities in American history—both those that preceded industrialization and those that were created or influenced by it—agriculture has had arguably the greatest impact on the ecology of the nation. Not only has it shaped the dietary trends of Americans, it has also been the single most important factor dictating land-use practices in U.S. history. Indeed, strictly in terms of land area affected, the plow changed greater swaths of American territory than any other force. These changes paved the way for a level of agricultural and ranching productivity that made the United States the envy of the world. But the changes also took a heavy toll on regional wilderness ecosystems and natural resources adjacent to farmland, such as rivers and streams. As one historian noted, "The environmental history of North America is unintelligible without agriculture because husbandry embodied the force of settlement, created cultural landscapes, sustained the entire population, and produced commodities for trade and manufacturing. Environmental change did not cease after land had been cleared and farmed for a generation. Deforestation, erosion, the destruction of habitat—farmers caused them all" (Stoll 2002).

Agriculture and Environment in Early America

When the first generations of American colonists carved agricultural livelihoods out of the wilderness of the New World, they largely discarded the farming and land-use practices that had served their forebears so well back in England. Essentially, the seemingly limitless and fertile land resources that existed in America made it easy for them to embrace an array of wasteful and shortsighted cultivation practices and abandon the sustainability-based land-use practices that their English ancestors, who had limited land at their disposal for cultivation, had perfected. Under this English system, farming families had obeyed the dictates of the so-called three-field system, in which all cultivated land under their hand was divided into three large fields, one of which was left fallow each growing season in a regular rotation.

In colonial America, this practice was, quite accurately, seen as financially limiting, given the abundant land available for cultivation. As a result, the standard practice of most early American farmers was to squeeze every last bit of productivity out of existing fields, regardless of whether this approach exhausted the soil's nutritional bounty, and then simply clear new land for cultivation. This approach would have used up any soil in relatively short order, but since the quality of New England soil was generally less than ideal for farming to begin with, the pace of abandonment and new land clearing became particularly brisk.

This mind-set, which increasingly saw land as a disposable commodity rather than a resource that could be used for generations through attentive stewardship, actually created a shortage of farmland in many parts of New England in the eighteenth century. This development led some New Englanders to belatedly adopt a more sustainable approach to their existing acreage. Many farmers took greater care to apply fertilizer to existing fields to replenish the soil, and numerous fields were turned over to crops that demanded less nourishment. Significantly, it was during this time that a strain of genuinely conservationist thought took root in the minds of some American farmers. These early conservationists, many of whom were stalwarts of the New England communities in which they toiled, embraced sustainability and nature preservation as philosophical goals in and of themselves, not just as tools to be employed toward greater financial fortune (Logsdon 1994; Stoll 2002).

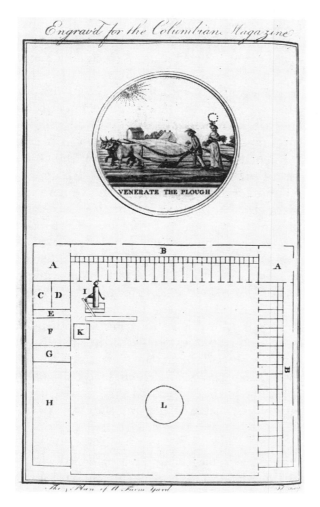

This eighteenth-century print shows a plan for a farmyard, as well as a vignette titled "Venerate the Plough." (Library of Congress)

The Plow and Early Territorial Expansion

The impact of agriculture on the forests and streams of the North American continent increased exponentially in the late eighteenth and early nineteenth centuries, a stretch of decades in which the young United States went on an unparalleled binge of territorial acquisition and expansion. It was during this period that federal and state governments joined hands with private enterprise to develop a comprehensive and efficient transportation infrastructure for the transport of a wide variety of goods—but most especially the transport of crops to market. This network included massive canals and bridges, local roadways, harbors at coastal locations (including major river mouths), and—from the 1830s on—railroad lines.

As young America's transportation network grew and its territorial limits marched steadily westward, the federal government took decisive action to encourage agricultural expansion into the wilderness. The legislation that resulted included the Basic Land Ordinance of 1785, which was instrumental in spurring settlement of the Great Lakes region; the Harrison Frontier Land Act of 1800 (also known simply as the Land Act) and subsequent amendments, which provided for the sale of large tracts of public land at a modest price; and the 1841 Preemption Act, which gave settlers on the western frontier the first right to buy the land on which they had put down stakes as soon as the federal government got around to surveying it. Under the terms of this law, the price was only $1.25 per acre for a maximum purchase of 160 acres. In 1854, the Graduation Act further lowered prices on unsold land on the western frontier.

In settled America, though, most of the nation's farmers remained careless caretakers of the natural resources on which they subsisted. Some settled regions of the country, whether in New England, the South, or points farther west, managed to implement land cultivation systems that were both sustainable and stable, and surrounding communities enjoyed greater levels of sustainability and stability as a direct result.

> Uninspired by distant river valleys, disdaining those statesmen who urged Americans to break the continent to the plow, an important minority of farmers and planters decided to dig in, preferring to rethink agriculture rather than remake their world on the frontier.... Improvement suggested a way for communities to hold or slow the extension of plowland into fields, forests, and waters, and it offered an opposite kind of change from the blaze and shift of nineteenth century America. (Stoll 2002)

But other regions of the country, including lands that had been settled for only a generation or two, struggled to arrive at a system of land husbandry that was not wasteful or needlessly destructive to remaining natural ecosystems in the vicinity. For example, countless rivers and streams continued to be choked and fouled by erosion from adjacent crop fields, with associated damage to spawning fish and other aquatic species dependent on healthy riverine systems. In some states, land clearing for cultivation reached such feverish levels that the ecological character of the entire state was forever changed. In Arkansas alone, for instance, an estimated 9 million acres of marsh and swamp forest—home to previously vibrant and complex communities of wildlife and native vegetation—were converted to farmland during the nineteenth century. And of course, shortsighted land-use policies left vast tracts of ruined fields in their wake. "In many of the settlements around us, the natural fertility of the soil has been exhausted," lamented an 1823 report of the Pennsylvania Agricultural Society. "Comparatively little new grounds remain to be brought under cultivation. To refertilize the old must be our resource; and the necessity is every day becoming more imperative" (quoted in Stoll 2002).

This state of affairs did not escape the notice of men such as George Perkins Marsh or Henry David Thoreau, who ranked among America's earliest conservationist voices. Thoreau, for example, vehemently criticized the wasteful land practices of his farming neighbors. Writing in his seminal work *Walden,* he declared that "by avarice and selfishness, and a groveling habit . . . of regarding the soil as property, or the means of acquiring property chiefly, the landscape is deformed, husbandry is degraded with us, and the farmer lives the meanest of lives" (Thoreau 1973).

Plowing Up the Western Frontier

Many farmers who pursued wasteful and unsustainable cropping practices, however, paid only a limited price for their behavior. Once the fields they tended were played out and exhausted, many of them simply packed up their families, their farming tools and seeds, and their other belongings and headed west, where vast new tracts of wilderness seemed to be thrown open to the plow with each passing year. Some historians have characterized this early American relationship to the land and its soil as essentially parasitic in nature: "A symbiotic relationship would be the best that could be hoped for, but American farmers tended to drain the body that hosted them, and the vector always pointed to fresh blood in the West" (Stoll 2002).

George Perkins Marsh

Born in Woodstock, Vermont, on March 15, 1801, George Perkins Marsh is considered by many environmental scholars to be America's first environmentalist, as the term is generally understood today. Marsh graduated from Dartmouth in 1820 and taught for several years before establishing a successful law practice in Burlington, Vermont. He then entered politics as a Whig, serving in the U.S. House of Representatives from 1843 to 1849. From there, he went on to serve for five years as the U.S. ambassador to Turkey.

George Marsh's 1864 work *Man and Nature; or, Physical Geography as Modified by Human Action* spurred the conservation movement in the United States for several decades. (Library of Congress)

Marsh returned to the United States in 1855. For the next several years, he indulged his restless intellect, writing books on subjects as diverse as the history of the English language and the economic benefits that would accrue from introducing the camel to American soil as a supplement to—or replacement for—the horse. He also continued his lifelong study of foreign languages, a passion that served him well when he was named the first U.S. ambassador to Italy in 1861. He served his country in that capacity until his death on July 23, 1882.

Despite Marsh's considerable diplomatic achievements, however, he is best known today for his books on the natural environment and humanity's careless degradation of woods, waters, and other resources. In 1864, he published *Man and Nature; or, Physical Geography as Modified by Human Action*, a book that is regarded today as one of the seminal harbingers of the conservation ethic that would emerge in the late nineteenth and early twentieth centuries. Following is an excerpt from this work, which has been described as the fountainhead of the American conservation movement:

The changes [to landscape], which these [farming and other land-clearing] causes have wrought in the physical geography of Vermont, within a single generation, are too striking to have escaped the attention of any observing person, and every middle-aged man, who revisits his birth-place after a few years of absence, looks upon another landscape than that which formed the theatre of his youthful toils and pleasures. The signs of artificial improvement are mingled with the tokens of improvident waste, and the bald and barren hills, the dry beds of the smaller streams, the ravines furrowed out by the torrents of spring, and the diminished thread of interval that skirts the widened channel of the rivers, seem sad substitutes for the pleasant groves and brooks and broad meadows of his ancient paternal domain. If the present value of timber and land will not justify the artificial re-planting of grounds injudiciously cleared, at least nature ought to be allowed to reclothe them with a spontaneous growth of wood, and in our future husbandry a more careful selection should be made of land for permanent improvement. It has long been a practice in many parts of Europe, as well as in our older settlements, to cut the forest reserved for timber and fuel, at stated intervals. It is quite time that this practice should be introduced among us. After the first felling of the original forest it is indeed a long time before its place is supplied, because the roots of old and full grown trees seldom throw up shoots, but when the second growth is once established, it may be cut with great advantage, at periods of about twenty five years, and yields a material, in every respect but size, far superior to the wood of the primitive tree. In many European countries, the economy of the forest is regulated by law; but here, where public opinion determines, or rather in practice constitutes law, we can only appeal to an enlightened self-interest to introduce the reforms, check the abuses, and preserve us from an increase of the evils I have mentioned.

Source

Marsh, George Perkins. 1848. *Address Delivered before the Agricultural Society of Rutland County, September 30, 1847.* Rutland: Herald Office, University of Vermont, Bailey/Howe Library. George Perkins Marsh Online Research Center.

The federal government, in league with state and territorial legislators and agencies, actively facilitated the rampant "improvement by agriculture" of the retreating western frontier. After all, it was an article of faith, whether one was a southern planter reliant on "King Cotton" or a midwestern grain farmer, that extraction of the continent's natural bounty to feed fellow citizens was practically a patriotic duty, especially since doing so had the added benefit of "civilizing" the wild territory within America's borders.

American legislators passed a fleet of laws meant to encourage settlement and cultivation across the country's midsection in the mid-nineteenth century. Of these, the Homestead Act of 1862 was more momentous than any previous legislation, even the Land Act of 1800 and the 1841 Preemption Act. The Homestead Act was specifically created to settle territory opened as a result of the passage of the 1854 Kansas-Nebraska Act. According to the terms of this act, any American citizen or immigrant alien who was at least twenty-one years old or the head of a family could, by paying a $10 claim fee, take possession of 160 acres of unsettled public land. After residing on and improving the parcel for five years, the settler automatically received final title at no additional cost. In addition, a provision in the act gave settlers the option of paying $1.25 an acre to receive title after only six months of residency—a provision that was utilized by more financially secure farmers.

By the 1860s and 1870s, the great westward migration was fetching up against the so-called Great American Desert—the Great Plains. Long-standing doubts about the suitability of this vast, semi-arid territory for farming quickly crumbled, done in by America's appetite for new lands and new commerce and its knack for wrapping perceived self-interest in patriotic trappings. Prominent promoters of western settlement such as William Gilpin, for example, trumpeted that the Great Plains were, rather than a desert, actually the "cardinal basis for the future empire now erecting itself upon the North American continent" (Gilpin 1890).

During the 1870s and 1880s, settlement of the plains accelerated, fueled by several years of above-average rainfall and a deep pseudo-scientific conviction that "rain follows the plow."

The notion that settlement was changing the climate on the flat, loamy, treeless plains rang irresistibly true to the subsistence farmer from the East who spent more time clearing his land of rocks and stumps than plowing and harvesting. [As a result] the breaking wave of settlement was eating up half a meridian a year; from one season to the next, settlements were thirty miles farther out. By the late 1870s, the hundredth meridian had been fatefully crossed. . . . On their way across the plains, travelers could see huge rolling clouds of dust on the southern horizon, caused by cattle drives from Texas to railheads at Dodge and Kansas City. The plains were being dug up; the buffalo were being annihilated to starve the Indians and make way for cows; the vanishing tribes were being herded like cattle onto reservations. (Reisner 1986)

This expansion of agriculture onto the Great Plains was the single greatest factor that drove America's enormous jump in agricultural capacity and productivity during the last three decades of the nineteenth century. An estimated 430 million acres of land were settled across the country during that time, bringing total U.S. farm acreage to more than 840 million acres. The total number of American farms underwent a corresponding increase during the same time, from 2.7 million in 1870 to 5.7 million by 1900. Between 1881 and 1885 alone, approximately 67,000 new homesteads were established in the Dakota Territory. The growth in acreage under cultivation, combined with the advent of tractors and combines and other machines, fueled impressive jumps in crop yields. Wheat production climbed from 250 million to 600 million bushels during the last three decades of the nineteenth century, and corn production rose from 1.1 million to 2.7 million bushels. Cotton production more than doubled during that time as well, rising to 10.1 million bales annually by the turn of the twentieth century (Bogue 1994).

John Wesley Powell and Farming in the West

The expansion of agriculture in the American West during the 1870s and 1880s, however, flew in the face of certain iron realities of climate and geography. The above-average rainfall registered across the plains and foothills of the West during that period sowed a false sense of security among the "sodbusters" of the era. And various land speculators—a term that came to encompass everyone from railroad barons to newspaper publishers to state and territorial lawmakers—did their utmost to advance the notion that rain follows the plow.

The Conquest of Arid America

Writing in the May 1895 issue of *The Century*, William E. Smythe exulted in the future "Conquest of Arid America." Starting from the premise that "the material greatness of the United States is the fruit of a policy of peaceful conquest over the resources of a virgin continent," Smythe praised the vigor and ambition of settlers and miners who had tamed the wilderness on the eastern half of the continent. But he cautioned that the job was only half done and that the United States would never achieve its potential greatness if it failed to bend the arid western lands west of the one-hundredth meridian to its will:

> Beyond the line where the armies of civilization have bivouacked, if not laid down their arms, sleeps an empire incomparably greater and more resourceful than the empire those armies have conquered. Here lie the possibilities of a twentieth-century civilization—a civilization new, distinctive, and more luminous . . . than any which has preceded it in the world's long history. . . .
>
> The one-hundredth meridian divides the United States almost exactly into halves. East of that line dwell sixty-four million people. Here are overgrown cities and overcrowded industries. Here is surplus capital, as idle and burdensome as the surplus population. West of that line dwell four or five millions. Here is a great want both of people and of capital for development. Here is the raw material for another war of conquest, of-

"God speed the plow," proclaimed Charles Dana Wilber, one of America's leading advocates of this myth. "By this wonderful provision, which is only man's mastery over nature, the clouds are dispensing copious rains. . . . [The plow] is the instrument which separates civilization from savagery; and converts a desert into a farm or garden" (quoted in Burns and Ives 1996).

Occasionally, however, this chorus of optimism was tempered by the discordant voice of a dissenter. And perhaps the most notable westerner who attempted to puncture this fanciful notion of "plow as rainmaker" was the famed explorer and geologist **John Wesley Powell.** But Powell's clear-eyed assessment of the West as an arid to semiarid region that would require sensible and sustainable irrigation measures to nurture a permanent agricultural presence was at odds

fering prizes far greater than those of the past, because natural resources are richer, and much more varied and extensive. The new empire includes, in whole or in part, seventeen States and Territories. It is a region of imperial dimensions. From north to south it measures as far as from Montreal to Mobile. From east to west the distance is greater than from Boston to Omaha. Within these wide boundaries there are great diversities of climate and soil, of altitude and other physical conditions. But everywhere the climate is healthful to an extraordinary degree, and in all, except the great plains region of the extreme east, the scenery is rugged and noble beyond description.

The one-hundredth meridian is not merely the boundary line of present development. It is much more significant as indicating the beginning of the condition of aridity. To the popular mind "arid" means only "rainless," and "rainless" is synonymous with "worthless." But "aridity," when properly defined and fully comprehended, is seen to be the germ of new industrial and social systems, with far-reaching possibilities in the fields of ethics and politics. It would be idle to attempt to predict how the American character will be modified and transformed when millions of people shall have finally made their homes in the arid regions, under conditions as yet untried by Anglo-Saxon men. But that millions will live under these conditions is inevitable, and that the new environment will produce momentous changes in methods of life and habits of thought is equally certain.

with the Manifest Destiny philosophy at work across the West, and railroad agents, real estate developers, western senators, and community boosters all did their utmost to drown out his prophetic warnings.

Powell was born on March 24, 1834, at Mount Morris, a town in western New York State. He received only a limited early education (his later feats as a geologist were founded on years of self-education), and his family led a somewhat nomadic existence through his adolescence. As a young man, he considered following his father into the organizational workings of the Methodist Episcopal Church, but in the late 1850s, his studies at various midwestern schools, including Oberlin and Wheaton, helped instill in him a deep and abiding interest not only in midwestern geology and botany but also in

Famed explorer John
Wesley Powell offered
prescient warnings
about sustainable water
use in the American
West. (Library of
Congress)

the cultural history and practices of the Native American tribes that were being harried from their ancient tribal grounds all across the West. This intellectual curiosity, combined with a great appetite for adventure, led him to row the entire length of the Ohio and Illinois rivers by himself in 1857 and 1858, respectively.

When the American Civil War broke out in 1861, Powell immediately joined the Union army as an enlistee from his adopted home state of Illinois. He rose to the rank of captain of artillery before losing his right arm at the Battle of Shiloh in April 1862. He returned to the front lines after a period of convalescence, and by war's end, he had been promoted to the rank of major of artillery.

After the war, Powell joined the faculty of Illinois Wesleyan College in Bloomington as a professor of geology and museum curator. Over the next several years, he organized ambitious nineteenth-century field trips of sorts with deserving students across the Great Plains and into the Rocky Mountains. It was during one of these forays, which received U.S. Army protection, that Powell became obsessed with the idea of running the canyons of the mysterious Colorado and Green rivers. In May 1869, his dream came true, as he launched a party of ten men and four boats. Over the next 900 miles, the party encountered an array of tremendous obstacles, from the loss of one of their boats and most of their provisions within days of their departure to a gauntlet of roaring cataracts on the Colorado. The party also shrank in size: one man quit after a mere 80 miles, and three others, convinced that a continued descent of the Colorado was suicidal, hiked out of the Grand Canyon only to be murdered after their emergence, either by Indians or Mormon settlers. Powell and the remaining members of his party, meanwhile, completed the first-ever descent of the Colorado through the Grand Canyon on August 29, 1869.

Powell's feat made him one of the era's foremost heroes of exploration. Two years later, he made a return expedition to the Colorado, from which he produced a variety of valuable maps and anthropological and geological research papers. Fees from lectures and grants from Congress enabled Powell to carry out additional expeditions into various parts of the unsettled West in 1874 and 1875. It was also in 1875 that Powell joined the U.S. Geological Society of the Territories, the forebear of the U.S. Geological Survey (USGS). In March 1881, Powell became director of the USGS, a position he held until 1894.

Powell's record as an administrator was admirable, but despite his clear abilities in that regard—and his heroic exploration of the Grand Canyon—he was a controversial figure. The controversy stemmed in large part from his many pronouncements about the arid West and its suitability for settlement. He made these statements throughout his career, but they were summarized most effectively in his 1878 *Report on the Lands of the Arid Region,* based on his firsthand impressions of the West.

Powell's 1878 report was essentially a blueprint for adaptation rather than conquest. Taking note of the region's fundamental aridity, he argued that the land simply would not be able to support agriculture over the long term without sustainable, community-based irrigation systems. Wallace Stegner, one of Powell's biographers, declared that had these warnings been heeded,

> he might have spared the West the dust bowls of the 1890s, 1930s, and 1950s, as well as the worst consequences of river floods. He might have saved the lives and hopes of all the innocents who put their straddlebugs on dryland homesteads in the Dakotas, Kansas, Nebraska,

and Montana. But the boosters and the politicians always proclaimed that rain followed the plow; free land and movement westward were ingrained expectations. Habit, politics, and real estate boosterism won out over experience and good sense, and that is part of the history of the West, and of western landscape. (Stegner 1991)

After retiring from the USGS in 1894, Powell divided his time between his scientific writings, his family, and work with the Bureau of Ethnology. He died from a cerebral hemorrhage in Haven, Maine, on September 23, 1902, and was buried at Arlington Cemetery.

Ranching and Meatpacking

In terms of sheer acreage affected, cropping was easily the greatest force that impacted the ecological complexion of the United States in general and the West in particular. But ranching and the associated industry of meatpacking wreaked significant ecological changes on the American landscape in their own right.

The westward migration of the American population was directly responsible for the emergence of a thriving cattle industry. Prior to the 1850s, only eastern Texas and western California, of all the U.S. land west of the Mississippi River, had anything approaching a cattle industry. During the second half of the nineteenth century, however, an immense cattle industry developed in the region, and beef eclipsed pork as America's most popular meat. By 1880, more than half of the nation's cattle population was located west of the Mississippi, and by 1900, an estimated 35 million cattle were grazing on the western prairies. These beasts, however, were much harder on the vegetation and erosion-vulnerable riverbanks than the buffalo herds they replaced (and the grazing habits of the sheep that began competing with them for forage in the last two decades of the nineteenth century were even more destructive to grassland ecosystems).

The prosperity of both cattle- and sheep-ranching operations in the West in the 1860s, 1870s, and early 1880s was predicated, in large part, on access to the open range that prevailed on federal public lands. This state of affairs enabled ranchers to graze their herds on federal lands without paying even nominal grazing fees. Instead, a hierarchical system was maintained in which range rights were allocated on a first come, first served basis. Some of the larger western operations staked out hundreds of thousands of acres for their cattle herds under this system.

Farming pressure from new arrivals, though, put enormous pressure on this system in the last few decades of the nineteenth century, and the acreage of rangelands available for ranchers inevitably began to shrink, despite angry condemnation from ranching interests. Desperate to stave off economic disaster, western ranchers built fences around "their" range rights on public lands and became adept at securing essential water rights by snapping up land adjacent to rivers and streams. This strategy showed that the ranchers understood, earlier than many overly optimistic farmers, that access to water was the key to long-term economic survival in the semiarid West.

In the meantime, beef's ascension to primacy in the dietary habits of Americans—and the immigration-fueled explosion in the overall U.S. population—increased the economic significance of the nation's meat trade. And as the meatpacking industry grew in size, its environmental footprint grew larger as well. Industrial-sized feedlots and slaughterhouses alike generated ever greater quantities of dung, blood, and viscera that were commonly dumped into the nearest waterway, and the working conditions that prevailed in the slaughterhouses of Cincinnati (the hog-butchering capital of the country through the mid-nineteenth century), Omaha, Kansas City, and Chicago were truly deplorable.

Of all the great American meatpacking centers of the late nineteenth century, the City of the Big Shoulders was by far the most fantastically impressive, in its own blood-drenched fashion. By 1890, the Chicago meatpacking workforce had risen to an estimated 25,000 men, women, and children, who processed approximately 14 million animals a year. This productivity enabled meat trade titans such as Gustavus Swift and Philip Armour to rake in $200 million or more on a yearly basis. Their corporate slaughterhouses even became unlikely tourist attractions for a brief period, despite—or perhaps because of—the squalor and awful smells that permeated the facilities.

Like all other sectors of nineteenth-century agricultural enterprise, the meatpacking industry was profoundly affected by technological advances. Perhaps the foremost of these innovations was refrigeration—and specifically the introduction of the refrigerated railroad car in 1867. Within a few years, long-distance rail shipments of refrigerated dressed beef were commonplace among industry leaders who could absorb the high capital costs necessary to launch such operations. This development enabled numerous participants in the meat trade to expand their operations, with attendant increases in pollution to local lands and waterways.

A Heavy Price Paid on the Plains

The West-based beef trade also benefited from the years of above-average rainfall that fell across the region in the late 1870s and much of the 1880s, for this additional precipitation made it easier to generate quality corn and other feed for use in regional feedlots. But as indicated earlier, the extended cycle of higher rainfall was most notable in the development and ecology of the West because it was such a potent lure to farmers from the eastern states. The seeming confirmation that rain did indeed follow the plow prompted thousands of native-born farmers and recent immigrants from Europe to make their way out to the plains, mostly to plant wheat. In western Kansas alone, the population soared from 38,000 people in 1885 to 139,000 in 1887 (Steinberg 2002).

But in the 1890s, the hubris and rationalizations that drove pell-mell settlement of the Great Plains met extended drought. These drought years could have been weathered by many newly transplanted farming families and communities if they had husbanded their limited water resources and placed greater emphasis on ranching instead of cropping—as the prescient John Wesley Powell had counseled. But they had instead heeded the call of the boosters, who had waved off suggestions that nature might impose limits on farming practices in the semiarid West. They were thus left exposed when drought settled over the land. As a result, the populations of states such as Nebraska and Kansas declined by between one-quarter and one-half during the decade. Even California, which was enjoying a tremendous increase in its overall population, saw its agricultural population merely tread water by middecade (Reisner 1986).

As the new century dawned, annual rainfall levels returned to normal, and regional farmers belatedly pursued practices that increasingly—though still insufficiently—acknowledged the region's climatic realities. Irrigated agriculture became integral to farming across the region; the number of irrigated acres in the eleven westernmost states, for example, jumped from 7.3 million acres to 17.4 million acres over the first two decades of the twentieth century. This turn to irrigation, though, especially in tandem with the growing water needs of expanding towns and cities in Arizona, California, Colorado, Montana, Utah, and other western states, began to take an environmental toll on waterways in the region. Indeed, it was at that time that unsustainable rates of withdrawal and dam erection first became a major environmental issue (today, overtaxed rivers across the West have experienced marked deterioration of riverine habitat and major declines in migrating fish species due to steadily escalating rates of diversion and river corridor alteration). In addition, many farmers paid greater heed to dryland farming techniques, such as the use of drought-resistance grain crops, deep plowing, and other water-conserving measures.

These changes in agricultural practices paid significant dividends initially. Buoyed by high wheat prices and the penetration of gasoline-powered machines such as tractors, trucks, and combines into all aspects of farming operation, farmers of the Great Plains were able to grow greater quantities of wheat and other crops than ever before. When the onset of World War I further heightened demand for wheat, plains farmers eagerly cast about for additional land to plow up and plant. Their collective gaze settled on the millions of acres of prairie grassland that had evaded "improvement" to that point. From 1914 to 1919, an estimated 11 million acres of grassland in the states of Kansas, Colorado, Nebraska, Oklahoma, and Texas were destroyed so that wheat farmers could increase their yields: "Life on the plains became tied to economic imperatives in distant lands, as the soil wealth of the plains was creamed off to feed people across the globe" (Steinberg 2002).

But the wheat bonanza proved relatively short-lived. A glut on the world wheat market drove prices down precipitously during the 1920s, and the onset of the Great Depression in 1929 devastated all sectors of the American economy, including agriculture. Worst of all, the feverish rush to convert wildlife-rich prairie habitat into cultivable fields set the stage for arguably the worst episode of environmental calamity in the nation's entire history.

By the late 1920s, years of myopic farming practices had shattered the landscape of the Great Plains. In 1879, about 10 million acres of plains grasslands had been plowed up for farming; by 1929, the total was 100 million acres (Great Plains Drought Area Committee 1936). In addition, most of the soil on this acreage had been broken down and exhausted by repeated plowing and constant cultivation from

Myopic land-use practices led to the infamous Dust Bowl years in Oklahoma and other parts of the Great Plains. (Library of Congress)

farmers and overgrazing by cattle and sheep outfits. Consequently, when drought conditions returned, the landscape was prostrate and beyond help. Soil that had been protected by resilient grasslands for thousands of years baked under the sun, creating vast tracts of dirt that were vulnerable to the perennial winds of the region. Thus was the Dust Bowl born.

Drought conditions returned to the plains in the summer of 1931 and locked down over the region for eight years. During that time, agricultural production plummeted—to negligible levels in many areas—and immense, deadly dust storms became a recurring nightmare. At its peak, the Dust Bowl covered 100 million acres of the plains, with the southern plains states of Oklahoma, Texas, New Mexico, Colorado, Kansas, and Nebraska the hardest hit. Hundreds of millions of tons of topsoil-turned-dust were carried off by the winds, often coalescing into black clouds that rolled across entire states. Some people literally suffocated in these dusters, as the storms were called, and others saw their lives snuffed out by years of dust inhalation that became known as dust pneumonia. The environmental devastation was biblical in scope, and it elicited expressions of brokenhearted wonder from witnesses (Lowitt 1984; Watkins 1999).

By 1935, an estimated 850 million tons of topsoil had been blown off the southern plains—nearly 8 tons of dirt for every resident of the United States. The disaster created almost a million refugees from the region, with Kansas, Oklahoma, and Texas suffering the greatest exodus (Egan 2006). In 1936, a committee specifically created by the administration of President Franklin D. Roosevelt delivered a frank and accurate assessment of the underlying causes of the environmental catastrophe unfolding on the Great Plains. "The basic cause of the present Great Plains situation is an attempt to impose upon the region a system of agriculture to which the Plains are not adapted," declared the authors of the report, titled *The Future of the Great Plains.* "The Great Plains has climatic attributes which cannot be altered by any act of man, although they may be slowly changed, for better or worse, by natural weather cycles which we cannot yet predict" (Great Plains Drought Area Committee 1936).

The Father of Soil Conservation

Onto this pulverized landscape strode **Hugh Hammond Bennett,** who is today widely regarded as the father of soil conservation in the United States. Born on April 15, 1881, in North Carolina into a farming family with a 1,200-acre cotton plantation, he graduated from the University of North Carolina in 1903. Within weeks of graduating, he landed a job with the U.S. Department of Agriculture's Bureau of Soils as a soil surveyor. He thus became part of a team that undertook the first comprehensive soil survey of U.S. territory in the nation's history.

Bennett's formative experiences on his family's cotton plantation and his wide travels with the Bureau of Soils convinced him that erosion and nutrient depletion were approaching epidemic levels across large agriculture-oriented swaths of the country. He rose through the ranks of the Department of Agriculture, and from 1909 to 1928, he served as the country's supervisor of soil surveys. By the time the Dust Bowl hit, Bennett "knew more about the crust of the United

Hugh Bennett on the Relationship
between Soil and Wildlife

Hugh Bennett, the father of soil conservation in the United States and the nation's first head of the Soil Conservation Service, was a tireless advocate for America's wildlife. In the following excerpt from a 1935 speech, he urged a group of early American conservationists to understand that one of the Soil Conservation Service's greatest mandates, to his mind, was wildlife protection and preservation:

> We have been more prodigal of our heritage of natural resources than any other people in the world. True, other civilizations have waned and expired because of erosion, but their lands were utilized for centuries before they finally had to be abandoned. Much of our ruined land knew the plow for scarcely a generation.
>
> We have been living in a fool's paradise with respect to the security of our most basic asset. Since colonial days we have, unquestionably, been guilty of the most colossal soil wastage the world has ever witnessed in a like space of time. We have permitted tens of thousands of our farmers to become tillers of subsoil—bankrupt farmers of bankrupt land. Moreover, this ruin of the soil is permanent so far as we and our sons and their sons are concerned; for nature needs centuries to build a single inch of soil that, through human misuse and abuse, may be carried away by a single rain or wind storm. We have continued to plow up and plant the short-grass country of the plains, regardless of soil character and without thought of the permanency, under natural conditions, of the native cover of nutritious grasses, or of its value for livestock and wildlife. Actually, the activities of man have caused the creation of numerous small and large areas of desert in that region during the present year.
>
> As indicated, the effects of erosion on agriculture, and hence on our national and individual prosperity, are more or less obvious. But how, you may ask, is wildlife concerned with human economics? It may even be argued theoretically that the abandonment of a field and its reversion to a wild state is to the advantage of wildlife, and that when people are less prosperous they have less money with which to buy ammunition, and therefore shoot less game.
>
> Both arguments are fallacious. The present depression has

amply demonstrated that thousands of people in time of economic stress turn to the woods, fields and waters to relieve the strain on a diminishing larder. As for the worn-out fields, it is noteworthy that the volunteer growths of weeds and brush on badly eroded land often are not of kinds valuable to desirable wildlife species.

It is not intended to imply, however, that the great reduction in farm wildlife is one of the direct results of erosion. In fact, erosion and decreasing wildlife reserves are fellow symptoms of the same disease. The underlying malady is the reckless denudation of soil resulting from the stripping off of the protective cover of vegetation.

When white men first set foot on American shores, they found no gutted fields and impoverished farms. Such cultivation as was practiced by the Indians had not been extravagant of soil. Unlike white men, the Indians did not use a field until it was dissipated by erosion, and then clear another from a supposedly limitless and inexhaustible supply of land.

We can now boast the banishment of our last frontier, and we have made the sad discovery that our land is neither limitless nor inexhaustible. It is a matter of very simple arithmetic to figure out how long we can stand the annual destruction of 200 thousand acres of good farm soil. Even today we do not have enough good farm land; a considerable part of our aggregate production is from soil made hopelessly poor by erosion—land that yields so poorly the operators have been forced down to the level of bare subsistence. What we are going to do about it, however, is a real problem.

Obviously, we can not return to pre-settlement conditions. The Nation has its very roots in agriculture, and if it is to persist, its agriculture must go on. But we can not raise our corn and cotton in the woods, nor grow our wheat on unbroken prairie. If we would continue to grow these crops, however, we must be prepared to compromise with nature.

Source

Bennett, Hugh H. 1935. "Wildlife and Erosion Control." Speech presented before the 31st Annual Convention, National Association of Audubon Societies, New York, October 29.

Hugh Bennett, "Father of Soil Conservation." (Library of Congress)

States—from close personal inspection—than perhaps any person alive in the early twentieth century" (Egan 2006).

By the 1920s, Bennett had become incredibly frustrated by the drumbeat of official sanctions for exploitive farming practices. He believed that prevailing practices on the Great Plains, in the South, and even in the Northeast were wasteful, economically counterproductive over the long term, and enormously destructive to area wildlife. This led him to cowrite, with William R. Chapline, an influential Department of Agriculture report called "Soil Erosion: A National Menace" and to become a highly visible presence at congressional hearings and meetings on farming and land conservation issues.

When the Roosevelt administration cast about for someone to spearhead the interdiction effort on the Great Plains during the Dust Bowl years, Bennett was the obvious choice. Using his prodigious communication abilities and his deep knowledge of land-use issues, he helped shape and implement a wide variety of New Deal initiatives designed to reverse the ecological devastation and rescue economically destitute and emotionally battered farming families.

As the head of the newly minted Soil Conservation Service, Bennett established thousands of local soil conservation districts, set up specific erosion and flood control projects for various counties and states, implemented programs to replant native grasses and trees that could serve as windbreaks, introduced crop-reduction programs that withdrew an estimated 9.6 million acres of wheat land and 10.3 million acres of cotton land from cultivation, and educated American farmers about the benefits of contour tillage and other cultivation practices (Eisenhower 1934; Watkins 1999).

Despite Bennett's stewardship, an estimated 750,000 landowners lost their farms and savings during the Great Depression, and American farming did not return to pre-Depression levels in terms of income until 1941, when the nation once again found itself in a war economy (Horwitz 1980). But without Bennett's decisive leadership, the toll would have been much greater, and the Great Plains (and other agricultural regions of the country, to a lesser degree) would not have been set on the road to ecological recovery.

Bennett remained the nation's leading authority on soil conservation issues for the next two decades. One of his greatest qualities was his ability to help his audiences understand the complex interplay of environmental forces on and around their farms—and to take a second look at the importance of wildlife and other natural resources to their lives. In 1948, the Inter-American Conference on Conservation of Natural Renewable Resources nominated him for the Nobel Prize in recognition of his contributions to humanity. He died in Falls Church, Virginia, on July 7, 1960.

Sources

Berry, Wendell. 1977. *The Unsettling of America: Culture and Agriculture.* San Francisco: Sierra Club Books.

Bogue, Allan G. 1994. "An Agricultural Empire." In *The Oxford History of the American West,* edited by Clyde A. Milner II, Carol A. O'Connor, and Martha A. Sandweiss. New York: Oxford University Press.

Brink, Wellington. 1951. *Big Hugh: The Father of Soil Conservation.* New York: Macmillan.

Burns, Ken, and Stephen Ives. 1996. *New Perspectives on the West.* On-line companion Web site to the Public Broadcasting System documentary *The*

West. Originally broadcast September 1996. Available on-line at www.pbs. org/weta/thewest/program.

Cowdrey, Albert E. 1983. *This Land, This South: An Environmental History.* Lexington: University of Kentucky Press.

Cronon, William. 1991. *Nature's Metropolis: Chicago and the Great West.* New York: W. W. Norton.

Cunfer, Geoff. 2005. *On the Great Plains: Agriculture and Environment.* College Station: Texas A&M University Press.

Donahue, Brian. 2003. "The Resettling of America." In *The Essential Agrarian Reader: The Future of Culture, Community, and the Land,* edited by Norman Wirzba. Lexington: University of Kentucky Press.

Egan, Timothy. 2006. *The Worst Hard Time.* Boston: Houghton Mifflin.

Eisenhower, Milton S., ed. 1934. *1934 Yearbook of Agriculture.* Washington, DC: U.S. Department of Agriculture.

Flores, Dan. 2003. *The Natural West: Environmental History in the Great Plains and Rocky Mountains.* Norman: University of Oklahoma Press.

Gilpin, William. 1890. *The Cosmopolitan Railway: Compacting and Fusing Together All the World's Continents.* San Francisco: History.

Great Plains Drought Area Committee. 1936. "Report of the Great Plains Drought Area Committee, Aug., 1936." Available on-line at www. newdeal.feri.org.

Hargreaves, Mary W. M. 1957. *Dry Farming in the Northern Great Plains, 1900–1925.* Cambridge, MA: Harvard University Press.

Hillstrom, Kevin, and Laurie Collier Hillstrom. 2003. *North America: A Continental Overview of Environmental Issues.* Santa Barbara, CA: ABC-CLIO.

Horwitz, Elinor Lander. 1980. *On the Land: American Agriculture from Past to Present.* New York: Atheneum.

Logsdon, Gene. 1994. *At Nature's Pace: Farming and the American Dream.* New York: Pantheon.

Lowitt, Richard. 1984. *The New Deal and the West.* Bloomington: Indiana University Press.

MacDonnell, Lawrence J. 1999. *From Reclamation to Sustainability: Water, Agriculture and the Environment in the American West.* Niwot: University Press of Colorado.

Reisner, Marc. 1986. *Cadillac Desert: The American West and Its Disappearing Water.* New York: Viking Penguin.

Shover, John L. 1976. *First Majority, Last Minority: The Transforming of Rural Life in America.* De Kalb: Northern Illinois University Press.

Skaggs, Jimmy M. 1986. *Prime Cut: Livestock Raising and Meatpacking in the United States, 1607–1983.* College Station: Texas A&M University Press.

Stegner, Wallace. 1991. "Thoughts in a Dry Land." In *A Western Harvest,* edited by Frances Ring. Santa Barbara, CA: John Daniel.

Steinberg, Ted. 2002. *Down to Earth: Nature's Role in American History.* New York: Oxford University Press.

Stoll, Steven. 2002. *Larding the Lean Earth: Soil and Society in Nineteenth-Century America.* New York: Hill and Wang.

Thoreau, Henry David. 1973. *Walden.* Princeton, NJ: Princeton University Press.

U.S. Department of Agriculture. N.d. "Hugh Bennett." Available on-line at www.nrcs.usda.gov/about/history/bennett.html.

Walsh, Margaret. 1982. *The Rise of the Midwestern Meat Packing Industry.* Lexington: University of Kentucky Press.

Watkins, T. H. 1999. *The Hungry Years: A Narrative History of the Great Depression in America.* New York: Henry Holt.

Worster, Donald. 1978. *Rivers of Empire: Water, Aridity, and the Growth of the American West.* New York: Pantheon Books.

———. 1979. *Dust Bowl: The Southern Plains in the 1930s.* New York: Oxford University Press.

Immigration's Impact

Nicole Mitchell

From the time America was first colonized until the start of the American Revolution, over 1 million immigrants journeyed to the country. In 1785, the U.S. Congress passed an act allowing land in the Northwest Territory—which included the future states of Ohio, Michigan, Illinois, Indiana, and Wisconsin—to be sold at public auction. With the purchase of the Louisiana Territory in 1803, even more land became available for settlement. With these great additions of territory, American leaders encouraged European immigrants to settle the vast landscape. In fact, the American Emigrant Company was established in 1865 to import new laborers from Europe. Between 1820 and 1860, more than 6 million people immigrated to America (Hoobler and Hoobler 2003). Many had dreams of creating a better life for themselves and their families. Others sought refuge in the new nation from turmoil in their homelands. No matter where they came from, immigrants played an important role in the development of agriculture in America, as well as in the emerging meatpacking industry.

General studies of the American agriculture industry largely ignore the contributions of the country's immigrants. The 1911 *Report of the Commission on Country Life,* for instance, made no mention of immigrant farmers. Before the Civil War (1861–1865), African, German, and Irish immigrants were some of America's most productive agricultural laborers. Soon after coming to the new country, German immigrants began establishing agricultural communities. These

German farming districts were especially prevalent in the North during the 1830s and 1840s. After the Civil War, many of these immigrants headed to the South, hoping to make a living by growing tobacco in the middle colonies such as Virginia initially and then cotton in the lower South.

African American Slave Labor

African slaves were some of the first immigrants to the newly formed country, for almost as soon as the earliest colonists arrived in America, they began importing slaves from Africa. The first load of slaves arrived in the colony of Virginia in 1619, though the trade did not boom until after 1660. By the time of the American Revolution in the 1770s, there were approximately 500,000 African Americans in the colonies, most of whom were held in slavery. It is estimated that four or five Africans were taken to America for every one European who arrived. The slave trade from Africa proved to be one of the primary methods for bringing immigrants to the new country. By the end of the eighteenth century, one out of every five Americans was either an immigrant from Africa or a descendant of an African immigrant (Daniels 2001). The sudden growth in the number of slaves occurred due to the development of the plantation system in the southern colonies.

Though slavery existed in all of the colonies, it was in the South where the institution really flourished. The great majority of southern slaves were used as rural agricultural workers. With the expansion of the colonies into the South, the plantation system of agriculture was introduced and was used primarily for growing such labor-intensive crops as rice, tobacco, and cotton. African slaves soon proved to be the main source for such labor, and the plantation economy in the South created an "insatiable demand for labor to grow cash export crops" (Daniels 2001). Since most plantation crops, such as cotton, tobacco, and corn, "demanded sustained attention during a long growing season," slavery was the most economical labor system to employ (Earle 1978). Crop production in the South tended to be more specialized than that in the North. In addition, slaves could be used more profitably in agriculture rather than in industry. Colonies in the North, by contrast, had little use for slave labor. Northerners

Slaves of Confederate General Thomas F. Drayton at his plantation on
Hilton Head Island, South Carolina, May 1862. (Library of Congress)

who participated in agricultural pursuits tended to grow crops such
as wheat, corn, fruits, and vegetables—crops that did not require as
much time and effort to plant and harvest. Northern farmers typically employed wage labor, since it was cheaper, and wage laborers
were not needed for the whole year. Thus, there was virtually no
need for slave labor in the North.

Southern slavery, however, was vital to the northern economy.
Agriculture in the South essentially provided the raw materials for
America's principal industries. Textile manufacturing in the North,
for instance, depended on southern cotton production. Though a few
textile mills were established in the South, the vast majority tended to
be found in the North. Southerners were generally more interested in
planting various crops than engaging in industry; as a result, rather
than investing in industry, southern planters continued to buy more
land and more slaves, hoping to produce even more of the staple
crops that could be exported to the North. In fact, most of the cotton

produced was exported for use in northern textile mills. Cotton, largely the result of slave labor, soon became America's most valuable crop, generating more revenue than any other.

Plantation systems of agriculture were first used in the mid-Atlantic colonies, such as Virginia, to harvest tobacco. Initially, American planters employed indentured servants from Europe to produce their crops. When the number of indentured servants began to decline, planters resorted to using slaves, and with more and more slaves, owner-planters were able to substantially increase the production of their crops. They typically used their land as collateral to buy more slaves, hoping to increase production even more. Eventually, planters no longer had a need to purchase slaves from Africa because the slaves living on plantations reproduced.

Plantation labor systems steadily expanded into the South. Though individual yeoman farmers still planted and produced various crops with the aid of their family members, planters who used slave labor were generally able to produce more crops. Of course, the largest plantations typically employed the greatest number of slaves, ranging from the tens to the hundreds. Cotton plantations rapidly spread across the southeast into Arkansas and Texas. With the cotton boom in the 1850s, planters needed greater numbers of slaves to plant and harvest more cotton. In time, large plantations essentially forced out yeoman farmers. Planters who owned these large plantations had more capital and resources to obtain the best land and produce the most crops, and yeoman farmers simply could not compete.

Meanwhile, because slaves were worked at lower rates than free workers would expect to be paid, there was virtually no opportunity for white labor. Until the Civil War, slaves and black freedmen did most of the agricultural work in the South, and slaves practically "monopolized" any prospects for white agricultural labor (Berlin and Gutman 1983). It was simply more profitable to use slave labor, for most slaveholding planters produced larger crop yields than those who did not own slaves. The more profitable cotton became, the more entrenched the use of slaves became.

The plantation system using slave labor was eventually brought to a halt with President Abraham Lincoln's issuance of the Emancipation Proclamation in 1863 and the Union's victory in the Civil War two years later. The abrupt end of the system gave way to the practice of sharecropping. Blacks now wanted land of their own to farm, but planters did not wish to give up their land so easily. Therefore, the planters basically just divided up their land into smaller share-cropped farms. Rather than owning their own land and growing their own crops, poor whites and ex-slaves began farming small plots of land that belonged to the large planters. Generally, tenants borrowed farm implements from the planters as well. Under the sharecropping system of agriculture, tenants essentially rented both the land and the tools from planters. At the end of the year, whatever crops had been harvested were given to the owner-planters. In turn, the planters would allocate a portion, or "share," of the crops to the workers. This share was, for all intents and purposes, the tenant's wage. Planters especially supported the sharecropping system, since it allowed them to pay their workers with a share of the crops rather than in hard cash.

European Immigrant Farmers

Though many immigrants to America never ventured outside the cities where they landed, a large number hoped to become farmers. More than half of the immigrants who journeyed to the new country during the colonial period had been farmers while living in Europe, and many of these people sought the same occupations in America. By 1790, farming and agriculture accounted for the majority of the country's income. Many immigrants who first arrived in America as indentured servants later ended up becoming small landowners. A great number of these indentured servants were Irish immigrants. Though Irish immigrants initially settled in the middle colonies, such as Pennsylvania, many migrated southward into North and South Carolina. From there, they continued migrating in a southwesterly direction, to areas such as Mississippi and Texas, where land was abundant and the soil was fertile. Though most Irish in the South settled in the cities, some hoped to become frontier farmers, believing the propaganda that America was a "country without landlords, where there was land for those who wanted it" (Daniels 2001).

In the years between 1850 and 1860, the Irish population in the South grew by more than 55 percent. In the period before 1845, Irish who migrated to the South were most likely to pursue a life of farming, and during that time, a number of Irish immigrants took full advantage of the surge in cotton production in the South and South-

Eighteenth-century indentured servitude contract. Indentured servitude was a form of serfdom people entered into in order to pay their way to the English colonies in North America. (Library of Congress)

Verbindniß eines Lehrjungen.

THIS INDENTURE witnesseth, that JOHN Nemo, by the Consent of : : : : : hath put himself, and by these Presents, with the Consent aforesaid, doth Voluntarily, and of his own free Will and Accord, put himself Apprentice to Philip Sharp of Bristol, to learn his Art, Trade and Mystery, and after the Manner of an Apprentice to serve him, his Executors and Assigns from the Day of the Date hereof, for, & during, & to the full End & Term, of (die Jahre) next ensuing: During all which Term, the said Apprentice his said Master faithfully shall serve, his Secrets keep, his lawful Commands every where readily obey. He shall do no Damage to his said Master nor see it to be done by others, without letting or giving Notice thereof to his said Master, he shall not waste his said Masters Goods, nor lend them unlawfully to any. He shall not commit Fornication, nor contract Matrimony, within the said Term: At Cards, Dice, or any other unlawful Games he shall not play, whereby his said Master may have Damage. With his own Goods, nor the Goods of others, without Licence from his said Master, he shall neither buy nor sell. He shall not absent himself Day nor Night from his said Masters Service without his Leave: Nor haunt Ale-houses, Taverns, or Play-houses; but in all Things behave himself as a faithful Apprentice ought to do, during the said Term. And the said Master shall use the utmost of his Endeavour to teach, or cause to be taught and instructed the said Apprentice in the Trade or Mystery of a Taylor, and procure and provide for him sufficient Meat, Drink, Apparel, Lodging and Washing, fitting for an Apprentice, during the said Term of : : : Years

west. One such man was Frederick Stanton of New Orleans, Louisiana. Abandoning his career as a physician and moving to Natchez, Mississippi, in 1818, he quickly became a leading cotton planter. By the 1850s, Stanton owned more than 15,000 acres of land, comprising six different plantations, in both Louisiana and Mississippi (Gleeson 2001). Another prominent Irish farmer was James McCann of South Carolina. Though he found the cotton business in South Carolina to be difficult due to low crop yields, he did not give up on his plans to harvest cotton. He moved to Mississippi in the 1840s, where he eventually became the owner of a 200-acre farm. McCann urged other Irish immigrants to follow suit, telling them that cotton was the only sure path to financial security (Gleeson 2001).

Instead of venturing off on their own to establish single plantations, many Irish immigrants in the South banded together to form small communities. In that way, they were able to work in concert to "exploit the South's fertile land" (Gleeson 2001). One such community was that of Locust Grove, Georgia. Mortimer Griffin, who migrated to Locust Grove in the late 1820s, was a successful Irish planter. Not long after moving to the community, he bought more than 1,000 acres of land there. He soon began growing cotton and eventually purchased even more land in the area. By 1860, he had acquired 400 acres in south Georgia in addition to more than 300 acres in Mississippi (Gleeson 2001).

Like Griffin, many other Irish settlers in the South ventured farther west into Mississippi and Texas in search of "virgin land for continued cotton growth." A number of small towns were developed by Irish migrants who succumbed to the "lure of land [available for cotton farming] in the Old Southwest" (Gleeson 2001). Many, including Maunsel White of Louisiana, established large sugar plantations as well. Though a good number were lured to the Southwest in hopes of establishing large plantations of their own, many others simply became overseers on plantations that belonged to other planters; indeed, young, single Irishmen constituted a sizable proportion of the overseers on large rice and sugar plantations. And overseers on these types of plantations earned far higher salaries than their peers on other plantations.

During the last twenty years of the nineteenth century, hordes of immigrants settled in the South. Though southerners had generally been wary of "foreigners," they soon began recruiting immigrants in order to furnish a labor force, for by only using "the present labor supply the South [had] about reached the limit of cotton production though the demand for cotton [was] increasing" (Fleming 1905). Because of their desire to produce more cotton, southerners began to encourage immigrants to venture south to work on their plantations. Plantation owners effectively led the movement to bring in immigrants to supplement Negro labor.

Immigrants were now more willing to settle in the South than they had been in preceding years, an attitude due most likely to the fact that "prices of farm lands [were so] high in the North and West . . . that it [was] practically impossible for the average poor man to look forward to owning [his own land]" (Fleming 1905). Unlike farmland in other areas, land in the South was relatively inexpensive. And states all across the South and Southwest utilized countless immigrants on their farms, even employing immigration agents to entice more of these people to the area. This great flux of immigration was spurred by "land companies in the middle West [who would] buy large tracts of land . . . and induce colonies to settle [there]" (Fleming 1905).

Trends in Rural Immigration

During the great episodes of immigration in the late 1700s and early 1800s, several trends began to emerge. English farmers were more apt to settle in villages throughout New England, whereas other immigrant farmers, including the Dutch, German, Swedish, and Scottish-Irish, tended to settle in more rural areas. Scandinavians and Japanese were also more likely to settle in the country and more rural farming areas. Conversely, immigrants from Ireland, China, and Italy were inclined to settle in the cities and more urban areas.

By the middle of the nineteenth century, farmers made up more than 60 percent of the nation's workforce. And in the mid-1840s, America experienced the massive immigration of farmers seeking agricultural land. Persons from Scandinavia especially wanted to farm and tended to settle in the Midwest. Initially, Swedish immigrants overwhelmingly settled in the Wheat Belt states, such as Minnesota, Nebraska, and both Dakotas. Norwegian immigrants to the United States were also likely to settle in rural farming areas in the Midwest.

Immigrants from Poland and Czechoslovakia also settled in the Midwest territories, including Texas. Polish farmers formed agricultural communities all across the Midwest, in places such as Texas, Nebraska, and Illinois, and "in certain sections of [the country,] their numbers changed the face of the farm population." By 1900, more than 25,000 Poles were engaged in farming (Gladsky 1988). Germans, however, were by far the largest group of immigrants to the Midwest. In fact, such large numbers of German immigrants settled in the cities of Milwaukee, St. Louis, and Cincinnati that the area soon became known as the German Triangle (Hoobler and Hoobler 2003). By 1870, only one out of four German immigrants was employed in farming, though large numbers of German farmers settled in the Midwest. There were also scattered German agricultural settlements in the far west (Daniels 2001).

With the passage of the 1862 Homestead Act, settlers who agreed to farm the land for at least five years were granted 160 acres each.

Many immigrants were attracted to the Midwest due to the fairly inexpensive price of land; others ventured west in hopes of striking it rich by finding gold in California. It was not until more than twenty years later, however, that farmers began progressively settling on the Great Plains and in the West. With most of the "good" land already developed in the East, those who wished to establish their own farms had no course but to move farther west. Between 1880 and 1914, most of the immigrants to America came from southern and eastern Europe, and during that time, more and more immigrants were becoming farmers. Norwegians, in particular, almost always established agricultural settlements. This great increase in cultivated land significantly boosted the nation's agricultural productivity.

Seasonal farmwork first became an option for immigrants during this period of rapid agricultural expansion, for many large farms began to hire nomadic laborers to help harvest the year's crops. It was these seasonal farmworkers who helped progress the industrialization of agriculture. One immigrant who took part in this newly emerging seasonal farmwork was Norwegian Andrew Hanson. Emigrating to the United States in the early years of the twentieth century, Hanson first sought work on a farm owned by fellow Norwegians (Higbie 2003).

Laborers migrated continuously all over the middle and western states looking for work on farms. Though they were indispensable to farming, many of these workers shuffled between agricultural and industrial jobs. People who had recently migrated to cities in search of work in factories made up a significant portion of harvest or seasonal workers, and generally speaking, they rarely remained in one job for longer than a month. Reduced wages was a prime reason why seasonal farm laborers left one farm to find work elsewhere. In addition, no matter their place of origin, immigrants desired to own land of their own rather than work as farm laborers.

Asian American Farmworkers in California

Immigrants to America also made important contributions to the development of the agriculture industry in California. By the early 1890s, significant numbers of Japanese immigrants were settling in the California area; the greatest influx occurred in the following decade, between 1900 and 1908. Most of these Japanese immigrants sought various jobs in the agricultural sector. In fact, two-thirds of these new immigrants worked in agriculture, and many of them were tenant farmers. Over time, more and more Japanese immigrants began "concentrat[ing] in California, especially in the areas where the acreage of labor-intensive crops was being expanded" (Higgs 1978).

The typical trend was for these immigrants to become agricultural proprietors. By 1919, Japanese farmers in California contributed more than 10 percent of the state's farm income. Ultimately, so many Japanese immigrants became land and farm owners in California that the state, along with ten other states in the West, passed laws to prohibit the Japanese from owning or, in some cases, leasing agricultural land (Daniels 2001). Many Japanese immigrants, however, found ways to get around this law. One such method was to buy land in the names of their children who had been born in America and were therefore not subject to the law. In 1924, Japanese were prevented from entering the country.

Like the Japanese, the Chinese emigrated to America in tremendous numbers between 1850 and 1882, settling particularly in New York and California. Although they were later restricted from entering the United States under the Chinese Exclusion Act of 1882, Chinese immigrants in earlier years had "played a vital entrepreneurial role in California agriculture, introducing new crops and pioneering distribution systems" (Daniels 2001). After the passage of laws prohibiting certain groups from immigrating to America, the United States began soliciting Mexican laborers to help fill the huge void in the agriculture industry caused by the lack of immigrants. Mexican workers were especially needed to help farm the expanding agricultural lands across the Southwest. These Mexicans essentially filled the farm jobs that Chinese and Japanese immigrants had vacated.

Immigrants in Meatpacking

As in the agriculture industry, immigrants also left their mark on and made important contributions to the American meatpacking industry. After the Civil War, Chicago became the largest meatpacking center in the United States. One of the first entrepreneurs to establish a meatpacking company in Chicago was German immigrant Nelson Morris (1838–1907). Soon after arriving in Chicago, Morris gained employ-

Meat cutters at an Armour packinghouse in Chicago, ca. 1893. (Library of Congress)

ment at a local stockyard before founding his own livestock business in 1859. When the city's Union Stock Yards opened in December 1865, Morris was one of the first to locate his firm there, which allowed his meatpacking business to have direct railroad connections. Locating his packinghouses in the Union Stock Yards district also helped put the more scattered packinghouses out of business. In the late 1870s, Morris established packinghouses in other cities, including Kansas City and St. Joseph. In 1883, he formed a partnership with fellow meatpacker Nathaniel Fairbank to both produce and ship canned meats. By 1888, Morris had successfully become the third-largest meatpacker in America (Carstensen 1999), prospering alongside such entrepreneurs as Gustavus Swift and Philip Armour.

Irish immigrant Michael Cudahy (1841–1910) also helped to develop America's meatpacking industry. After emigrating to America in 1849, Cudahy settled in Milwaukee, Wisconsin, where he soon began working for Layton and Plankinton, a local meatpacking company. By 1866, he had become the chief meat inspector for the Milwaukee Board of Trade, a position that allowed him to study how meat was preserved. His employers quickly recognized his talents and continued to promote him. In 1875, well-known meatpacker Philip Armour hired Cudahy to supervise both the slaughtering and meatpacking processes in the Armour Union Stock Yards plants.

Once in Chicago, Cudahy continued his work in the study of meat preservation, using refrigeration to store fresh meat. By lowering the temperature in packinghouses, fresh meat was soon available year-round, as these facilities no longer had to close down during the warm summer months. Cudahy's refrigeration system fundamentally "revolutioniz[ed] the meat-packing industry . . . [and enabled] meat packers to significantly expand the geographical boundaries of their markets" (Buenker 1999). His work in refrigeration soon led to the practice of using refrigerated railroad cars. In 1887, Cudahy partnered with his younger brother and Armour to form a branch of the company in Omaha, Nebraska. By the time he bought out Armour's shares in 1890, the Cudahy Packing Company had helped make Omaha the third-largest packing center in America (Buenker 1999).

Author Upton Sinclair's groundbreaking 1906 novel, *The Jungle,* paints a vivid portrait of immigrant life in America's meatpacking industry. In addition to taking leading roles in the development of this industry, immigrants also formed meatpacking's main labor force. By the late 1800s and early 1900s, Chicago had become a "patchwork quilt of vibrant ethnic neighborhoods" populated by thousands of immigrants willing to put in long hours of hard labor for meager wages (Barrett 1983). The first workers in the Union Stock Yards were primarily Irish and German immigrants. The packinghouse population shifted in the late 1890s when Poles, Lithuanians, and Slovaks began pouring in from the nations of southern Europe. By 1905, Polish immigrants were the largest foreign-born group employed in Chicago's packinghouses. Polish, Lithuanian, and Slavic immigrants all typically performed unskilled jobs, such as cleaning the dressed carcasses and transporting animal parts from the killing floor to various other departments. The majority of these unskilled positions were temporary, depending on how much work was needed and the amount of livestock received each day. Unskilled jobs were generally filled by poor, recent immigrants rather than native-born workers.

German, Irish, and Bohemian immigrants, however, rose through the ranks from unskilled jobs to work as full-fledged butchers. The 1880 census found that 36 percent of the butchers were German and 14 percent were Irish. Germans were also the primary workers in the sausage rooms, "where it was easier to mechanize work, to introduce piecework, and to employ women and children" (Keil and Jentz 1988). By 1880, German and Irish workers "enjoyed a virtual monopoly on the more skilled and better paying positions in the packinghouses" (Halpern 1997).

Women workers were at first typically employed in the meatpacking industry only when male workers were on strike. Women were also given more menial tasks to complete, such as meat trimming (cutting fat from the meat), because "only foreign-born women of the European peasant type accustomed to farmwork in the old country [were] willing to do work of this character" (Abbott and Breckinridge 1911). Eastern European immigrant women were also hired to work in the sausage rooms, linking and tying the sausages. In many cases, these new immigrant women began taking the place of other workers.

Communities in the stockyards initially developed according to nationality. By 1870, Packingtown had grown into a neighborhood of more than 5,000 workers, mostly Irish immigrants. Just ten years later, large numbers of both Irish and German workers lived in Packingtown (Halpern 1997). As newer immigrants joined the packinghouse workforce and began living in Packingtown, older immigrant families, including both Irish and Germans, moved on to other neighborhoods.

Some labor unions were also established on the basis of national origin, including the "Bohemian meat-cutters, Hebrew meat-cutters, and German sausage-makers" (Thompson 1907). In particular, the Amalgamated Meat Cutters and Butcher Workmen union had its ties in the Irish community (Barrett 1983). The Packinghouse Employees' Union, formed in 1889, was composed of several thousand workers "from a wide range of ethnic groups, including Germans, Poles, Bohemians, and Scandinavians" (Barrett 1983). Several other labor associations were formed, such as the Blackthorn Club of cattle butchers; though primarily made up of Irish cattle butchers, all other nationalities were welcomed as well. The U.S. commissioner of labor, Ethelbert Stewart, observed in 1904 that unions brought immigrants together. Stewart noted that it was only in the union that "the

Slav mixes with the Lithuanian, the German, and the Irishman" (Barrett 1983).

Though African Americans had toiled in the meatpacking industry in Kansas City since the 1880s, they had not worked in large numbers in Chicago. In the early1900s, however, some African Americans from the South migrated to Chicago, entering the city's meatpacking labor force. Then, after the beginning of World War I in 1914 essentially ceased all immigration from Europe to the United States, African Americans flocked to industrial cities in the North, gaining employment in the meatpacking industry as a result of the shortage of immigrant labor. In just ten years, from 1910 to 1920, the African American population in Chicago increased by more than 65,000 people. By 1918, more than 6,000 of these African Americans labored in the Chicago packinghouses. The majority of these workers, however, were restricted to unskilled labor; in fact, in 1922, 99 percent of the African American workers in Chicago's packinghouses were employed at unskilled jobs (Barrett 1983). Though European immigrants usually obtained jobs in the "cutting rooms," African American workers generally worked on the slaughtering floor.

Immigrants from all over the world populated the workforce that built and sustained America's agriculture and meatpacking industries from their earliest days. Though not typically thought of as such, African slaves were some of America's first immigrants, supplying a labor force for plantations across the South, and descendants of these original immigrants later migrated to Chicago and other northern cities for work in industrial factories. America's expansion would never have proceeded at the pace it did without the efforts of the immigrant workforce, both slave and free. No matter their place of origin, these men and women had a tremendous impact on the country's developing agriculture and meatpacking industries.

Sources

Abbott, Edith, and S. P. Breckinridge. 1911. "Women in Industry: The Chicago Stockyards." *Journal of Political Economy* 19, no. 8 (October).

Andreas, Carol. 1994. *Meatpackers and Beef Barons: Company Town in a Global Economy.* Niwot: University Press of Colorado.

Barrett, James R. 1983. "Immigrant Workers in Early Mass Production Industry: Work Rationalization and Job Control Conflicts in Chicago's Packinghouses, 1900–1904." In *German Workers in Industrial Chicago, 1850–1910:*

A Comparative Perspective, edited by Hartmut Keil and John B. Jentz. De Kalb: Northern Illinois University Press.

———. 1987. *Work and Community in the Jungle: Chicago's Packinghouse Workers, 1894–1922.* Urbana: University of Illinois Press.

Berlin, Ira, and Herbert G. Gutman. 1989. "Natives and Immigrants, Free Men and Slaves: Urban Workingmen in the Antebellum American South." In *Economics, Industrialization, Urbanization, and Slavery*, edited by Paul Finkelman. New York: Garland.

Berthoff, Rowland T. 1951. "Southern Attitudes toward Immigration, 1865–1914." *Journal of Southern History* 17, no. 3 (August).

Brandfon, Robert L. 1964. "The End of Immigration to the Cotton Fields." *Mississippi Valley Historical Review* 50, no. 4 (March).

Buenker, John D. 1999. "Michael Cudahy." In *American National Biography.* New York: Oxford University Press.

Bushnell, Charles J. 1901. "Some Social Aspects of the Chicago Stock Yards." *American Journal of Sociology* 7, no. 2 (September).

Carstensen, Fred. 1999. "Nelson Morris." In *American National Biography.* New York: Oxford University Press.

Daniel, Cletus E. 1981. *Bitter Harvest: A History of California Farmworkers, 1870–1941.* Ithaca, NY: Cornell University Press.

Daniels, Roger. 1990. *Coming to America: A History of Immigration and Ethnicity in American Life.* New York: HarperPerennial.

———. 2001. *American Immigration: A Student Companion.* Oxford: Oxford University Press.

Earle, Carville V. 1989. "A Staple Interpretation of Slavery and Free Labor." In *Economics, Industrialization, Urbanization, and Slavery*, edited by Paul Finkelman. New York: Garland.

Fink, Deborah. 1998. *Cutting into the Meatpacking Line: Workers and Change in the Rural Midwest.* Chapel Hill: University of North Carolina Press.

Fite, Gilbert Courtland. 1981. *American Farmers: The New Minority.* Bloomington: Indiana University Press.

Fleming, Walter L. 1905. "Immigration to the Southern States." *Political Science Quarterly* 20, no. 2 (June).

Gladsky, Thomas S. 1988. "The Immigrant on the Land: Polish Farmers and New England Novelists." *New England Quarterly* 61, no. 3 (September).

Gleeson, David T. 2001. *The Irish in the South, 1815–1877.* Chapel Hill: University of North Carolina Press.

Hahamovitch, Cindy. 1997. *The Fruits of Their Labor: Atlantic Coast Farmworkers and the Making of Migrant Poverty, 1870–1945.* Chapel Hill: University of North Carolina Press.

Halpern, Rick. 1997. *Down on the Floor: Black and White Workers in Chicago's Packinghouses, 1904–54.* Urbana: University of Illinois Press.

Halpern, Rick, and Roger Horowitz. 1996. *Meatpackers: An Oral History of Black Packinghouse Workers and Their Struggle for Racial and Economic Equality.* New York: Twayne.

Higbie, Frank Tobias. 2003. *Indispensable Outcasts: Hobo Workers and Community in the American Midwest, 1880–1930*. Urbana: University of Illinois Press.

Higgs, Robert. 1978. "Landless by Law: Japanese Immigrants in California Agriculture to 1941." *Journal of Economic History* 38, no. 2 (March).

Hill, Howard Copeland. 1923. "The Development of Chicago as a Center of the Meat Packing Industry." *Mississippi Valley Historical Review* 10, no. 3 (December).

Hoobler, Dorothy, and Thomas Hoobler. 2003. *We Are Americans: Voices of the Immigrant Experience*. New York: Scholastic.

Keil, Hartmut, and John B. Jentz, eds. 1983. *German Workers in Industrial Chicago, 1850–1910: A Comparative Perspective*. De Kalb: Northern Illinois University Press.

———. 1988. *German Workers in Chicago: A Documentary History of Working-Class Culture from 1850 to World War I*. Urbana: University of Illinois Press.

Luebke, Frederick C. 1998. *European Immigrants in the American West: Community Histories*. Albuquerque: University of New Mexico Press.

McQuillan, D. Aidan. 1990. *Prevailing over Time: Ethnic Adjustment on the Kansas Prairies, 1875–1925*. Lincoln: University of Nebraska Press.

Page, Brian, and Richard Walker. 1991. "From Settlement to Fordism: The Agro-Industrial Revolution in the American Midwest." *Economic Geography* 67, no. 4 (October).

Peck, Gunther. 1996. "Reinventing Free Labor: Immigrant Padrones and Contract Laborers in North America, 1885–1925." *Journal of American History* 83, no. 3 (December).

Rosenbloom, Joshua L. 1998. "Strikebreaking and the Labor Market in the United States, 1881–1894." *Journal of Economic History* 58, no. 1 (March).

Sosnick, Stephen H. 1978. *Hired Hands: Seasonal Farm Workers in the United States*. Santa Barbara, CA: McNally and Loftin, West.

Thompson, Carl William. 1907. "Labor in the Packing Industry." *Journal of Political Economy* 15, no. 2 (February).

Trotter, Joe W., and Earl Lewis, eds. 1996. *African Americans in the Industrial Age: A Documentary History, 1915–1945*. Boston: Northeastern University Press.

Wells, Miriam J. 1984. "The Resurgence of Sharecropping: Historical Anomaly or Political Strategy?" *American Journal of Sociology* 90, no. 1 (July).

Societal Impact

Leigh Kimmel

Although the Industrial Revolution was slow to come to the agricultural sector, once it arrived, it completely transformed America's rural culture. To understand the extent to which the mechanization of agriculture changed everything, one must examine what the countryside looked like before the Industrial Revolution. Early America was largely rural, even bucolic. Thomas Jefferson regarded the yeoman farmer as the foundation of a free republic, and although he himself was a southern planter who owned a large spread worked primarily by slaves, he strove to create policies that would favor the small landowner who worked his own ground. The epitome of this policy was the Homestead Act, which promised free land to any man or woman who worked on it and lived on it.

For the first five decades of the new Republic, the labor of agriculture was not all that different than it had been in previous centuries, right back to the beginnings of agriculture in the Neolithic period. Innovations in agricultural methods came slowly and incrementally, over generations. Hoe agriculture gave way to wooden scratch plows, then to iron plows, and ultimately to the self-scouring steel plow. Sickles gave way to scythes, then to cradle scythes. Each innovation made it possible for the people working the land to support more of their nonproductive counterparts.

The first revolutionary innovation in American agriculture came in 1831, when Cyrus McCormick introduced the mechanical reaper. Where formerly it required whole crews of men with cradle scythes

187

to harvest a field of wheat, now it could be done by two men—one to drive the reaper and one to bind the sheaves as they were cut. Some historians have suggested that the men who were freed from farm labor by the reaper and were then able to fight in the Union army were a significant contributing factor to the Union victory in the Civil War. The development of the threshing machine—which separated grain from straw quickly and cleanly with far less waste than traditional methods, such as beating with the flail and treading by oxen—further increased American farmers' effective productivity.

But all of these mechanical devices were dependent on animal traction for their energy. The reaper and its successor, the binder, were drawn by horses, and the threshing machine's mechanical separators were powered by horses walking on either a treadmill or a sweep, a device rather like a carousel. The limitations of horsepower in the latter were particularly noticeable, since any variation in the horses' pace would adversely affect the quality of the separation process, resulting in grain lost in the straw-stack. Given the variations in equine temperaments, maintaining a steady speed was often easier said than done. Furthermore, horses required rest, so the threshing machine had to be stopped periodically to switch the weary team for a fresh one. As a result of these difficulties with animal power, threshing was one of the first agricultural processes for which there was interest in applying mechanical power.

From Horses to Horsepower

Early steam engines were large and clumsy things, which meant that a stationary task such as threshing was relatively easy to convert to steam power. A threshing machine was so large and expensive, however, that only the wealthiest farmers, who operated enormous acreages with hired help, were able to purchase their own. The usual practice for ordinary farmers was to join together with a number of neighbors to purchase a threshing machine. It was then moved from one farm to another during threshing season, with everyone in the threshing cooperative working together to get each farmer's grain threshed as rapidly as possible. As a result, a typical stationary steam engine on a foundation was not suitable for their purposes.

At first, manufacturers put a sort of wheeled cart under the steam engine so that it could be pulled from farm to farm by the horses that previously had provided the threshing machine's power. Yet the existence of the steam locomotive made it clear that a steam engine could be made to propel itself. Once inventors found a solution to the problem of driving the wide wheels necessary for moving such a heavy load on dirt roads instead of rails, the portable steam engine was transformed into a steam traction engine.

The steam traction engine was not a true tractor. With its huge size and relatively primitive steering, it was really not suitable for providing power in the field. Most steam traction engines were 10 to 12 feet tall, weighed 20 tons, required an acre just to turn around at the end of the row, and took a whole team of men to operate safely. At minimum, a steam traction engine took one person to operate the boiler while a second drove. Inattention to the boiler could be deadly, for the primitive safety devices of the time left steam traction engines vulnerable to boiler explosions if the pressure within them was allowed to rise too high. Even so, some early experimenters put them to work plowing on the largest farms of the Great Plains, and they even used flexible steam lines to run secondary steam engines to operate the separators on some of the earliest experimental combine harvesters.

As a result of the early difficulties, however, the steam traction engine made relatively little change in the average American farm. The typical small farmer continued to rely primarily on horses for row-crop agriculture, and thus, the size of farms was limited by the amount of acreage a farmer could work with a team of horses.

That situation changed with the development of the internal combustion engine. Smaller and lighter than the giant steam engines of the nineteenth century, these tractors were actually practical on the average farmer's establishment. When Henry Ford produced his small tractor, the Fordson, he often commented that his only competition was the horse. However, not every farmer was immediately won over by the practicality of exchanging his or her team of horses for a tractor. Farmers often developed a bond with their horses, which was not surprising given that one of the essential parts of working with these animals was learning their individual temperaments to manage them most effectively. Having made this investment, farmers were often reluctant to make the change to tractors.

A woman selling a Fordson tractor, ca. 1921. (Library of Congress)

Furthermore, they were a conservative lot, and they tended to resist change until it was proven beyond a doubt that it was beneficial. Their ancestors had farmed with horses, so horses would be good enough for them as well.

A few early tractor manufacturers, trying to sell reluctant and old-fashioned farmers on the virtues of the tractor, equipped their machines with an optional rein drive. This curious apparatus allowed a farmer to walk behind a tractor and guide it with leather reins, just as it had always been done with a team of horses. However, in the end, it was the simple practicalities of the tractor that won farmers over. Tractors did not grow tired and need to rest periodically. If a tractor broke down, getting it back in operation was a matter of swapping out the broken part for a new one from the implement dealer, rather than coping with the uncertainties of veterinary treatment. Tractors were not bad-tempered or ornery, as some horses were. And most important of all, the tractor enabled one man to do far more than he could accomplish with horses.

The first and most obvious change that resulted from the use of tractors instead of horses was the consolidation of small fields into larger ones. With horses, the length of the field was determined by the distance a team of horses could pull before needing to rest. It was generally considered good practice to rest one's horses at the end of the row, not in the middle. By contrast, even relatively small tractors needed a larger turning radius than a team of horses, so it was to the farmer's advantage to reduce the amount of times he needed to turn his tractor. In addition, a tractor could work more land in a day than a team of horses could, so it made sense to work larger fields and avoid having to waste time moving between many little fields.

Because the farmer could work more land in the same amount of time, it became possible for him to work a larger acreage by himself, without hired help. Successful farmers sought to acquire additional acreage; less successful ones often ended up getting out of the business altogether in order to take jobs in town. As a result, the proportion of the population involved in production agriculture steadily diminished, whereas the urban and suburban population came to represent a steadily increasing share of American society. By World War II, the number of working farmers had been reduced enough as a result of mechanization that there could be no question of returning to horses in order to save fuel for the war effort. There were no longer enough horses left to do the work, and going back to horse-drawn agriculture would require more men—men who were badly needed in uniform. As a result, the government's rationing boards made fuel for agriculture a priority, so that farmers were able to get as much as they needed.

The trend toward mechanized agriculture only increased after the war, which accelerated the changes taking place on American farms. In order to farm larger acreages, farmers needed larger equipment, which required larger capital investments. And to justify those capital investments and maintain a reasonable standard of living in a world where increased production had driven the per unit price of grain downward, farmers had to increase their acreages. Farming was no longer a way of life but a business, and farmers had to learn how to think and operate like entrepreneurs rather than traditional agriculturalists.

Life Down on the Farm

In addition to the direct effects that industrialization had on the process of farming, the Industrial Revolution also had its effect on the lifestyle of farm families. For the first century of the American Republic, the life of the farmer and his family was lonely and isolated, filled with heavy labor from dawn until dusk. Unlike the traditional European peasant, the American farmer did not live in a village but on an isolated farmstead surrounded by the fields he worked. Often, the nearest neighbor would be a half hour's brisk walk away, and trips into town were at most weekly affairs, to attend church and possibly purchase essentials.

A whole series of technological innovations worked together to completely change that situation. The first was the introduction of small gasoline engines that could be put to use in a multitude of tiresome tasks around the farm. The great steam engines that ran threshing machines and pumped water from deep wells were not suitable for smaller tasks because their power could not be effectively subdivided. With the development of 1- and 2-horsepower gasoline engines, however, it became possible to mechanize the work of grinding corn for chickens, churning butter, turning the agitator on a washing machine, and otherwise lightening the load of the farmer and his family. As a result, farming was no longer such a continual back-breaking effort.

The development of the gasoline engine also led to the development of the automobile. The earliest production automobiles were luxury items, made one by one for the very wealthy. Henry Ford changed everything with his development of the assembly line and a scientific approach to mass production, systematically finding ways to increase efficiency and reduce the price of an automobile so that everyone could own one. Though farmers using horses would be reluctant to ask their beasts to take them into town after working a long day in the fields, there were no such qualms about hopping into a car or truck (or even a suitable tractor if the family was not wealthy enough to own a separate car or truck) and heading for town to visit friends or to participate in such social activities as a dance. Distance no longer isolated the farmer from the cultural events of the big city.

The telephone also helped tie farmers together and connect them with town and the wider world. Although early telephone companies focused primarily on serving the cities and larger towns, where the high concentration of wealthy customers made the installation of telephones a profitable affair, many farm communities did not wait around for the telephone company to bring service to them. Once telephone technology passed out of the experimental stage and any reasonably savvy person could assemble a basic telephone circuit, farmers strung their own lines from house to house, setting up independent rural exchanges. Because it was not feasible to give each telephone its own connection with the central switchboard, all the telephones in the system were attached on a single connection known as a party line.

The rural party line developed an informal etiquette all its own. Because of the way a party line was wired, all phones on the line would ring when the central switchboard connected a call. As a result, a code of short and long rings was developed to indicate which subscriber was being called. Although anybody on the party line who picked up the receiver could answer the call or listen in on a call in progress, it was considered poor manners to do so. The rule, however, was often observed as much in the breach as the keeping. Listening in on the business of one's neighbors via the party line was so common that it was even given a name: "rubbernecking." It was not unknown for neighbors to chime in with answers to a question raised by the original callers. However, it was considered rude in the extreme to call attention to the presence of other parties listening in.

Even with all its problems and limitations, the party line was often a lifesaver for rural families. Tornado warnings could be passed to everyone on the circuit, giving them a vital extra few minutes to take cover, which might well make the difference between life and death on the plains. As rural party lines were connected with town switchboards, it also became possible to summon a doctor to deal with urgent medical emergencies; patients were saved who formerly may well have died while someone was riding to town to fetch the doctor.

The next major life changer on the farm was the broadcast radio, which provided a window on the wider world in the form of news and big-city cultural programming, such as operas, theatrical productions, and lectures. For the first time, farm families were able to hear breaking news stories, such as the wreck of the airship *Hindenburg*, in real time instead of learning about them days later during a visit to town. The broadcasting of popular shows such as *Amos and Andy* or *The Shadow* helped to tie rural families more firmly into a broad national culture, although often at the expense of local cultures.

Because many farms in the 1920s were not yet electrified, radios were often powered by batteries. Farmers frequently used the large wet-cell batteries that normally powered electric fences. Batteries were expensive, though, so it was essential to make them last as long as possible. Thus, it was not uncommon to find the entire family crowded around the radio, straining to hear the faint sounds produced by a battery on its last life.

Electricity was a relative latecomer to the rural scene. Even as late as the 1920s, electric companies did not regard rural areas as profitable enough to merit the amount of wire that would have to be strung in order to bring service to them. As a result, only a few farms along the edge of towns and urban areas received power from transmission lines. A few more farm families were able to own generators and produce their own electricity. This situation changed in the 1930s, however, with President Franklin D. Roosevelt's Rural Electrification Administration, one of the programs intended to bring the country out of the Great Depression.

But all these changes were only peripheral to the greatest change worked on rural society by the Industrial Revolution, namely, the integration of the rural population into the consumer economy that was developing in the cities. Until the late 1900s, farmers and their families made most of the things they used on a regular basis. Store-bought items, such as tools, were rare and precious things, to be kept in service as long as possible. But the development of factories and mass production led to an abundance of inexpensive products that could be purchased by a farmer who had the necessary cash. Although the local general store might continue to carry only a restricted range of essentials, the development of catalog merchandising by Montgomery Ward and Sears, Roebuck and Company brought a virtual cornucopia of worldly goods as close as the farmer's mailbox.

Richard Warren Sears was born on December 7, 1863, in Stewartville, Minnesota. His parents, James Warren and Eliza A. Sears, were both of English ancestry. His father was a wagon maker and reasonably wealthy until he lost most of his money in a stock market venture when Richard was about fifteen. Two years later, James died, leaving his son to support the family, which he did by working in the general offices of the Minneapolis and St. Louis Railway.

An ambitious young man, Sears soon concluded that there would be more opportunities for advancement in a smaller town. He subse-

Richard Sears of Sears, Roebuck and Company, the largest mail order business in the early twentieth century. (Library of Congress)

quently got himself transferred to Redwood Falls, Minnesota, where he did chores in exchange for his board and slept in the station loft in order to make his salary stretch further. Always alert for a possibility to turn a profit, he dealt in various goods on the side, even buying wild berries and venison from the local Native American tribes.

A fortuitous accident formed the foundation of his fortune. A local jeweler had refused to accept a shipment of watches, and as a result, the package of watches was left sitting in the station. Since no freight had been paid, Sears wrote to the wholesaler for instructions and was given permission to dispose of them as he saw fit. He then wrote letters describing the wares and offering them for sale at bargain prices. Soon, he sold them all. The profit he turned on them provided the seed money for a new mail-order business venture, the - R. W. Sears Watch Company. In a single year, he did so much business that he was able to move to Chicago, and by 1889, he sold the business for a handsome profit and set himself up as a banker.

However, banking proved less promising than Sears had hoped, and he soon sought something more challenging. Prevented from launching a business in Chicago for three years by a noncompetition agreement he had signed as part of the sale of his former company, he returned to Minneapolis. There, he looked up an old business partner, A. C. Roebuck, and set up a new mail-order jewelry business.

By 1893, the noncompetition agreement had expired, and Sears was able to move his business back to Chicago. It grew rapidly, and he began to add other lines of products to his mail-order business. Throughout the early years, he wrote all the advertising copy for his catalog himself, even when it grew from a booklet listing twenty-five models of watches to a substantial book of over a thousand pages. He experimented with various types of catalog listings, seeing what kinds of phrasings would draw the most business. Sears's personal life proved happy. On June 20, 1895, he married Anna Lydia Mackstroth of Minneapolis, with whom he had two sons and two daughters. All survived their father. In 1909, he retired from the business and went to live on a farm north of Chicago, where he died on September 28, 1914, just as World War I was starting.

Trouble on the Farm

The changes brought by the Industrial Revolution put increasing pressure on the rural economy. Even as farmers were becoming steadily more integrated into, and thus dependent on, the money economy, cash was getting more difficult to come by. The years following the American Civil War were marked by a general economic downturn, but it hit farmers particularly hard, in large part because so many of them had shifted from subsistence agriculture to cash crops. Since the new way of farming required large outlays of capital up front, many farmers became trapped in a pernicious cycle of indebtedness.

The situation was especially onerous in the South, where the newly freed African Americans wanted to translate their legal freedom into meaningful economic independence, whereas the white landowners wanted to maintain the old social and economic relations of slavery, leaving the freedmen's new status purely symbolic. After much struggling, a new system was worked out that was not particularly satisfactory to either side but was more tolerable than continued struggle, particularly after the federal government ceased even a pretense of Reconstruction.

Sharecropping, as this new arrangement was called, kept the freed-men working for the landowner but without the hated gang system of the old plantation. Under the gang system, slaves had worked un-der the direct supervision of the planter or his overseers, rather like employees in a factory but subject to corporal punishment and with-out the option of quitting. Under the new system, the arable land of the former plantation was parceled up into small units, and each freedman and his family tended the fields assigned to them. Further-more, the freedmen were no longer constrained to dwell in central-ized quarters but instead were free to locate their homes on the plots they farmed. Their dwellings might be nothing more than shanties, often even cruder in construction than those they had used as slaves (since the landowner no longer had an economic interest in their well-being, only in the product of their labor), but many sharecrop-pers found the sense of being a little farther away from the landlord's watchful eye was worth the decrease in quality of housing.

Technically, the sharecropper was a sort of employee of the landowner and thus under his supervision. However, instead of being paid in cash for his labor, the freedman was given a share of the crop he had produced. In theory, the sharecropper would be able to sell his crop share, but the reality was different and cruel. The landlord did not provide tools or seeds, so the sharecropper had to borrow money to purchase them. Furthermore, such little necessities as he and his family might need during the growing season had to be pur-chased on credit from the landlord's furnishing merchant, a rural variation on the company store system. In order to secure that line of credit, the sharecropper pledged the crop share he was promised as payment for his labor. By setting an artificially high price for supplies and an artificially low price for the cotton or other crops being pro-duced, landlords were able to ensure that the sharecropper would have no money ahead when "settle up" time rolled around at the end of the crop year. In a bad year, the sharecropper might well end up owing the landlord money, which meant he could not leave that land-lord until the debt was repaid. In effect, sharecropping became a form of debt peonage.

As long as the victims of this system were black, it was easy for a society in which racism was ubiquitous to ignore their plight. As the Gilded Age wore on, however, many white yeoman farmers on the hardscrabble small farms of the South began to experience the same economic difficulties as their fellow farmers in the North and West.

Unlike the farmers in other regions, though, southern white yeoman farmers who needed to borrow money for production expenses were generally required to pledge their harvest as surety for the loan. As a result, they soon became entangled in the same trap of sharecropping as the freedmen. This is not to suggest there was any sense of solidarity between white and black sharecroppers—far from it, as many of the white farmers rendered landless and debt-bonded considered it a special humiliation that they should be bound to the same odious terms as the members of a despised race.

Throughout the country, there was a growing sense that the American democratic ideal had been betrayed and that power was increasingly becoming concentrated in the hands of a few. The kings and aristocrats from whom the immigrants had fled were now being replaced by the industrial magnates, robber barons, and large landowners who used various legal tricks to structure the economic situation in their favor. Wheat farmers on the Great Plains resented the ways in which they were taken advantage of by the railroads' pricing structures, which gave favorable rates to large shippers while paying paltry prices for small farmers' grain harvests. There was an angry sense that the other trusts existed in order to maximize profits at the expense of the ordinary citizen. The American countryside was rapidly becoming ripe for revolt.

The tradition of political activism in response to perceived injustice was a cornerstone of American democracy, going back to the Revolutionary War. Throughout the nineteenth century, various small third parties had periodically arisen to address a single issue. But the political movements that arose in the decades after the Civil War had one critical difference. Rather than remaining isolated and fading away as the immediacy of their issue faded, they took advantage of new communications technologies and the generalized increase in political awareness in rural America to forge connections with one another and with organizations of the urban proletariat, building a larger coalition that would ultimately be known as the Populist, or People's, Party.

The rural roots of the Populist movement lay in the Grange, founded in 1864 by Oliver Hudson Kelley, a Bostonian by birth who had homesteaded in Minnesota and experienced the worst of rural life. He envisioned a voluntary organization of farmers similar to the self-assistance organizations then common in American society. Founding such an organization was simple: one drew up a constitution and a list of criteria for membership and then set about seeking members. If one's vision had a broad appeal, the organization soon grew and became self-perpetuating, with an interlocking system of federal, state, county, and local bodies. If its appeal was limited, it would soon wither as the enthusiasm of the original organizers waned.

Kelley's vision of the Grange was an organization uniting farmers in a manner somewhat similar to the Freemasons, complete with a system of "degrees" and secrets. However, the practical benefits of membership as touted to prospective members lay in the cooperative buying power the Grange could exert. Although each individual farmer might be at the mercy of the big corporations, such as the railroads and the various trusts, a sufficiently large pool of buyers would be able to pressure the corporate interests into reducing their prices to a more equitable level. The Grange's business agencies actually did enjoy some success, until they met real competition in the form of catalog merchants such as Montgomery Ward and Sears, Roebuck, which recognized that one could make a substantial profit by selling large volumes at cut-rate prices. On major capital purchases such as threshing machines and other farm machinery, the Granges in several states actually ended up going into manufacturing for themselves in an effort to respond to high prices.

In the South, the Grange showed a darker side, aligning with the planters in an effort to "redeem Dixie" by undoing the last vestiges of Reconstruction. They might not have been able to literally reenslave the freedmen, but they would use the law or outright force to restore what they considered to be the proper social order—the absolute subjugation of the African American. More than one important Grange leader also held office in the Ku Klux Klan. As a result, many small farmers in the South turned to other organizations, such as the Cotton Pickers' Association, the Agricultural Wheel, and the Knights of Labor, a quasi-secret society that originally arose among the urban proletariat and was a precursor to the modern labor union.

By the 1880s, the Farmers' Alliance, a looser organization without the quasi-Masonic trappings, was doing financial battle with the railroads and particularly with the notorious robber baron Jay Gould. As members of the Farmers' Alliance began to forge links with the Knights of Labor and other, similar organizations, the beginnings of the Populist Party began to take definite shape. By 1890, the most pressing question was whether the Populists should ally themselves with the Democratic Party—which in the North was seen primarily as the party of the working class against the wealthy and powerful who now ran the Republican Party—or whether the Populists should remain independent and run as a third party. Those who favored the merger argued that joining forces with the Democrats would give them additional leverage against the political weight the plutocrats could bring to bear. Those who opposed it argued that the specifically Populist character of their aims would be submerged by the compromises inherent in such a merger, particularly in the "solid South" where the Democrats were the party of the planters, arrayed against the yeoman farmer and the poor tenant.

The 1890s were the high-water mark of the Populists. Camp meetings, rather like the religious revivals of the Second Great Awakening but of a secular, political nature, were used to draw new members into the Populist Party. Farmers might travel for miles by horse and buggy to hear their speakers expound on the evils of monopolistic corporate capitalism and the way in which it had betrayed the ideals of Jefferson and the other Founding Fathers. The Populist Party even ran some candidates for federal office and won a few minor state and local elections. But by the middle of the 1890s, the Populists had pretty much run out of steam as a viable third party on the American political scene. The strongest parts of the Populist movement became absorbed into the Democratic Party; those that refused to compromise became isolated and eventually broke up altogether.

The last great act of the Populists came in the 1896 election, in which they conominated the Democratic candidate for president, **William Jennings Bryan,** whose youth and speaking skills earned him the nickname "Boy Orator of the Platte." Bryan was born on March 19, 1860, in Salem, Illinois, a small rural town in the southern part of the state. He was raised in an atmosphere of morality and righteousness that grew from the Second Great Awakening. Those values remained the lodestone of his moral compass, even as the world that had created them gave way to the twentieth century.

Bryan's education was typical for a young Protestant man of his time, relying heavily on the *McGuffy Reader* series, with its strong emphasis on clean living, hard work, and virtues that both complemented and reinforced the moral lessons learned in Sunday school. He showed an aptitude for public speaking early on, although those youthful orations were heavily derivative of his reading. But most important to his future career was his sense that politics was no

Populist politician William Jennings Bryan. (Library of Congress)

stranger to religion and that it was the duty of the God-fearing Christian to seek to make the world a better place through political means.

At the age of fifteen, young Bryan had exhausted his hometown's education opportunities, and he left his family home to attend high school and college in nearby Jacksonville, Illinois. While studying at Jacksonville's Illinois Wesleyan College, Bryan briefly flirted with agnosticism in the vein of Robert Ingersoll before joining the local Presbyterian church. This momentary wavering of his moral compass left him with a deep conviction that college students were particularly at risk for being led astray by modernist philosophies. While in Jacksonville, Bryan also met and wooed Mary Baird, but he was not able to marry her until he completed his law degree. This effort took him to Union College of Law in Chicago, a place very much unlike the rural small towns of downstate Illinois with which he was familiar. Although he had to live on a shoestring budget, he was able to complete the two-year course and return to Jacksonville to start his law practice and wed his fiancée.

But Bryan continued thinking about some of the things he had seen in Chicago—such as the wealth enjoyed by the captains of industry and the squalor endured by the immigrant workingmen. After a few years of tepid success, he decided to move to Nebraska and become involved in politics. He was particularly interested in questions of monetary policy and especially the theory of bimetallism (using both gold and silver as monetary standards), which was proposed as a solution to the problem of contractions in the money supply caused by the rapid increase in the American population. By that time, Bryan had honed his voice to perfection, and his skill in public speaking got him elected twice to the U.S. House of Representatives, in 1890 and 1892. However, a bid for the Democratic nomination to the Senate in 1894 failed.

Two years later, Bryan turned everything around with his famous "Cross of Gold" speech at the 1896 Democratic National Convention, which won him its presidential nomination. The Populist Party, convinced that he shared their ideals, also made him their candidate. However, Bryan still lost to William McKinley, the Republican candidate. After a brief period of military service during the Spanish-American War, he ran for president again in 1900, only to be beaten once again by McKinley. As a result, he sat out the 1904 election, instead applying his energies to his newspaper, *The Commoner,* and to a world tour. In 1908, he made his third and final bid for the presidency, only to lose to William Howard Taft.

In 1912, Bryan actively supported Woodrow Wilson, and as a reward, he was made secretary of state. However, as America's slide toward involvement in World War I became increasingly clear, he finally tendered his resignation and then worked as a private citizen to keep the country neutral. Once a formal declaration of war was made, Bryan set aside his peacemaking efforts and supported the war, although he continued to devote much of his energies to Progressive agendas, such as alcohol prohibition and women's rights. In the postwar period, he opposed America's retreat into isolationism, arguing that it was essential for long-term peace for the United States to ratify the Versailles Treaty and become a member of the League of Nations.

Bryan's last years were marked by his deep opposition to the teaching of the Darwinian theory of evolution in public schools. Bryan believed that evolutionary theory was contributing to a growing devaluation of human life in American society. He became convinced that only by returning to a belief in the literal truth of the biblical creation narrative could the nation's fundamental moral sense of humanity be restored. His final act was his participation in the famous Scopes Monkey Trial, in which science teacher John Scopes was accused of violating the Butler Act, a Tennessee law that prohibited the teaching of evolution as scientific fact. Although the trial technically ended in victory for Bryan's side, since Scopes was convicted (he paid a $100 fine), the grand moral regeneration that Bryan had hoped for did not come to pass. In fact, many Americans condemned Bryan and his supporters for suppressing rational thought in favor of superstition. Bryan died on July 26, 1925—a mere six days after the trial's conclusion—while still in Dayton, Tennessee.

Although the Populist Party effectively ceased to exist as a political organization by the turn of the twentieth century (and with it, the Farmers' Alliance and the Grange), the idea of farmers working together lived on. The twentieth century saw the development of the Farm Bureau movement, which ultimately became a natioinwide association. State and local Farm Bureau organizations formed cooperatives for purchasing chemicals and other supplies and for providing affordable insurance to farm families. Although there was some initial resistance to the Farm Bureau movement, particularly in the period immediately after World War I when the fear of a Communist infiltration of unions was particularly high, the Farm Bureau has become an accepted part of rural society. In most areas, it worked together with the Co-operative Extension Service, an outreach program of the land-grant agricultural universities, to teach improved practices in field and home. Only with the sharp decline in the farming population in the last decades of the twentieth century did the Farm Bureau and the Co-operative Extension Service diminish in importance.

From Farm to Table

The Industrial Revolution's effects on agriculture stretched beyond the rural landscape to reach all the way to the urban dwellers who ate the products of the farmer's toils. Previously, the farmer's products were consumed relatively close to the farm that produced them, often by persons who knew the farmer. Generally, there were no more than one or at most two layers of middlemen standing between farmer and consumer. Butchers would buy live animals, slaughter them, and reduce them to cuts, which they sold. The local miller would buy the farmer's grain, grind it to flour, and sell it directly to homemakers or possibly to bakers. As long as everyone knew the people with whom they were trading and communities were reasonably small, simple word of mouth kept everyone honest. The persistently dishonest might have to be dealt with by the local sheriff.

The growth of the cities, driven by industrialization and the factory system, led to a lengthening of the supply chains that connected producer and consumer. Sometimes several layers of middlemen were involved, and rarely did the consumer have any real sense of who provided the food in the store or how it got there. This was particularly true of canned and otherwise processed and preserved foods. Adulteration of foods with various substances became an easy way for the unscrupulous to expand their profits at the expense of the consumer. Such substances as chalk and talcum powder were ground into flour, and "strawberry jam" might well be made of fragments of apples and grass seed, all colored the right hue with chemicals of unknown safety.

But it was in the slaughterhouses that the most stomach-turning abuses abounded. The large-scale meatpacking operations were largely staffed by immigrants, many of whom spoke little English, so it was difficult to communicate safety procedures to them. Although some meatpackers, such as Gustavus Franklin Swift's company, were meticulous about cleanliness, many others emphasized profits instead. In fact, some saw no problem with the presence of all manner of filth and vermin in the areas in which animals were being slaughtered and meat was being processed. As a result, contamination was a frequent occurrence, but few consumers realized how badly tainted their food might be or that it might well be the cause of their various stomach ailments.

It was only when a brash young socialist writer produced a fictionalized exposé of the horrific conditions in the slaughterhouses that there was a hue and cry for change. Although Upton Sinclair wrote *The Jungle* primarily in hopes of bettering the conditions of the workers, it was the gruesome images of poisoned rats being chopped into sausage and workers falling into the lard-rendering machines to be sent out as "fine leaf lard" that made the deepest impres-

Muckraking journalist and
novelist Upton Sinclair.
(Library of Congress)

sions on his readers, who demanded that the federal government in-
vestigate the safety of their food supply.

Upton Sinclair was born on September 20, 1878, in the squalor of
a Baltimore boardinghouse, but his family soon moved to New York.
By the time he reached adulthood, he had moved so many times that
he could no longer remember all the places he had once called home.
His father was an alcoholic who could not hold a steady job and was
continually seeking a new start in hopes that he would have better
luck. The elder Sinclair's chief contribution to his son's life was providing a negative example of the effects of strong drink, a theme that
would appear in many of the latter's adult writings. Sinclair was far
closer to his mother, although he was stubbornly reticent about exactly how that relationship had affected him.

A slim and sickly child whose frequent moves prevented him from
putting down lasting roots or developing strong friendships, Sinclair
learned early in life to take refuge in reading. Particularly when visiting his mother's family, he was able to delve through veritable trea-

sure troves of books and to build from them a vital life of the mind that enabled him to survive the misery of his physical surroundings. After discovering Shakespeare through his uncle's library, he began to compose poetry.

Sinclair's literary career started early, with astonishing success. After a friend introduced him to the lucrative world of writing formulaic fiction for the popular press, he put himself through college on his output. Still flush with his early success, he married the lovely Meta Fuller and set forth on his grand ambition: to write a novel that he described as what Percy Bysshe Shelley would have written had he chosen the novel as his medium. Shortly after the birth of a son, David, Sinclair's success came crashing down when *Springtime and Harvest* was rejected by one publisher after another. Its rejection began a chain of failures that sent Sinclair on a downward spiral to the nadir of his life. He had even lost his facility at writing entertaining potboilers. His wife and son went to live with his father-in-law, who forbade him from any contact with them on the basis that he was refusing to support them as a man ought, by taking regular employment. After an attempt to find solace in an extended wilderness sojourn that nearly killed him, Sinclair was reduced to living with his own parents, although his father's worsening alcoholism disgusted him.

Sinclair's anger at the establishment, which he regarded as having spurned his genius, finally opened the way for him to re-create himself. The poet would become a muckraking journalist, exposing the ills of society and the corruption of the elites who fostered them. This resolution brought him into contact with the socialists, who suggested he should write an exposé of the meatpacking industry. Sinclair went to Chicago to research the situation on the ground. His poverty stood him in good stead, for his clothes were so shabby he could easily pass for a worker in one of the meatpacking plants. The simple expedient of carrying a lunchpail and saying the right things often got him into places he never could have entered had his true intentions been known.

In 1906, Sinclair published *The Jungle,* the story of a Lithuanian immigrant family's travails both in the workplace and in the brutal streets of Chicago. Although Sinclair dedicated the novel to the workers whose lot he hoped it would improve, it was the visceral images of contaminated food that moved people to action. As a result of the popular demand that something be done about the safety of the nation's food supply, Congress passed the Pure Food and Drug Act of 1906, which created the predecessor of the modern Food and Drug Administration.

Although Sinclair's position was now permanently ensured, his marriage to Meta was already beyond repair. While on a trip to Battle Creek, Michigan, to visit the famous sanitarium there, he encountered Mary Craig Kimbrough, a young woman who determinedly worked her way into his company until she could win his heart. Deciding that it was time the country's archaic divorce laws be reexamined in a more modern light, Sinclair sued for divorce from Meta. The resulting battle went all the way to the New York Supreme Court, and when his petition was denied on a technicality, Sinclair went to the Netherlands to obtain a divorce in 1912. Free of Meta, he was able to wed Mary Craig, with whom he would live in reasonable happiness into old age.

For the next several decades, Sinclair enjoyed the success brought by the fame of *The Jungle*. Although none of his later novels achieved a similar level of sales, he was able to use them to address other social ills, even touching on issues of sex education at a time when the Comstock Laws made it illegal to transmit any information about sexuality or birth control via the mail. He appeared on the Chautauqua circuit, a program of traveling lecturers that was quite popular in the 1920s and 1930s. As a socialist, he took a particular interest in the experiment of socialism taking place in the Soviet Union. When Franklin Delano Roosevelt was elected to the presidency and set the nation on his New Deal, Sinclair saw it as a hopeful step in the right direction.

Sinclair's star began to fade after World War II. This was the era of McCarthyism and the suspicion of communist infiltration of America's intellectual elite, and he was just the sort of person targeted by the notorious senator's campaigns. Furthermore, his second wife's health was in steady decline, which meant that he had to spend increasing amounts of his time nursing her. After her death on April 26, 1961, Sinclair was married for a third time, to Mary Elizabeth Willis. This seventy-nine-year-old widowed great-grandmother proved to be an excellent match for the eighty-three-year-old Sinclair, and they enjoyed a happy life together.

Near the end of his years, Sinclair was a guest at the White House when President Lyndon B. Johnson signed the Wholesome Meat Act of 1967. Also present was consumer advocate Ralph Nader, and in a sense, one could see the event as the passing of the torch to a new generation. Sinclair died on November 25, 1968. Succeeding generations of schoolchildren heard his name primarily in connection with the role of *The Jungle* in the passage of the Pure Food and Drug Act, but they learned little or nothing about his activism in socialist causes.

In Search of Wellville

Even as the battles for clean food were being fought in the slaughterhouses and the halls of Congress, another battle for wholesome food was being fought on a more subtle stage. The question was less about overt contamination than about what sorts of foods were most conducive to good health. Although it did not directly relate to the development of industrialized society, this growing interest in nutrition and healthy eating was largely a result of the new affluence of society that resulted from industrialization. Mechanization made food cheap and abundant, banishing the specters of crop failure and mass starvation that had hung over preindustrial societies. At that point, Americans' concerns about food could move beyond "What do we have available to eat?" to explore "What ought we be eating?"

The Gilded Age marked the beginning of society's interest in dieting as a deliberate and systematic change in one's eating habits in pursuit of a specific goal. The earliest diet gurus, such as Sylvester Graham, operated on a concept of health drawn largely from the ancient Greeks' ideas of the four humors and of disease being the product of their falling out of balance with one another. According to these schemes, "hot" foods were to be avoided because they excited the "animal passions" (sexuality), always a source of disgust for the Victorians. In addition to the obvious spices, these foods also included almost any kind of meat, as well as rich sauces and desserts. By contrast, "cool" foods such as vegetables and cereal grains were supposed to foster a calm and contented temperament conducive to good health and stable functioning in society.

As the era progressed, the interest in proper diet and health began to take on a more scientific aspect. Purely philosophical categorizations of the nature of foods gave way to an idea that one needed to experiment and observe the physiological effects of foods in order to

Battle Creek Sanitarium. (Library of Congress)

develop a healthful diet. Although a true scientific understanding of the value of a balanced diet would not develop until the first decades of the twentieth century, one notable health institute was already devising a systematic program of dietary experimentation and improvement.

That institution was the Battle Creek Sanitarium, or the "San," as it was affectionately known by those who came to it in search of good health. Under the tutelage of John Harvey Kellogg, it became not just a place for celebrities and the wealthy to go in search of a cure for what ailed them (as it was portrayed by T. Coraghessan Boyle in the historical novel *The Road to Wellville*) but also a laboratory kitchen for transforming the diet of the American public. Kellogg realized that it was not enough simply to tell Americans what they ought to be eating, without making a healthy diet palatable enough that they would actually follow through and eat it. Throughout his long career, Kellogg developed over eighty different grain-based foods that were intended to be both wholesome and tasty.

However, it would be his brother W. K. Kellogg who would transform the San's dietetic prescriptions into a lasting institution on the American societal landscape.

William Keith Kellogg was born on April 7, 1860, in Battle Creek, which was already becoming known as a "health town" due to the strong presence of Seventh-Day Adventists, who promoted an abstemious lifestyle as a path to physical and spiritual health. Kellogg was deeply fascinated with the numerological significance of his birth position as the seventh son of a seventh son, and throughout his life, he considered the number seven particularly lucky for him. On the whole, however, his childhood was rather grim, filled with hard work and overshadowed by the Civil War. He later claimed that he never learned to play, and one of his wishes in endowing his foundation would be to make the lives of children happier, that they might be more productive as adults. Undiagnosed nearsightedness, combined with a headmaster who believed that regular beatings improved a boy's concentration, made schooling a particularly unpleasant experience for him, but it was not enough to quench his interest in learning through observation and experimentation in the natural world.

By his teen years, Kellogg had become a salesman for the products of his father's broom factory. His success led him to a stint working for his half brother Albert, until the latter's factory failed. He also went to Texas to teach an associate how to run a broom factory properly during 1879, but by the end of the year, he was back in Battle Creek, where his brother was running the sanitarium. The following year, he married Ella Davis, and the last vestiges of boyhood gave way to his new adult status.

The next two decades were grim, filled with constant frustration and worries about money. He came to describe himself as his brother's "flunky," and he resented John Harvey's success. However, it was his assistance with his brother's food experiments that would form the foundation for his own fortune. John Harvey was looking for a more easily digestible substitute for bread and thought he had found it in a sample of shredded wheat that was sent to him by an admirer in Denver. When a copy of the machine used to make shredded wheat failed to arrive, the Kellogg brothers set to experimenting on their own. Fed up with laboriously scraping the rollers, Will decided to set up a knife apparatus to do the work. The resulting product peeled off in neat flakes, which soon proved popular with the San's patients.

John Harvey Kellogg's understanding of medical ethics prohibited him from attaching his name to a commercial product. As a result, it was Will whose name and signature went on the first box of flaked cereal when it went on the market beyond the San. Initially, his business was confined to similar institutions around the country and done almost entirely by mail order. Later, various small jobbers began selling Kellogg's cereals.

His strained relations with his brother came to a head when it was decided to expand the cereal company and give it its own building. Suddenly, the financing of the building became Will's responsibility. Through some quick borrowing, he was able to raise the necessary money, but he never could forgive John Harvey's high-handedness. In 1901, he quit working for his brother and cleaned out his desk at the sanitarium. Exactly six months later, a fire on February 18, 1902, destroyed several important buildings at the San. Unable to totally ignore his brother's plight, Will offered his services for free until the San's debts were discharged. At the same time, the rise of multiple competing firms producing flaked cereals cut into the profits of Will's own company, on which he was depending for his own finances. By the end of 1902, the situation was looking exceedingly bleak.

Things began to turn around when a St. Louis businessman, Charles D. Bolin, visited the San and saw commercial potential in Will's cornflakes, which had not yet been pirated by rival companies. He helped Will found an independent firm, the Battle Creek Toasted Corn Flake Company, to market the product beyond the health food circle. In a bold preemptive strike against would-be imitators, the packaging bore Kellogg's signature with the logo "none genuine without this signature." Suddenly, Will's life, which he had despaired of ever making anything of, turned completely around.

His success, however, put him even further at odds with his brother, who had overcome his scruples about commercial marketing and begun pushing his own line of foods. Only in 1921, after an ugly series of court battles, did Will finally secure the right to use the family name for his own line of products. In addition to the break with his brother, he found disappointment in his son and grandson, both of whom proved utterly unsuitable to take over the business. Ultimately, he made arrangements for corporate leadership and set up a charitable foundation to administer the dispersal of most of his fortune.

Kellogg's later years were troubled by health problems. Always nearsighted, he developed glaucoma and effectively went blind by 1937. He retired from the company on his eightieth birthday and spent the last eleven years of his life traveling, aided by a group of devoted assistants and a German shepherd dog. He died on October 6, 1951; his grave is marked by a bronze sculpture of a robin tugging at a worm. His company continued to grow and prosper long after his passing and has become one of the largest food companies in the world. More important, his efforts effected a permanent transformation of the American breakfast from a primarily meat-based to a grain-based one.

The New Industrial Countryside

However slowly the Industrial Revolution may have come to agriculture, it eventually led to a complete transformation of not only the rural community but also all that flowed from it. From being the mainstay of democratic society, the yeoman farmer has dwindled to such a minute portion of the population that by the close of the twentieth century, the Bureau of the Census ceased to produce statistics on the percentages of the American populace directly involved in agriculture. In many areas, the few farmers who have remained in business are operating vast acreages and enjoy a level of material wealth comparable to their city cousins, yet there are more than a few parts of the rural landscape that have been left out of this explosion of wealth. There, crushing poverty is the rule, made all the more severe by the isolation of the countryside, which cuts residents off from many of the amenities and diversions enjoyed by the urban poor.

Sources

Aldrich, Lisa J. 2002. *Cyrus McCormick and the Mechanical Reaper.* Greensboro, NC: Morgan-Reynolds.
Ashby, LeRoy. 1987. *William Jennings Bryan: Champion of Democracy.* Boston: Twayne.

Atherton, Lewis. 1954. *Main Street on the Middle Border*. Bloomington: Indiana University Press.

Berger, Samuel R. 1971. *Dollar Harvest: The Story of the Farm Bureau*. Lexington, MA: Heath Lexington Books.

Blandford, Percy W. 1976. *Old Farm Tools and Machinery: An Illustrated History*. Fort Lauderdale, FL: Gale Research.

Clemen, Rudolf Alexander. 1923. *The American Livestock and Meat Industry*. New York: Ronald Press.

Colby, Edna Moore. 1968. *Hoosier Farmers in a New Day*. Indianapolis: Indiana Farm Bureau.

Danbom, David B. 1995. *Born in the Country: A History of Rural America*. Baltimore, MD: Johns Hopkins University Press.

Davidson, Osha Gray. 1990. *Broken Heartland: The Rise of America's Rural Ghetto*. New York: Free Press.

Dregni, Michael, ed. 1998. *This Old Tractor: A Treasury of Vintage Tractors and Family Farm Memories*. Stillwater, MN: Town Square Books.

———. 1999. *This Old Farm: A Treasury of Family Farm Memories*. Stillwater, MN: Voyageur Press.

Duncan, Cynthia M. 1999. *Worlds Apart: Why Poverty Persists in Rural America*. New Haven, CT: Yale University Press.

Ertl, P. W. 2001. *The American Tractor: A Century of Legendary Machines*. Osceola, WI: MBI Publishing.

Fetherston, David. 1996. *Farm Tractor Advertising in America, 1900–1960*. Osceola, WI: Motorbooks.

Gray, R. B. 1975. *The Agricultural Tractor, 1855–1950*. St. Joseph, MI: American Society of Agricultural Engineers.

Haber, Barbara. 2002. *From Hardtack to Home Fries: An Uncommon History of American Cooks and Meals*. New York: Free Press.

Halberstadt, Hans. 1996. *The American Family Farm*. Osceola, WI: Motorbooks.

Harmon, Daniel E. 2002. *The Food and Drug Administration*. Philadelphia: Chelsea House.

Harris, Leon. 1975. *Upton Sinclair: American Rebel*. New York: Thomas Y. Crowell.

Hoge, Cecil C., Sr. 1988. *The First Hundred Years Are the Toughest: What We Can Learn from the Century of Competition between Sears and Wards*. Berkeley, CA: Ten Speed Press.

Howard, Robert P. 1983. *James R. Howard and the Farm Bureau*. Ames: Iowa State University Press.

Hull, I. Harvey. 1952. *Built of Men: The Story of Indiana Cooperatives*. New York: Harper and Brothers.

Hunnicutt, Benjamin Kline. 1996. *Kellogg's Six-Hour Day*. Philadelphia: Temple University Press.

Klancher, Lee. 2003. *Tractor in the Pasture: Rusting Icons of Rural America*. St. Paul, MN: Motorbooks.

Kyvig, David E. 2002. *Daily Life in the United States, 1920–1939: Decades of Promise and Pain.* Westport, CT: Greenwood Press.

McCormick, Cyrus, III. 1931. *The Century of the Reaper.* Boston: Houghton Mifflin.

McMath, Robert C., Jr. 1993. *American Populism: A Social History, 1877–1898.* New York: Hill and Wang.

Powell, Horace B. 1956. *The Original Has This Signature—W. K. Kellogg.* Englewood Cliffs, NJ: Prentice-Hall.

Root, Waverly, and Richard de Rochemont. 1997. *Eating in America: A History.* New York: Ecco Press.

Shearer, Stephen R. 1992. *Hoosier Connections: The History of the Indiana Telephone Industry and the Indiana Telephone Association.* Indianapolis: Indiana Telephone Association.

Sinclair, Upton. 1906. *The Jungle.* New York: Harper.

Swift, Louis F. 1927. *The Yankee of the Yards: The Biography of Gustavus Franklin Swift.* Chicago: Shaw.

Swinford, Norm. 2000. *A Century of Ford and New Holland Farm Equipment.* St. Joseph, MI: American Society of Agricultural Engineers.

Turner, Paul. 1947. *They Did It in Indiana: The Story of the Indiana Farm Bureau Co-operatives.* New York: Dryden Press.

Gilded Age Art and Literature

Roger Matuz

Those who labor" in the earth," wrote Thomas Jefferson, "are the chosen people of God, if ever he had a chosen people, whose breasts he has made his peculiar deposit for substantial and genuine virtue" (Jefferson 1832). That image of the American farmer has persisted into the twenty-first century, even as most Americans born on a farm since 1880 eventually left it in favor of an urban locale, as those who continued to "labor in the earth" increasingly relied on machines to help them do their work, and as independent farmers faced such dire natural and economic challenges that many were supplanted by large corporate farms supervised by land managers.

During the Gilded Age, the amount of land dedicated to agriculture greatly increased in the United States, while the number of farmers significantly decreased. Farmers made up 60 percent of the population in 1860; in 1910, they comprised 30 percent of the population. During that fifty-year span, the United States was transformed from a largely agricultural and rural country to a modern industrial nation.

The effect of industrial progress on agriculture was well represented in literature and art. Works of art rooted in rural life generally focus on the individual, self-reliant farmer and family life on the farm, as well as the challenges of nature. After the Civil War, farmers were more often depicted in literature as battling against prevailing social and economic forces, and representations of farm life grew increasingly quaint—urban culture had become so predominant that works set on farms were routinely categorized as regional literature. Meanwhile, industrialism was often portrayed as having disrupted pastoral life. "[Again] and again, our writers have introduced the same overtones," noted one historian, "depicting the machine as invading the peace of an enclosed space, a world set apart" (Marx 1964).

By the 1920s, continual advances in farm machinery and "the application to agriculture of the financial, cultural, and ideological methods of industrialism," as one scholar described it (Fitzgerald 2003), contributed to the transformation of farming by individuals into a largely systematic and businesslike agriculture industry, or agribusiness. Bankers and emerging professionals in engineering and economics increasingly became the decisionmakers, and banks and corporations increasingly became the landowners.

As late as 1880, some 80 percent of American farms were individually or family owned, and less than 5 percent of the 5 million farms in the United States spanned over 600 acres. Those numbers changed rapidly. When natural and economic disasters hit at the end of the 1920s—the drought that turned the Great Plains into the Dust Bowl and the stock market crash that turned the Roaring Twenties into the Great Depression—many of the remaining independent farmers were dispossessed of their land. They joined the swollen ranks of migrant workers, who faced difficult working conditions, low wages, and little job security. Art of rural-based, social protest emerged in the 1930s, exemplified by John Steinbeck's novels *In Dubious Battle* and *The Grapes of Wrath*. California, with expansive tracts of fertile land, became emblematic of twentieth-century American agriculture, with corporate farms spanning thousands of acres staffed mostly with seasonal migrant workers.

The Farmer: An American Ideal

The idealistic image of the American farmer as a hardworking, self-reliant, self-made man uncorrupted by social life was projected in the eighteenth century by J. Hector St. John de Crèvecoeur in his 1782 *Letters from an American Farmer*. The author was born in France, emigrated to England at age nineteen, served in the Canadian militia, toured the American colonies as a surveyor, and settled on a farm in New York State. His letters, a series of essays based on his experiences in the States, highlight the work ethic and individual responsibility of farmers as a prototype of the American character and the promise of a social system free of rigid class structures. Comparing the opportunities for a man in America and in Europe, he wrote, "Here [in America] the rewards of his industry follow with equal steps the progress of his labour," expressing a sentiment that made his book popular on both continents.

Although St. John de Crèvecoeur included anti-intellectualism as an admirable trait in Americans, Thomas Jefferson came to represent the gentleman farmer—a learned man who applied principles of science and horticulture in managing his farm. Jefferson's 1787 *Notes on the State of Virginia* described the land and its people, as well as the author's thoughts on political, historical, and natural systems.

Both St. John de Crèvecoeur and Jefferson envisioned an end to slavery in America, but of course, Jefferson himself was a slaveowner. The invention of the cotton gin and its production in the mid-1790s tremendously increased the quantity of cotton that could be processed in a day, making widespread cultivation of cotton lucrative in the South and increasing the demand for slave labor.

The plantation system of the South was represented in literature in what became known as the plantation novel as well as in writings by abolitionists. George Tucker's *The Valley of the Shenandoah* (1824) established the plantation novel with its tale of the fall of a once-prosperous and respected family. Typical of the subgenre, the focus of this work is largely on codes of honor and social situations involving the plantation-owning family, rather than on the work being performed on the plantation. The evils of slavery and the agricultural work of slaves were documented by abolitionists, most famously in the autobiography *Narrative of the Life of Frederick Douglass, an American Slave* (1845) and in Harriet Beecher Stowe's novel *Uncle Tom's Cabin* (1852). These works contributed greatly to a more vocal, activist, and uncompromising abolitionist movement.

In New England, meanwhile, several experiments in communal living were attempted, with the goal of combining the virtues of farmwork and intellectual development. Bronson and Abigail Alcott, along with their four daughters, joined a communal living experiment at Fruitlands, a farm in Harvard, Massachusetts, in 1843. The

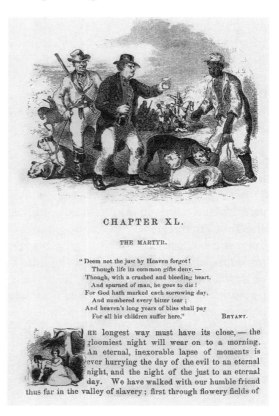

An illustration from *Uncle Tom's Cabin*, an antislavery novel that took the nation by storm when it was published in 1853. (Library of Congress)

daughters had been encouraged to keep journals beginning at a young age as part of their learning experience. One of these girls, Louisa May Alcott, would later become famous as the author of *Little Women* (1868) and seven novels that followed in the "Little Women" series. Her observations on Fruitlands, written when she was nearly eleven years old, were published many years later in *Louisa May Alcott: Her Life, Letters, and Journals* (1889). She described life at Fruitlands as a kind of vacation but noted the experiment failed because the adults were not prepared for the demands of farming.

George Ripley founded Brook Farm in Massachusetts as a means for merging ideas, spiritual values, and physical events—a union of mind, body, and spirit where physical labor contributed to mental well-being and health. Nathaniel Hawthorne lived there from April to November 1841. In fact, his novel *The Blithedale Romance* (1852), in which a utopian community is undone by the self-interests of its members, is loosely based on Brook Farm. Henry David Thoreau described a more individualistic method for enlightenment and spiritual growth in *Walden, or Life in the Woods* (1854), in which a modest garden served him during a period when he lived a life of labor and reflection with only the basic necessities of food, clothing, and shelter.

Most of the literary works addressing farm life that were published during the Gilded Age are categorized as regional literature. "With the increasing move toward urbanization and industrialization following the war and the concurrent diminishing of regional differences," Anne Rowe stated in the *Encyclopedia of Southern Culture*, "it is not surprising that there was a developing nostalgia for remaining regional differences" (Wilson and Ferris 1989). The small farms so prevalent in the Northeast during colonial times and the early Republic, for example, had largely receded by the Civil War, as great urban settings became cultural centers. The southern states, of course, were involved in physical and social reconstruction following the end of the Civil War. The prairie had been settled steadily westward, but a new rush of pioneers arrived after the war, and many moved on to the western frontier. The Homestead Act of 1862 and quickly spreading railroads opened up new territories and possibilities.

Northeast Regionalism

Northeastern cosmopolitan writers such as William Dean Howells, Henry James, and Edith Wharton are most frequently cited as being among the literary giants of the Gilded Age, but rural life in the region was well represented by several popular writers of the time. Most significant among them was Sarah Orne Jewett, whose works were set in the countryside and coastal villages of Maine that were becoming dominated by textile mills and canneries. Glimpses of the concerns, characteristics, and idiom of the people inhabiting those areas are presented in *A Country Doctor* (1884) through the experiences of Nan, a girl who frequently accompanies her foster father, a country doctor, on his rounds—just as Jewett had done with her own father in her youth.

Doris Owen, the heroine of Jewett's novel *A Marsh Island* (1886), initially is content with her life on the farm and her prospects with a local blacksmith. But then, a wealthy artist from the city comes to stay with the Owen family to paint scenes of their farm and the surrounding countryside, and Doris's outlook changes when they enter a romance. The contrast between what rural and urban locales offer to the characters is central to the work. The rural/urban theme is explored in Jewett's short stories as well: "A White Heron" (1886) is a children's story about a girl who finds meaning in her interactions with the natural world while growing up on an isolated farm in Maine; "Fame's Little Day" (1895), by contrast, humorously depicts a well-meaning country man duped by a city slicker.

Alice Brown and Mary Wilkins Freeman are often grouped with Jewett as northeastern regionalists. Brown's stories, especially those in *Meadow-Grass: Tales of New England Life* (1895) and *Tiverton Tales* (1899), typically feature middle-aged protagonists whose attempts to embrace new experiences conflict with the social expectations of their community. The title character of "Farmer Eli's Vacation" (1893), for example, is deeply attached to his New Hampshire farm and traditional methods of farming. When he decides to go on the journey he has always wanted to make—a 6-mile trip to see the ocean—he is left awestruck and speechless. The story ends ambiguously, as Farmer Eli returns to the farm and a work routine that had given him a sense of purpose and added meaning to his life. Mary Wilkins Freeman explored the effects of modernization on the culture and economy of rural New England.

Southern Regionalism

Following the Civil War, American readers showed great interest in works that evoked the life and dialects of remote southern settings. Joel Chandler Harris's tales narrated by a slave, Uncle Remus, became immediately popular in periodicals of the late 1870s. Collected and published in late November 1880, *Uncle Remus: His Songs and His Sayings* sold 7,500 copies by the end of the year. The stories almost always begin behind "the big house" on the plantation where Uncle Remus is a slave. Harris had lived on a plantation for four years beginning in 1862, working at age thirteen as an apprentice on a weekly newspaper, *The Countryman.* He spent many evenings listening to tales told by Uncle George Terrell, Old Harbert, and Aunt Crissy, slaves who later became the models for Uncle Remus, Aunt Tempy, and other characters in the Uncle Remus fables.

Mary Noailles Murfree evoked life among the mountaineers of east Tennessee in dozens of stories published in magazines, beginning in the late 1870s. The stories were collected in *In the Tennessee Mountains* (1884), which became an instant best-seller. Murfree's colorful characters include shiftless men, millers, blacksmiths, moonshiners, preachers, and women whose lives are dominated by childbearing, child rearing, and work in the home and the field. In the decade following the turn of the century, John Fox Jr. was popular for his novels *The Little Shepherd of Kingdom Come* (1903) and *The Trail of the Lonesome Pine* (1908). Set in the mountains of Kentucky, Tennessee, and Virginia, the novels depict hardscrabble individuals who turn chores into entertainment, including bean-stringing and corn-shucking parties.

The plantation novel made a comeback near the end of the nineteenth century in the works of Thomas Nelson Page. His story "Marse Chan" appeared in a periodical in 1884, and his novel *Red Rock* was published in 1898. These works feature "beautiful southern maidens, noble and brave slave-owners, and happy, contented slaves," noted Anne Rowe in the *Encyclopedia of Southern Culture* (quoted in Wilson and Ferris 1989). Margaret Mitchell would refer to Nelson's works when defending her own novel, *Gone with the Wind* (1936), from critics who viewed it as an unrealistic picture of plantation life: "My God, they never read the gentle Confederate novel of the [1890s], or they would know better." Mitchell's novel, which won the Pulitzer Prize and was adapted into a blockbuster film, breaks the stereotype of the southern belle unable to fend for herself even as it captures the end of a way of life in the South.

Ellen Glasgow broke new ground with her strong female characters and her critical approach to traditional southern social expectations. *The Voice of the People* (1900) exposes the effects of economic class distinctions between the urban and rural South, which become evident in the relationship of a farmer's son and the daughter of a wealthy family. The pair are briefly engaged but prove unable to transcend class lines. Dorinda Oakley, the protagonist of *Barren Ground* (1925), overcomes social pressures to become a successful farmer and independent woman. One critic noted that the novel exposes "gender assumptions of an American culture whose understanding of farming is rooted in an agrarian myth that defines farmers exclusively as men" (Conlogue 2001). The novel's title is ironic: betrayal and an accident have left Dorinda without husband or child, and the land she farms seems fallow, yet she proves heroic in becoming a successful farmer and a woman shaping her own destiny. Contributing to her success is her use of modern, industrial methods of agriculture rather than more traditional kinds of farm management in the South.

Midwest Regionalism

Hamlin Garland's *Main-Travelled Roads* (1891), the most powerful work of social protest against the economic pressures facing farmers of the late nineteenth century, challenged the romantic ideal of the American farmer. The six stories in this collection show the drudgery of farm life in the upper Midwest, including hard work in the fields, often in bad weather; roughshod homes and clothing; and little in the way of intellectual stimulation. None of the stories romanticizes farm life, yet the characters continue to strive against increasingly harsh demands. The stories counter what one critic called the American "Garden of the World" myth—"the image of an agricultural paradise in the West, embodying group memories of an earlier, a simpler and, it was believed, a happier state of society" (Smith 1950).

Similarly tough circumstances are confronted by characters in the prairie around Red Cloud, Nebraska, in Willa Cather's novels *O Pioneers!* (1913) and *My Ántonia* (1918). The works are especially noteworthy for their portrayals of women and immigrants attempting to establish settlements and farms on the prairie. *O Pioneers!* centers on Alexandra, the oldest child of Swedish immigrants who holds the family together after the death of their father. Tragedy ensues despite the heroic efforts of the protagonist, but her untiring work and astute land-management decisions result in a successful homestead. Alexandra chooses to invest in the techniques of industrial agriculture, which frees her from male dominance to work the land successfully. "Fortunate country," concludes a passage late in the novel, "that is one day to receive hearts like Alexandra's into its bosom, to give them out again in the yellow wheat, in the rustling corn, in the shining eyes of youth" (Cather 1998).

Born in Virginia, Cather was nine years old when her family moved to Webster County, Nebraska, in 1883. Two years later, the family resettled in Red Cloud, the town that recurs in several of her novels. While she attended the University of Nebraska, Cather became a theater critic and columnist for the *Nebraska State Journal* and the *Lincoln Courier.* After graduating, she worked in Pittsburgh and then New York, where she served as managing editor for *McClure's* magazine. While there, she met Sarah Orne Jewett, known for her stories set in her native Maine. Jewett encouraged Cather to develop a more personal style, and by 1913, when she turned thirty, Cather published *O Pioneers!* and became regarded as a major writer.

The title character of Cather's novel *My Ántonia* is an immigrant farm girl who was seduced and abandoned with child, endured the suicide of her father, and struggled through additional hardships before emerging triumphant and establishing a successful farm. Like *O Pioneers!* this novel depicts prairie life as harsh and tragic, but the protagonist possesses the stamina and passion needed to endure. Cather's poem "Prairie Spring" (1912) builds a similar sense of the harshness and remoteness of the prairie before hope and desire emerge: "Against all this, Youth / Flaming like the wild roses . . . Singing and singing, / Out of the lips of silence, / Out of the earthy dusk" (Cather 1998).

An immigrant woman is the focus of Edna Ferber's novel *So Big* (1925), which the author stated was inspired by "the sight of a face in a crowd, a farm woman going to market." Ferber's varied career included coauthoring the Broadway musical *Showboat* and writing several novels that were later adapted to film, including *Cimmaron* and *Giant.* The protagonist of *So Big* marries a lackluster farmer whose death leaves her to support a son and a debt-ridden farm, which she struggles to improve. The novel was awarded the Pulitzer Prize for Literature.

The immensely popular works of Laura Ingalls Wilder and Carol Ryrie Brink are lighter in approach than those of Garland, Cather, and Ferber, yet they, too, stress the hardiness needed to survive prairie life. "Once upon a time, sixty years ago, a little girl lived in the Big Woods of Wisconsin, in a little gray house made of logs," begins *Little House in the Big Woods* (1932), the first of Wilder's seven-book "Little House on the Prairie" series. Wilder began writing her books while in her early sixties, recalling her early life and her family's journeys from Wisconsin in the late 1860s to Missouri and Kansas, back to Wisconsin, and then west again to establish a more permanent home. Brink Newbery Medal–winning novel *Caddie Woodlawn* (1935) is set in pioneer times in Wisconsin.

Immigrants on the Farm

Cather and Ferber were among several writers whose works in rural locales addressed interactions between immigrants and their offspring and others in the Midwest. Over 23 million immigrants entered the United States between 1860 and 1910. Many of German, Scandinavian, and Irish descent began arriving in midcentury and fanned out to the midwestern farmland.

The experiences of Norwegian Americans living in rural areas of Minnesota and South Dakota were the focus of the novels of Ole Rölvaag, who emigrated from a small Norwegian fishing village. His main characters face conflicts as they try to maintain their self-identity while adapting to new social and physical surroundings. *Giants in the Earth* (1927), a popular and critical success, follows a daring man and his timid wife, both second-generation Norwegian Americans, in their struggle to survive as early pioneers in the rough environment of South Dakota. As the husband becomes obsessed with prospering as a farmer, the wife grows increasingly isolated during a series of failures, most of which result from the harsh environment of long, frigid winters and brief, scalding summers.

Giants in the Earth forms a trilogy with two later novels, *Peder Victorious* (1929) and *Their Fathers' God* (1931). The title character of *Peder Victorious* rebels against both his mother's stern religious beliefs and the local community, whereas *Their Fathers' God* has Peder and his wife living on a farm begun by their parents—the protagonists of *Giants in the Earth*—that is now prosperous. When a prolonged drought threatens all the farms in the area, conflict arises between husband and wife and between Peder and the larger community.

Wallace Stegner's first novel, *Remembering Laughter* (1937), is set on the Iowa plains, where he lived as a boy. Scottish immigrants Alec Stuart and his wife, Margaret, struggle to establish a farm. Their tough life together is brightened when they are joined by Margaret's sister, Elspeth, but a love triangle develops and undermines the lives of the extended family. Stegner went on to become one of the premier novelists and essayists of the American West in his fifty-year career.

Cover of an 1850s dime novel featuring frontiersman Kit Carson. (Library of Congress)

The Old West

The romanticized Old West—the site of small and raucous towns, sheriffs and gunslingers, miners and ranchers—first became popular through dime novels. Cheaply produced, these small paperbacks could be printed quickly and distributed in massive editions at newsstands and dry goods stores. Such larger-than-life western characters as Wild Bill Hickok, Buffalo Bill, Kit Carson, and Calamity Jane were introduced to readers across the country as dime novels flourished during the second half of the nineteenth century.

The first western to meet higher literary standards was Owen Wister's *The Virginian: A Horseman of the Plains* (1902). While detailing the title character's attempts to champion justice in the Old West, the novel provides more realistic and detailed portraits than the dime novels of western settlers and their heroic attempts to establish themselves on the frontier. Still, the novel fed the more romanticized version of the Old West, introducing such memorable lines as "This town ain't big enough for both of us" and "When you call me that—smile!"

Frank Norris, a central figure in the Progressive reform movements that arose in the 1890s, won acclaim for his novel *McTeague* (1899), set in San Francisco. He then set his sights on exposing socioeconomic ills in the San Joaquin Valley as revealed in the tensions between the Southern Pacific Railroad and the region's wheat growers. Norris planned a trilogy of novels, but only two, *The Octopus* (1901) and *The Pit* (1903), were completed before his death in 1902. He was inspired to write the trilogy after researching the Mussel Slough Tragedy of May 11, 1880, in Kings County, California. This clash between local settlers and agents of the Southern Pacific Railroad, who had been locked in a long and bitter dispute over land titles in the region, claimed the lives of seven men. The novel dramatizes these events while presenting the new agribusiness—the concentrated development of production, distribution, and consumption of an essential commodity (in this case, wheat). *The Pit* picks up the story as harvested wheat moves eastward. Less concerned with the agricultural development of the crop, this novel focuses on the shipping, buying, and selling of an agricultural commodity, revealing that what was meant by agriculture had taken on a much larger dimension than farming; it now involved numerous businesspeople far from the fields. Wheat speculators engaged in nefarious deals supplant the farmer in this novel of the business of agriculture. "A Deal in Wheat" (1902) was the title of Norris's work-in-progress that would have completed the trilogy.

Mary Austin focused much of her fiction on life in the arid Southwest, where her characters struggle to survive around the turn of the twentieth century, often discovering useful hints in remnants of Native American settlements of previous periods. Her stories portray uneasy interactions among white, Native American, and Hispanic people. Austin's novels also feature strong women who learn to adapt to the hot and dusty environment, reflected in the title of her first collection of stories, *The Land of Little Rain* (1903). *Lost Borders* (1909) includes stories, such as "The Ploughed

Lands," "Aqua Dulce," and "A Case of Conscience," that examine relationships between white men attempting to forge an existence in the frontier and Native American women whose descendants long lived in the region.

The Ford (1917) departs from Austin's typical Southwest setting by fictionalizing the environmental battle that occurred between the city of Los Angeles and the settlers of Owens Valley, east of the city. Priming for massive development and a rapid increase in population, the city began a long fight with settlers for water rights. In Austin's novel, city officials turn elsewhere, and the Owens Valley is spared. In reality, the city won the battle, and the Owens Valley gradually faded as an area for agriculture.

Austin herself was a colorful character, as shown in her autobiography, *Earth Horizon* (1932). She lived a hardscrabble life in the Southwest and later joined an artists' colony in Carmel, California. She built a wickiup in the coastal woods, where she lived and wrote, often wearing a deerskin dress.

Vardis Fisher, considered by many as the first important novelist from the Rocky Mountain region, wrote with often harsh realism about his Idaho heritage. *Toilers of the Hills* (1928) is set in antelope country, where Dock and Opal Hunter struggle to exist in the arid environment. Opal comes to hate and fear the area for constantly undermining their efforts, but through determination and cleverness, Dock becomes a successful dry farmer. Fisher later wrote an autobiographical tetralogy—*Tragic Life* (1932), *Passions Spin the Plot* (1934), *We Are Betrayed* (1935), and *No Villain Need Be* (1936)—that begins by depicting his youthful desire to leave Idaho; moves on through his progress as a writer in Chicago, New York, and Salt Lake City; and then comes full circle as he returns to his home area with a newfound respect for the land.

Southern Literature: 1920s and 1930s

Numerous major writers began emerging in the South during the 1920s and 1930s, a period known as the Southern Renaissance. Their works, often set in small towns, depict traditional ways of life being challenged by modernization and the effects of racism. These themes and the despoiling of nature are among the concerns in the works of

William Faulkner. His novel *Absalom! Absalom!* (1936) focuses on the monomaniacal passion of Thomas Sutpen to create a territory with himself as proprietor. He forms a bizarre plantation called Sutpen's Hundred with an architect he has taken captive and a group of African American workers he exploits. As many rumors spread about his behavior and actions, the novel questions the human capacity to know the truth about anyone or anything.

Caroline Gordon explored a tobacco tenant farmer's attempts to save his land and way of life during a prolonged drought in *The Gardens of Adonis* (1937). The farmer enters an agreement with the landowner's son to plant lespedeza clover, which requires little water and will help provide money during the drought. Tragedy occurs when the tenant's son attempts to reap an early harvest for a quick financial gain that will improve his social status.

In his novels *Tobacco Road* (1932) and *God's Little Acre* (1933), Erskine Caldwell depicted rural deprivation in the South as the contributing factor to social breakdown and tragedy. *Tobacco Road* is the more farm-based work, centering on a family on the brink of starvation living on once-fertile land. Years of agricultural mismanagement had made the land fallow so that it is no longer yielding enough to even pay for fertilizer for the next year's crop. The mismanagement is compounded into tragedy when the head of the family follows the questionable tradition of burning broom sedge off the fields as a quick, labor-saving technique.

The human deprivation presented in *Tobacco Road* and *God's Little Acre,* which are often categorized as works of southern gothic fiction, brought charges of sensationalism against Caldwell. The author responded by teaming with photographer Margaret Bourke-White to detail the poor conditions of rural life in the South. Caldwell wrote a series of shocking articles for the *New York Post,* many of which were collected and presented with photographs in *You Have Seen Their Faces* (1937). He also wrote *Tenant Farmer* (1935), a critique of the tenant-farming system.

A slice of African American life in the early twentieth-century South was vividly captured by Jean Toomer in *Cane* (1923), a work embraced by writers based in the North who formed the Harlem Renaissance. Blending narratives, poetry, drama, and prose poetry, *Cane* portrays African Americans in Georgia engaged in the difficult work of extracting sweet syrup from sugarcane, a labor Toomer uses as a metaphor for their lives. The stories in Julia Peterkin's collection

Green Thursday (1924) likewise involve a black plantation family's struggle for survival.

Paul Green's first collection of short stories, *Wide Fields* (1928), focused on what he called "the people who live hard by the ways of nature and not by civilization and its sophisticated arts." His tenant farmers display noble suffering in their struggles with nature. Green is best known for his folk plays, including *The Field God* (1927), in which a freethinking and idealistic farmer struggles against the narrow-minded religious community surrounding him; this includes his wife, who believes in a wrathful, Old Testament God.

Migrants and Agribusiness

"In sixty years a complete revolution has taken place in California agriculture," wrote John Steinbeck in a *Nation* magazine article in 1936 (Steinbeck 1936). Stating that the principal products of hay and cattle had been replaced by crops of fruits and vegetables, Steinbeck noted the newer crops required much more equipment and labor— and the labor was seasonal. Steinbeck also recognized that two predominant classes of farms had emerged in California: 5- to 10-acre operations held by small landowners and large-scale farms owned by speculative farmers (he cited newspaper tycoon William Randolph Hearst and former president Herbert Hoover among them), corporations, and banks, which acquired land by foreclosure. The small farmers, he continued, were likely to belong to traditional Grange groups, whereas the speculative farmers belonged to organizations that actively resisted attempts to unionize farm labor.

By 1936, severe drought in the Midwest had left thousands of farm families poverty-stricken. Many used their remaining resources to drive to California in search of jobs, and they arrived "so beaten and destitute," wrote Steinbeck, "that they have been willing at first to work under any conditions and for any wages offered" (Steinbeck 1936). Their plight was dramatized in his novel *The Grapes of Wrath*, published three years later.

Unlike many authors who addressed themes related to agriculture, Steinbeck was not born on a farm. He performed some farm labor to help pay his tuition at Stanford University, but his early works did not explore agricultural issues. A meeting with labor union organizers, however, inspired him to write *In Dubious Battle* (1935), a novel that pitted migrant workers against the two classes of farmers Steinbeck discussed in his *Nation* essay. In this novel, a small orchard owner is pressured by large-scale farm representatives to lower wages; a strike by migrant workers ensues, and violence erupts. Both the union leaders and the farm representatives use excessive claims and sensational symbols for their causes.

Steinbeck's *Of Mice and Men* (1937) focuses on ranch hands George and Lennie, who dream of earning enough money to buy a home with a few acres where they can tend a garden and raise rabbits. The novel, which was soon adapted to theater and film, shows the tension between ranchers and their hired help. Many of the hands face bleak lives, working long hours for low pay and then spending most of their earnings pursuing pleasure on weekends. Unlike them, George saves his money and looks after Lennie, who is physically imposing but mentally challenged. Ultimately, Lennie's inability to control his own strength crushes the pair's modest dream of becoming self-reliant landowners.

The Grapes of Wrath shows the devastating effects that prolonged drought had on farmers of the Midwest, many of whom were dispossessed of their land and enticed to California with the promise of jobs. The novel follows the Joad family as they leave Oklahoma and arrive in California, where they join an overabundant labor force. Tom Joad, the oldest son, and Jim Casy, a former preacher who joined the Joads on the trip, become involved in organized labor efforts. Amid many tragedies, part of the Joad clan endures, but Tom becomes a fugitive. His farewell to his mother, whose strength has made her the family leader, underscores the frustrations felt by those who lost their livelihoods as farmers and encountered hostility in trying to find work with decent pay: "I been thinkin' about our people livin' like pigs, an' good rich lan' layin fallow, or maybe one feller with a million acres, while a hunerd thousan' good farmers is starvin'." The novel's intercalary chapters, which alternate with the story of the Joads, cover various related topics—how the tractor changed the nature of farming, a description of a Dust Bowl storm, and contemplation of the California landscape and the way in which it was developed agriculturally.

The Grapes of Wrath proved a literary sensation. At the same time, however, associations of farmers in California appealed for a statewide ban of the book, *Collier's Magazine* treated it as communist propaganda, and Representative Lyle Boren of Oklahoma denounced the novel in Congress. Ruth Comfort Mitchell's *Of Human Kindness* (1940), written partly in response to *The Grapes of Wrath,* argued in favor of the industrial farm ideal while portraying rugged individualism and rural progress among California's farmers.

Meanwhile, *The Grapes of Wrath* was championed in the press by First Lady Eleanor Roosevelt, and it helped inspire social legislation that overturned oppressive migrant labor laws. Thus, *The Grapes of Wrath* joined such novels as Harriet Beecher Stowe's *Uncle Tom's Cabin* and Upton Sinclair's *The Jungle* as powerful works that helped inspire social activism. "Wherever human beings dream of a dignified society in which they can harvest the fruits of their own labor," wrote the editor of *Working Days,* Steinbeck's diary as he composed the novel, "*The Grapes of Wrath*'s radical voice of protest can be heard" (DeMott 1989).

Meatpacking

Chicago became the virtual center of the nation in the mid-nineteenth century as railroads began spreading westward and the Mississippi River blockade during the Civil War closed the north-south river trade route. An influx of meatpackers and livestock to the city led a consortium of nine railroad companies to purchase a 320-acre area of swampy land in southwest Chicago for $100,000 in 1864. This area became a new, modernized stockyard that served as a commercial link between the East and the West.

The Chicago stockyards preceded the American auto industry in becoming the first fully realized mass-production operation. Railroads brought the cattle, hogs, and sheep, and drovers herded them down two wide thoroughfares from the railroad cars to the pens. From there, the animals were led to the slaughterhouse, and the meat was transported to Packingtown, a term used both for the area of Chicago where the stockyards and slaughterhouses were concentrated and the poor neighborhoods that surrounded the stockyards. By the turn of the twentieth century, Chicago's meatpacking industry employed more than 25,000 people and produced 82 percent of the meat consumed in the United States. In addition to processing meat, the packinghouses made such by-products as leather, soap,

THE JUNGLE

BY

UPTON SINCLAIR

The title page of
The Jungle, Upton
Sinclair's famous
1906 novel. (Library
of Congress)

fertilizer, glue, imitation ivory, gelatin, shoe polish, buttons, perfume, and violin strings.

The working conditions in the industry were dreadful, especially on the killing floors of the slaughterhouse: laborers worked in stench while standing on blood-soaked floors, often for ten to twelve hours a day. Sanitary control in meatpacking was subordinate to speed and efficiency. A large supply of immigrant workers desperate to earn a living allowed the stockyard owners to keep wages as low as possible.

Upton Sinclair was encouraged by Isaac Marcosson, an editor of socialist periodicals, to write about the oppressive conditions and low wages being reported in Chicago and gave him $500 for serialization rights to his story. Marcosson and other socialists had been impressed by Sinclair's book *Manassas* (1904), which depicted growing hostilities between the North and South leading up to the Civil

War. Sinclair took the money, put a down payment on a New Jersey farm for his wife and new child, and set off for Chicago. He found a position as a meatpacking worker for seven weeks and observed the operation in Packingtown.

The manuscript he produced was rejected by four publishers as too graphic, especially the bloody slaughterhouse scenes. Author Jack London made a plea in the pages of the *Appeal to Reason* for funds to get Sinclair's manuscript published. Thanks to that effort, $4,000 was collected, which enabled Sinclair to have plates manufactured for publication, and he was signed by Doubleday, Page, and Company. *The Jungle,* as Sinclair's novel was called, became a bestseller, a topic of discussion in newspapers and magazines throughout the country, and a spur for federal regulation of the meatpacking industry as part of the Pure Food and Drug Act of 1906.

The Jungle follows members of a fictionalized Lithuanian immigrant family as they are systematically destroyed by the meatpacking industry. Health and safety violations are meticulously described through the uneducated, physically powerful Jurgis Rudkus, the head of the family. The novel begins with a hopeful event, the marriage of Jurgis and Ona. But the next six chapters reveal a series of injustices that destroy them—in their workplaces, at home where they are victimized by mortgage scams, and even in the food they buy in Packingtown stores, including the chalk-water masquerading as milk that they unwittingly feed to their children. Jurgis and Ona work harder and longer to keep up, leading to inevitable accidents that leave them vulnerable to dismissal. As Ona is about to give birth to another child, Jurgis goes on a drunken rampage, having learned his wife had been driven to prostitution. Forsaking his cares and attachments, he falls into crime and corruption.

Poetry of the Late Nineteenth Century

American poets of the Gilded Age who addressed the topic of agriculture often focused on the encroaching dominance of commerce and celebrated rural life. Sidney Lanier in the South, James Whitcomb Riley in the Midwest, and Edwin Markham in the West all won national acclaim for poems that represented their regions while also addressing larger, more universal concerns.

After having achieved some notice for poems published in periodicals following the Civil War, Lanier won national recognition when his volume *Poems* was published in 1877. Lanier had served the Confederacy in the Civil War, initially as an infantryman and then as a member of the mounted signal corps. He was captured in November 1864 and placed in the Union prison at Point Lookout, Maryland, where the terrible conditions affected his health and where he probably contracted the tuberculosis that affected him for the rest of his life and contributed to his death at age thirty-nine in 1881. The posthumously published *Poems of Sidney Lanier* (1884) added to his renown as one of the most beloved poets of his time. Despite the fact that his work expressed the dreariness of life in the South during the Reconstruction era, his poems consistently celebrated natural settings and humble, hardworking people.

A musician and composer, Lanier applied principles of music to his poetry. His theory for capturing the movement and sounds of the natural world is best exemplified in "The Marshes of Glynn," which describes the sea marshes near Brunswick, Georgia. Southern cornfields and the farmers who tended them were among the recurring symbols of the bond between humans and nature that was so significant in Lanier's work. "The Waving of the Corn" (1867) describes that bond as being distinct from urban life and its emphasis on commerce: "Green leagues of hilly separation roll: / Trade ends where yon far clover ridges swell."

"The Waving of the Corn" begins with an address to the plowman of a cornfield, praising him for his work. As the poet observes daily life on the farm, the actions of the farmer and his son, who appears from behind a hill, intermingle with descriptions of trees, cornstalks, and other vegetation swaying in a light breeze. Sounds are described—the boy whistling idly, crickets and bees humming, and the rustling of cornstalks. An integration of humans and nature emerges before the poem turns in its final verse to show urban life ("Ye terrible towns") as being separate and threatening. In urban settings, the speaker muses, time is never stopped to notice and appreciate simple and hard-earned bucolic pleasures, such as the waving of the corn.

Similarly lyrical descriptions of the natural world contrast with the concerns of business and commerce in "Corn" (1874). The poet passes through woods, describing the variety of vegetation ("A subtlety of mighty tenderness"), and emerges to find tracts of land dedicated to growing corn. The speaker muses that the poet, like the corn, gains sustenance from sun and rain, day and night, soil and air, to grow and mature in his craft ("So thou dost reconcile the hot and cold, / The dark and bright, / And many a heart-perplexing opposite"). The thick and sturdy cornstalks are contrasted with the ground where commerce thrives ("built on the shifting sand / Of trade"). The poem concludes in social protest against the view that farming is primarily a business, where crops are selected for planting based solely on the material wealth they might yield and the farmer is a servant to business values ("He staked his life on games of Buy-and-Sell, / And turned each field into a gambler's hell") (Lanier 1884).

Social commentary on the marginalization of agricultural workers is best exemplified in Edwin Markham's poem "The Man with the Hoe." Inspired by the similarly titled 1862 woodcut by French artist François Millet, Markham's poem first appeared in the *San Francisco Examiner* on January 15, 1899. It quickly became a sensation, embraced especially by labor unions and others with a progressive political agenda. It was also generally popular: "The Man with the Hoe" was published in more than 10,000 newspapers and magazines and in more than forty languages during the first three decades of the twentieth century. Markham became a major American poet literally overnight. Vividly describing oppressive demands on a field laborer who faces hard work, long hours, and low wages, "The Man with the Hoe" depicts the dehumanizing effects of business interests on the agricultural worker: "Who made him dead to rapture and despair, / A thing that grieves not and that never hopes, / Stolid and stunned, a brother to the ox?" (quoted in Nelson 2000).

Lighter and more celebratory verses on farmworkers and life on the farm are presented in the work of James Whitcomb Riley, the "Hoosier poet." Riley re-created midwestern dialect and expressions with inflections of the accents of Indiana's immigrants, including those of his own German ancestry. Often called a "dialect singer," Riley was popular as a performer of his works from the turn of the century to the onset of World War I, when his health began failing. Many of his poems were first published in periodicals, beginning in the 1880s, and then collected in such volumes as *Riley Child-Rhymes* (1899) and *Riley Farm-Rhymes* (1901).

"The Raggedy Man," first published in *Century Magazine* in 1890, lovingly describes a hired hand. The hired hand performs farm chores and tells stories to the boy narrator of the poem ("The

Raggedy Man, he knows most rhymes, / An' tells 'em, ef I be good, sometimes: / Knows 'bout Giunts, an' Griffuns, an' Elves, / An' the Squidgicum-Squees 'at swallers the'rselves"). Another poem, "When the Frost Is on the Punkin," first published in the *Indianapolis Journal* in 1882, is Riley's best-known tribute to farm living. In the poem's opening verses, the cold air of early autumn is welcomed ("They's something kindo' harty-like about the atmusfere / When the heat of summer's over and the coolin' fall is here"). The poem concludes by celebrating the bounties of harvesttime—apples filling the cellar, cider and apple butter aplenty, sausage for the family, and fodder for the animals.

Farmer-Poets

In the early twentieth century, Robert Frost and Carl Sandburg emerged as major poets. Both were often called farmer-poets, their works set in New England and the midwestern prairie, respectively. Frost excelled as a lyrical poet whose verses largely described rural settings to evoke natural wonders while musing on local and universal concerns. Sandburg wrote free verse that captured the vigor of urban and rural life. Both poets became nationally popular around the onset of World War I.

"Mowing," a poem in Frost's first collection, *A Boy's Will* (1913), is among many of his pieces in which the speaker is hard at work on the farm. Using a scythe to clear a field, the farmer is imposing a sense of order on the wild, natural world. He contemplates the value and results of his work ("earnest love that laid the swale in rows"), which will leave him with another chore—to make hay from the cut grass. *North of Boston* (1915), Frost's next volume, opens with a short poem, "The Pasture," in which the speaker announces two chores he is about to begin and invites the reader along ("I shant be gone long.—You come too"), uniting his farmwork with his profession as a poet.

The volume also includes the poem "Mending Wall," in which the speaker meditates on individualism and community. The poem was inspired by an annual springtime ritual—patching the walls of rock dividing farms—that follows the New England winter. The speaker wonders whether the natural elements created fissures in the wall to upset artificial boundaries created by humans. While the speaker is

Famed American
poet Robert Frost.
(Library of Congress)

considering what that "something is that doesn't love a wall," his neighbor begins mending the wall, secure in his belief that "Good fences make good neighbors."

"The Death of a Hired Man" is a dramatic narrative between a woman and her husband about how to treat an old, unreliable laborer who has returned to their farm. "After Apple-Picking," another of Frost's poems that promotes the value of farmwork, recounts an apple harvest so bountiful that the speaker tires into a dreamlike state. "Putting in the Seed," from *Mountain Interval* (1916), describes the farmer's passion for planting seeds and his anticipation for the coming day when the seedlings push through the earth. Perhaps the poem that best expresses Frost's decision to be a poet and farmer—professions out of the mainstream—is "The Road Not Taken": "Two roads diverged in a wood, and I— / I took the one less traveled by, / And that has made all the difference" (Newman 2000).

Carl Sandburg first won wide attention with his collection *Chicago Poems* (1916), containing pieces inspired by the bustle and excitement as well as the social problems of Chicago. In *Cornhuskers* (1918), his next collection, Sandburg moved to topics associated with the prairie. "I was born on the prairie," he announces in the opening lines of the first poem ("Prairie"), "and the milk of its wheat, the red of its clover, the eyes of its women, gave me a song and a slogan." The poem continues praising the life of a prairie farmer, noting that the prairie existed before cities were built and will survive long after cities have fallen. Other poems delight in the harvest ("Laughing Corn"), praise the good life lived by a dead farmer ("Illinois Farmer"), and describe the passing seasons as experienced on the prairie. Sandburg went on to write children's stories, folk songs, and a sprawling and acclaimed biography of Abraham Lincoln, along with poetry. Consistent with his vision is a theme that is prominent in both *Abraham Lincoln: The Prairie Years* (1926), a two-volume set, and the four-volume *Abraham Lincoln: The War Years* (1939): the values Lincoln learned growing up on the prairie served him through his triumphs and most difficult times on the world's stage.

Agrarian values were similarly championed by the Fugitives, a group of four southern poets who rebelled against what they called the "mannered sentimentality" of the Old South. Based at Vanderbilt University in Tennessee, John Crowe Ransom, Donald Davidson, Allen Tate, and Robert Penn Warren produced a poetry journal, *The Fugitive,* that ran from 1922 to 1925, and a collection, *The Fugitives: An Anthology of Verse,* that was published in 1928. Ransom's poem "Antique Harvesters" represents the group's agrarian outlook. The speaker calls friends and neighbors together to reap the harvest. Although the younger people in the group are dissatisfied with the crop yield, older members understand the significance of patches of land where troubling events had occurred but that are once again yielding food.

The four poets joined eight other southern writers (Frank Owsley, John Gould Fletcher, Lyle H. Lanier, Herman Clarence Nixon, Andrew Nelson Lytle, John Donald Wade, Henry Blue Kline, and Stark Young) in 1930 to produce *I'll Take My Stand,* a manifesto supporting the traditional, agrarian way of life in the South over the "progress" of industrialization. The twelve men went on to publish works in a variety of genres that supported the values of *I'll Take My Stand,* which were summed up by Ransom in the manifesto's "Introduction: A Statement of Principles": "If a community, or a race, or an age, is groaning under industrialism, and well aware that it is an evil dispensation, it must find the way to throw it off" (Twelve Southerners 1978).

Art and the Farm

American art prior to the Gilded Age was dominated by the work of portrait artists and landscape painters of the Hudson River school, a style that flourished from 1835 to 1870. Among those who painted farm scenes were Alvan Fisher and William Sidney Mount. Fisher's *View near Springfield along the Connecticut River* (1819) blends natural beauty and agricultural productivity. The harmonious, pastoral scene shows a slow-flowing river, herds of cattle, neat homes, rolling hills, and cultivated fields. Mount's rural-themed paintings include *Dance of the Haymakers* (1845), which celebrates the results of hard labor.

During the 1870s, Winslow Homer depicted idyllic scenes of farm life, nature's power in seascapes, and scenes related to fishing and hunting. Disillusioned by the state of the nation following the Civil War, Homer turned to nature: "The scandals, corruption, rampant venality, and moral decay that so deeply degraded democracy in Gilded Age America and disfigured it almost beyond recognition, made everything Homer believed have no hearing, no effect, and no direction," according to the curator of a retrospective exhibition of Homer's work at the National Gallery of Art (Cikovsky 1995). Homer's farm paintings include watercolors that interpret light and motion in evoking the beauty of quiet, otherwise ordinary scenes, such as *Boy in the Barnyard Feeding Chickens* (ca. 1872), *The Milk Maid* (1878), *The Pumpkin Patch* (1878), *The Rooster* (ca. 1878), and *Shepherdess and Sheep* (1878).

Grant Wood's *American Gothic* (1930) is probably the most famous American farm painting. Showing a tight-lipped, severe-looking couple—the woman wearing a prim gingham dress, the man in overalls and holding a pitchfork—the painting is both plain and ominous. Behind the couple is their Gothic Revival–styled home. According to the Web site of the Art Institute of Chicago (where the painting was first exhibited and where it is permanently displayed), "Some believe that

Wood used this painting to satirize the narrow-mindedness and repression that has been said to characterize Midwestern culture, an accusation he denied. The painting may also be read as a glorification of the moral virtue of rural America or even as an ambiguous mixture of praise and satire" (Art Institute of Chicago n.d.).

Wood's other farm paintings include *Old Stone Barn* (1919), *Woman with Plants* (1929), and *Young Corn* (1931). *Woman with Plants* depicts a farm woman in the front of the painting, similar to the couple positioned in *American Gothic,* with farmland stretching beyond her in the background. *Fertility* (1939) shows a burgeoning barn and densely packed cornfield as a testimonial to the agricultural productivity of Iowa. *Approaching Storm* (1940), one of Wood's final works, shows a farmer hard at work, surrounded by his bounty, while an ominous storm approaches—a painting often interpreted as foreshadowing America's involvement in World War II.

Thomas Hart Benton and John Stuart Curry are often associated by critics with Wood as exemplars of American regionalism. Curry chronicled rural life in Kansas. His *Baptism in Kansas* (1928), for example, shows a girl being baptized in a cattle trough, surrounded by the assembled guests and with a barn, farmhouse, and windmill in the background, while shafts of light emanate through glowing clouds. Curry also painted tornadoes tearing along the prairie and threatening family farms, as in his paintings *Tornado over Kansas* and *The Mississippi.*

Benton had established his reputation during the early 1920s and then rebelled against the established art world, calling himself an "enemy of modernism" after living in Paris and New York. He settled in Kansas City and worked as an instructor of drawing and painting at the Kansas City Art Institute, where one of his students was Jackson Pollock, who would later became famous as an abstract expressionist painter. Often distorting the skeletal and muscular features of figures in his painting, Benton conveyed a sense of strength and vibrancy in his works. Several of them depict everyday farm scenes of the contemporary Midwest and South. *Louisiana Rice Fields* shows industrialism on the farm, as men and machines (a smoke-spewing tractor and flatbed truck) are parts of busily efficient production.

Benton painted murals, collectively called *The Social History of the State of Missouri,* for the Missouri State Capitol building. *Pioneer Days,* on the north wall, portrays pioneers heading to Missouri by river and by land, then tilling the soil and raising log cabins among their first priorities. *Politics, Farming and Law in Missouri*, on the east wall, shows such farming scenes as a man pitching hay into a barn, a cow being milked, hog raising, and turkey farming. Smoke rising in the background indicates the beginning of industrialism in the cities of Missouri. The last farming scene is the interior of a one-room farmhouse, showing what life was like at the time and representing four generations of a farm family.

The Farm in Film and Television

By the time film developed into a mass medium, the transformation of American agriculture from individual farms to large-scale agribusiness was largely under way. Among films that showed farm families struggling against economic forces, rather than nature, was the early silent film *Clodhopper* (1917), in which a young man who fled the farm for the big city returns to reclaim the girl he loves and help his father save the family farm. Films in which heroes battle against economic and natural forces included *Our Daily Bread* (1928), in which a young couple succeed in difficult circumstances; *The Southerner* (1945), in which a laborer is given a piece of land by his uncle and struggles to make it profitable; and *The Green Promise* (1949), in which a daughter saves her family farm by using modern methods and machinery.

Comedies about the challenges of farm and ranch life included *The Purchase Price* (1932), in which a mail-order bride arrives on the frontier and causes problems for two male friends, and *The Egg and I* (1947), where newlyweds buy a farm to fulfill the husband's longtime dream only to discover many more challenges than expected. Nine films featuring Ma and Pa Kettle and their family are examples of a genre in which humor focuses on unsophisticated rural folk who nevertheless exhibit an enduring wisdom. The genre was popular in television as well, including the series *Green Acres,* which ran during the 1960s; more respectful fare emerged on television during the 1970s with family dramas such as *Little House on the Prairie* and *The Waltons.* Westerns have a longer history in serious television, exemplified by such series as *The Virginian* and *Bonanza.*

Numerous literary works addressing agricultural issues were adapted into acclaimed films, including *Of Mice and Men* (1939),

Gone with the Wind (1939), *The Grapes of Wrath* (1940), *Tobacco Road* (1941), and *God's Little Acre* (1958).

Farm Music

Farm life has been celebrated and defended in song from colonial times to the annual Farm Aid benefit concerts that began in the late 1980s. Farm life has been praised in virtually every American musical style, from children's songs such as "Old MacDonald Had a Farm" to Aaron Copland's suites for ballet. Copland's works include *Billy the Kid* (1938); *Rodeo* (1942), a tale of a ranch wedding that ends with the rousing "Hoedown"; and *Appalachian Spring* (1943), a pastoral suite in eight parts.

On Broadway, meanwhile, *Oklahoma!* broke box-office records when it opened in 1943. The first collaboration between Richard Rodgers and Oscar Hammerstein, *Oklahoma!* won a Pulitzer Prize for telling an emotional story through music, lyrics, and dance. As farmers and cattlemen fight over land use, a farm girl must decide whether a cowboy or a hired hand will be her beau. The musical features such classic songs as "Oh, What a Beautiful Mornin'."

Country music rose to national prominence in the late 1920s with national broadcasts from radio station WLS in Chicago (especially the *National Barn Dance* show) and WSM of Nashville, featuring the Grand Ole Opry. However, country music is only partly rooted in life on the farm, as Bill C. Malone noted in the *Encyclopedia of Southern Culture:* "The early entertainers were rural, for the most part, but not exclusively agricultural. Country music has always been a working-class music." Malone noted that many country music players worked in railroads, coal mines, textile mills, and sawmills; as cowboys and carpenters; and even occasionally as lawyers, doctors, and preachers (quoted in Wilson and Ferris 1989).

The changes and challenges accompanying the industrialization of agriculture were explored in songs ranging from light and amusing melodies to works of protest. "How Ya Gonna Keep 'Em Down on the Farm? (After They've Seen Paree)," written by Joe Young and Samuel M. Lewis with music by Walter Donaldson in 1918, addressed the massive flight of young, farm-born men and women to

Heartland troubadour Woody Guthrie, playing a guitar adorned with a sticker that reads, "This Machine Kills Fascists." (Library of Congress)

towns and cities for excitement and opportunity, a flight that had been occurring for three decades. Written as the United States entered World War I, the song quickly became a huge popular success.

Songs of celebration and protest are exemplified in the work of Woody Guthrie, as well as folksingers such as Leadbelly and Pete Seeger who were associated with him. Guthrie was born in Okemah, Oklahoma, and experienced firsthand the devastating effects of the drought that became known as the Dust Bowl. Guthrie had formed a band, the Corn Cob Trio, but the great Dust Storm, which hit the Great Plains in 1935, made it impossible for him to support his family. Guthrie was part of the mass migration of Dust Bowl refugees, collectively called Okies, who went west with their families in search of opportunities. Guthrie hitchhiked, rode freight trains, and even walked on his way to California, where he experienced scorn and antagonism on the part of residents opposed to the influx of outsiders.

Guthrie wrote "Dust Bowl ballads," including "I Ain't Got No Home," "Talking Dust Bowl Blues," and "Tom Joad." "Pastures of Plenty" combined protest and celebration: "Well, it's always we ramble that river and I / All along your green valley, I'll work till I die / My land I'll defend with my life, if it be / 'Cause my pastures of plenty must always be free." With a plain singing voice and a guitar brandishing the scrawled phrase "This Machine Kills Fascists," Guthrie became a modern-day troubadour, traveling the land expressing the problems and frustrations of those without political voice. "This Land Is Your Land," perhaps his most famous song, celebrated freedom and spoke for the dispossessed as well: "In the squares of the city, In the shadow of a steeple, / By the relief office, I'd seen my people / As they stood there hungry, I stood there asking, / Is this land made for you and me?" ("Woody Guthrie Biography" n.d.).

Guthrie's influence lived on after he died in the early 1960s in the work of Bob Dylan, among others. Two decades after Guthrie's death, Dylan inspired the concept of Farm Aid with a remark he made at a Live Aid benefit concert for Africa in 1986: "Wouldn't it be great if we did something for our own farmers right here in America?" Such popular singer-songwriters as Willie Nelson, Neil Young, and John Mellencamp helped found Farm Aid, a nonprofit farming advocacy organization that began publicizing the hardships of independent farmers and organized an annual concert to raise funds and awareness for their plight. In 1999, Young penned the song "Last of His Kind (The Farm Aid Song)":

> *Well I hate to say the farmer*
> *Was the last of a dying breed*
> *Living off the land*
> *And taking what he needs*
> *Don't say much for the future*
> *When a family can't survive*
> *I'd hate to say the farmer*
> *Was the last of his kind.* (Farm Aid n.d.)

Sources

Adams, Edward F. 1899. *The Modern Farmer in His Business Relations.* San Francisco: N. J. Stone.

Ambrose, Jamie. 1988. *Willa Cather: Writing at the Frontier.* New York: St. Martin's Press.

Art Institute of Chicago. N.d. "Grant Wood: American, 1891–1942." Available on-line at www.artic.edu/artaccess/AA_Modern/pages/MOD_5.shtml.

Austin, Mary. 1932. *Earth Horizon.* New York: Houghton Mifflin.

Burns, Sarah. 1989. *Pastoral Inventions: Rural Life in Nineteenth-Century American Art and Culture.* Philadelphia: Temple University Press.

Cather, Willa. 1998. *Three Novels: O Pioneers! The Song of the Lark, My Ántonia.* Introduction by Maureen Howard. New York: Carroll and Graf Publishers.

Cikovsky, Nicolai. 1995. *Winslow Homer.* Washington, DC: National Gallery of Art.

Conlogue, William. 2001. *Working the Garden: American Writers and the Industrialization of Agriculture.* Chapel Hill: University of North Carolina Press.

Cook, Sylvia Jenkins. 1991. *Erskine Caldwell and the Fiction of Poverty.* Baton Rouge: Louisiana State University Press.

Crow, Charles L., ed. 2003. *A Companion to the Regional Literatures of America.* Malden, MA: Blackwell.

DeMott, Robert, ed. 1989. *Working Days: The Journals of "The Grapes of Wrath."* New York: Viking.

Farm Aid. N.d. Available on-line at www.farmaid.org.

Fitzgerald, Deborah. 2003. *Every Farm a Factory: The Industrial Ideal in American Agriculture.* New Haven, CT: Yale University Press.

Foote, Stephanie. 2000. *Regional Fictions: Culture and Identity in Nineteenth-Century American Literature.* Madison: University of Wisconsin Press.

Jefferson, Thomas. 1832. *Notes on the State of Virginia.* Boston: Lilly and Wait.

Lanier, Sidney. 1884. "Sidney Lanier, 1842–1881." *Poems of Sidney Lanier,* edited by his wife [Mary D. Lanier]. New York: Charles Scribner's Sons.

Martin, Jay. 1967. *Harvests of Change: American Literature, 1865–1914.* Englewood Cliffs, NJ: Prentice-Hall.

Marx, Leo. 1964. *The Machine in the Garden: Technology and the Pastoral Ideal in America.* New York: Oxford University Press.

Nelson, Cary, ed. 2000. "Edwin Markham." In *Anthology of Modern American Poetry.* New York: Oxford University Press. Available on-line at www.english/uiuc.edu/maps/poets/m_r/markham/markham.htm.

Newman, Lea. 2000. *Robert Frost: The People, Places, and Stories behind His New England Poetry.* Shelburne, VT: New England Press.

Sarver, Stephanie L. 1999. *Uneven Land: Nature and Agriculture in American Writing.* Lincoln: University of Nebraska Press.

Simpson, Lewis P. 1975. *The Dispossessed Garden: Pastoral and History in Southern Literature.* Athens: University of Georgia Press.

Sinclair, Upton. 1981. *The Jungle.* Introduction by Morris Dickstein. New York: Bantam Classics.

Smith, Henry Nash. 1950. *Virgin Land: The American West as Symbol and Myth.* Cambridge, MA: Harvard University Press.

St. John de Crèvecoeur, J. Hector. 1912. *Letters from an American Farmer.* New York: E. P. Dutton.

Stanford's Dime Novels. N.d. Available on-line at http://www.sul.stanford.edu/depts/dp/pennies/home.html.

Steinbeck, John. 1936. "Dubious Battle in California." *Nation,* September 12. Available on-line at www.archive.thenation.com/summaries/v143i0011_10.htm.

———. 1992. *The Grapes of Wrath.* New York : Penguin Books.

Twelve Southerners. 1978. *I'll Take My Stand: The South and the Agrarian Tradition.* Baton Rouge: Louisiana State University Press.

University of North Carolina. *Documenting the American South.* Available on-line at http://docsouth.unc.edu/lanier/menu.html.

Wilder, Laura Ingalls. 1932. *Little House in the Big Woods.* New York: Harper.

Wilson, Charles Reagan, and William Ferris, eds. 1989. *Encyclopedia of Southern Culture.* Chapel Hill: University of North Carolina Press.

"Woody Guthrie Biography." N.d. *The Woody Guthrie Website.* Available on-line at www.woodyguthrie.org/.

Agriculture and Meatpacking in the Modern Era

Laurie Collier Hillstrom

Agriculture in the Modern Era

The face of agriculture in the United States has changed dramatically since World War II. The number of farms dotting the landscape has decreased significantly, as has the number of individuals who claim farming as their primary occupation. At the same time, the average size of an American farm has increased. In 1940, for instance, 30.5 million Americans (23.2 percent of the U.S. population) worked 6.1 million farms averaging 175 acres each (Fite 1996). By 2000, though, only 4.4 million Americans (1.6 percent of the population) earned a living as farmers, working 2.1 million farms averaging 434 acres each.

> In the last half of the twentieth century we came to see, reluctantly, that our favorite national family farm narrative was scarcely valid any-more. During that half century the number of American working farms decreased by two-thirds—roughly, from over six million to about two million. In the beginning we were a nation over 90 percent of whose people lived directly from the farm; today it is between 1 and 2 percent, and if that trend continues, the future of family farming does not imply a long or pleasant story. (Jager 2004)

Despite the declining numbers of farms and farmers, however, annual U.S. food production has increased steadily, while commodity prices have decreased. Production of corn, for example, grew from 38 bushels per acre in 1950 to 118 bushels per acre in 1990 (Fite 1996). Over the same period, the percentage of income an average American spent on food decreased from 30 percent to 10 percent (Jager 2004). Such statistics have prompted some industry observers to argue that the consolidation of American agriculture is part of a natural process that has resulted in improved efficiency.

> Farming in the United States since World War II has been in the throes of the same kind of transformation that revolutionized manufacturing during the eighteenth century and retail trade during the twentieth. Small-scale operations are just as outmoded on the land as they have become in the city. . . . The new family farm is merely a much larger and more efficient version of the older edition. (Hart 1991)

In addition to the consolidation of farms and the related decline in farm population, some of the major trends affecting American agriculture in the second half of the twentieth century include specialization, mechanization, vertical integration, and globalization. "Each is powerful alone, as a force in the farm economy, but each also combines with the others to create pressures for radical transformation on the farm" (Jager 2004). In fact, these trends have contributed to the development of a new industrial sector known as agribusiness, in which a few large companies control various aspects of farm production, from the manufacture of seeds and fertilizer to the processing and distribution of food. Agribusiness has come under criticism in recent years for garnering the lion's share of government subsidies, failing to use environmentally sustainable farming practices, and negatively impacting the rural economy.

Economically, the U.S. agricultural sector has in recent years been marked by increased federal expenditures in crop selection and stewardship decisions. The recent history of American farming has also been marked by a widening disparity among farmer incomes and increased consolidation of all aspects of the industry—manufacture, processing, and distribution—into fewer hands. "Market competition is limited. Farmers have little control over farm prices, and they continue to receive a smaller and smaller portion of consumer dollars spent on agricultural products. . . . Economic pressures have led to a tremendous loss of farms, particularly small farms, and farmers during the past few decades" (Gold 1999).

Declining Numbers of Farms and Farmers

The percentage of Americans who identified farming as their livelihood began to decline as the Industrial Revolution swept across the United States. In 1820, 71.8 percent of those in the working population were farmers, but this number had declined to 37.5 percent by 1900 (Gordon 2004). Although technology helped agriculture become more efficient and less dependent on labor during that time, the rise of various new industries also convinced large numbers of people to abandon the fields and seek their fortunes working in factories. The U.S. farm population peaked at 32 million in 1935, during the Great Depression, as millions of people who lost their factory jobs returned to the family farm (Hurt 2002). The number of farmers declined once again with America's entry into World War II in 1941, when people left the farms to join the military or work in war-related industries. The conflict marked the beginning of a period of prosperity for American farmers that lasted through the Korean War. The nation required greater food supplies to feed the troops and urban workers, so crop surpluses disappeared and commodity prices rose.

By 1950, the United States had 23 million farmers (15 percent of the population) working on 5.4 million farms. These farmers increased their use of machines by 15 percent and chemical fertilizers by 70 percent during the 1950s, contributing to a 23 percent increase in total farm output, and output per man-hour soared 157 percent (Fite 1996). As farmers became more efficient and increased their production in the postwar years, however, their efforts led to surpluses of crops, which depressed prices. Marginal producers went out of business, and control of their land passed to larger-scale enterprises. By 1960, the farm population had decreased to 15.6 million (representing 8.7 percent of the U.S. population) and the number of farms to 3.9 million, whereas the average size of a farm grew to 300 acres (Fite 1996).

Prosperity returned to the agricultural sector in the early 1970s. An upswing in worldwide demand for U.S. exports led to skyrocketing grain prices, which contributed to an increase of $40 billion in total farm receipts, from $52 billion in 1971 to $92 billion in 1974 (Fite 1996). Many farmers reacted to the increase in their annual income by purchasing additional land and new farming equipment— often on credit, at high interest rates. When the bottom dropped out on commodity prices in the mid-1970s, many farmers found themselves struggling under tremendous debt loads. In 1978, thousands of farmers participated in "tractorcades" organized by the American Agricultural Movement (AAM). They drove their tractors across the country and congregated in Washington, D.C., where they demanded increases in federal farm aid. The protests succeeded in gaining government price supports for commodities as well as payments for farmers to take land out of production in order to ease surpluses.

By 1980, there were 2.4 million farms in the United States (a decrease of 300,000 from 1970), averaging 426 acres each (an increase of 53 acres from a decade earlier) (Fite 1996). The agricultural sector experienced some recovery in the early 1980s, but farmers remained in a precarious financial condition due to high levels of debt. When both exports and prices dropped in the mid-1980s, a severe farm crisis was precipitated. Thousands of farmers went bankrupt, with 400,000 going out of business in 1985 alone (Casa 1999). The federal government attempted to alleviate the situation by approving large increases in support payments to farmers. Nevertheless, the farm population continued to decline. By 1990, there were 2.1 million farms in the United States, worked by 4.5 million farmers (representing 1.9 percent of the population). Of the 4.4 million farms that remained by 2000, about 50 percent were classified as residential/ lifestyle or retirement farms, whose owners reported a main source of income other than farming. In fact, farming was the primary occupation of only about 960,000 Americans (U.S. Environmental Protection Agency 2005). Despite having so few farmers, however, the United States still managed to lead the world in agricultural exports at the turn of the twenty-first century (Gordon 2004), largely due to increased efficiency and mechanization.

Improvements in Agricultural Technology

American agriculture has undergone a great deal of technological change since World War II. In fact, the period from 1945 to 1970 is often referred to as the second American agricultural revolution. One of the first significant developments in that era was the introduction of the mechanical spindle cotton picker by International Harvester in 1942. Widely adopted in the 1950s, this machine decreased the need for labor throughout the Cotton Belt of the South, reducing the number of labor hours required to harvest 100 pounds of cotton from forty-two in 1945 to five in 1965. By 1968, 96 percent of cotton crops were harvested through mechanical means ("History of American Agriculture" 2005). The machine's adoption led to the replacement of thousands of tenant farmers, most of whom left the farms to find better-paying factory jobs. Mechanical harvesting of cotton also contributed to a large-scale demographic change in the farming population of the South. When cotton growing was labor intensive, African Americans worked tens of thousands of farms across the region. Unable to afford mechanical cotton pickers, however, most of these farmers abandoned the fields for factories in the 1950s and 1960s. By 1990, minorities accounted for only 3 percent of resident farmers across the United States, and the majority of nonwhite farm employees were seasonal migrant workers (Fite 1996).

The use of tractors increased significantly in the postwar years, reducing the need for horses and forage and thus freeing up more land to raise crops. In 1954, tractors outnumbered horses and mules on American farms for the first time ("History of American Agriculture" 2005). The more successful farmers also invested in such emerging technologies as twine binders, self-propelled combines, and corn pickers in the decades following World War II. These inventions helped reduce the number of labor hours required to harvest 100 bushels of corn from twelve in 1945 to three in 1975 ("History of American Agriculture" 2005). Electricity also spread quickly through farming communities during these years, increasing from 35 percent of all farms in 1940 to 50 percent by 1945 and 98 percent by 1960 (Hurt 2002).

Another technological development favored by American farmers in the decades following World War II was chemical fertilizers. The average annual usage of these chemicals increased from 6.6 million tons between 1930 and 1939 to 32.4 million tons between 1960 and 1969. The application of chemical fertilizers led to significant increases in agricultural output, so that an individual farmer who supplied food for 10.7 people in 1940 was able to supply food for 75.8 people thirty years later. At the same time, mechanical farming equipment led to enormous increases in agricultural efficiency across the United States, along with significant decreases in the demand for farm labor. An average farm required one worker for every 27.5 acres in 1890; a century later, a single worker could farm 740 acres (U.S. Environmental Protection Agency 2005).

Even though both output and efficiency increased, some observers expressed concerns about the evolution of American agriculture in the postwar era. These critics claimed that other factors should be included in assessing the success of the agriculture industry.

> Since farming has traditionally required long hours of repetitive exhausting toil, the fact that the mechanization of agriculture has "released" millions of farmers from the necessity of working the land, while consumers enjoy a super-abundance of relatively inexpensive food, is often cited as irrefutable evidence of progress. . . . Today not only the farmer but people from all areas of public and private life are questioning our confidence in the belief that ever expanding productivity equals progress and success. They see the family farm and our once-healthy rural economy severely threatened. They are concerned as consumers about the wholesomeness of the food grown by big-business agriculture and about the ecological damage caused by modern farming methods. They have grown sharply critical of the "efficiency" of modern agricultural technology, in which it has become more profitable to use toxic chemicals than natural fertilizer and biological means of pest control and high energy consuming machines instead of people. (Horwitz 1980)

In fact, agriculture is one of the biggest consumers of petroleum in the U.S. economy. Certain critics question whether shortages of fossil fuels could someday contribute to shortages of food, making the mechanization of farming a national security issue.

Technology Squeezes Out Small Farmers

Although the widespread adoption of agricultural technology led to greater efficiency and higher crop-production levels on farms, as well as lower prices for consumers, it also increased the overall cost of operating a farm. The price of agricultural equipment rose steadily over time; a tractor that cost $2,400 in 1950 would cost upward of $7,000 by 1970. Farmers justified such expenditures by noting dramatic production increases. For instance, average corn production increased from 38 bushels per acre in 1950 to 87 bushels per acre in 1970. Over the same period, however, the market price of a bushel of corn actually decreased from $1.50 to $1.00 (Fite 1996). Farmers found that they had to invest in new technologies in order to lower production costs and increase efficiency. But as more and more farmers acquired the technology, they flooded the market with surplus crops. Oversupply then drove down commodity prices, forcing farmers to seek even greater efficiencies. They adopted better land-use practices (such as crop rotation and no-till farming methods); planted improved strains of crops; and applied higher levels of chemical fertilizers, herbicides, and pesticides.

Over time, however, the cycle of higher costs and lower returns squeezed smaller and less efficient farms out of business. Critics claim that it also led farmers toward a single-minded pursuit of efficiencies at the expense of stewardship of the land. "This narrowed concentration upon needed efficiencies . . . will tend to suppress or postpone other long-term concerns, such as sustainability, health of the soil, the energy source, waste byproducts, the landscape, the community, the environment" (Jager 2004).

These costs have not been reflected in the price of food. As noted earlier, an average American spent over 30 percent of his or her income on food in 1950, but by 2000, this figure had dropped to around 10 percent. Over the same period, the amount of income that farmers received from the sale of food products declined from fifty cents out of every dollar spent to less than twenty cents: "Consumers spend less of their income on food than ever, and farmers receive a smaller percentage of that lesser portion" (Jager 2004). Some critics argue that much of the difference went to corporate agribusiness.

While the farmers growing cereal grains—wheat, oats, corn—earn negative returns and are pushed close to bankruptcy, the companies that make breakfast cereals reap huge profits. In 1998, cereal companies Kellogg's, Quaker Oats, and General Mills enjoyed return on equity rates of 56 percent, 165 percent, and 222 percent respectively. While a bushel of corn sold for less than $4, a bushel of corn flakes sold for $133. In 1998, cereal companies were 186 to 740 times more profitable than the farms. Maybe farms are making too little because others are taking too much. (Christison 2000)

Modern American agribusinesses are armed with fleets of sophisticated machines, such as these wheat combines. (Corel)

Toward the end of the twentieth century, the transformation of agriculture into a large-scale industrial enterprise seemed complete. Farms classified by the U.S. Department of Agriculture (USDA) as large (with annual sales exceeding $250,000) accounted for 8 percent of all farms in the United States in 1997, yet these farms produced an impressive 72 percent of total American farm output. In fact, a mere 46,000 farms accounted for 50 percent of that year's total sales (USDA 2005).

> There is no question about the fact that the large corporate farm offers unfair competition to local farmers. Their farming endeavors may actually be run at a loss with losses written off against gains in other areas of the business. Large operations also receive cheaper inputs because of advantages in purchasing machinery and supplies in large quantities, and in easier credit terms. They are also the farms that employ crews of migratory workers, who receive lower wages than does a local hired hand employed by a family farm. (Horwitz 1980)

Large growers also collected the lion's share of government farm subsidies.

Government Subsidies Favor Large-Scale Producers

Federal subsidies for agriculture got started with the New Deal programs of President Franklin Delano Roosevelt. Although countless family farms struggled through the Depression and Dust Bowl years, these programs allowed many farmers to remain on their land. The New Deal also brought electricity to many rural areas and launched early soil conservation programs. As the United States pulled out of the Depression, however, the government found that its policies tended to create surpluses of many commodities.

America's entry into World War II led to increased demand, which helped reduce the surpluses and created prosperous times for many farmers. But the war years also saw severe shortages in farm labor, a situation that large-scale growers in the West urged the federal government to address. In response, Congress established the bracero program, which allowed western farmers to import Mexican immigrant laborers and pay these workers substandard wages. Between 1942 and 1947, 219,000 Mexican immigrants entered the United States to work primarily in the fields and groves of California. The growers soon became dependent on the program and convinced Congress to extend it after the war ended. Although the bracero program was criticized for driving down farm wages, preventing workers from gaining needed reforms, and forcing domestic workers out of the fields, it remained in place until the civil rights movement of the 1960s.

After World War II ended, farmers looked to the federal government for assurances that they would not endure precipitous drops in commodity prices in the postwar years. The government responded by passing the Agricultural Act of 1949, which provided high, guaranteed price supports for many basic crops—such as corn, wheat, cotton, and rice. Because the benefits were usually based on acreage and production, these subsidies tended to favor large producers over small family farms. As early as 1950, President Dwight Eisenhower informed Congress that "the chief beneficiaries of our price support programs have been the two million larger, highly mechanized

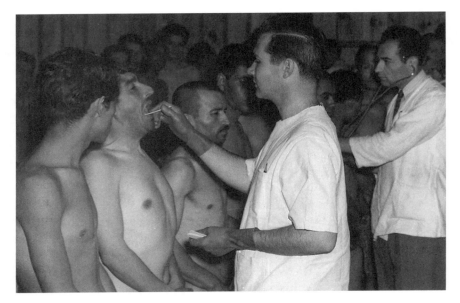

Migrant workers receive physical examinations as part of their application for work in the United States, ca. 1943. (Howard R. Rosenberg, "Snapshots in a Farm Labor Tradition," *Labor Management Decisions,* Winter–Spring, 1993)

farming units which produce about 85 percent of our agricultural output. The individual production of the remaining farms, numbering about 3.5 million, is so small that the farmer derives little benefit from price supports" (quoted in Horwitz 1980).

Eisenhower tried to implement a system of flexible price supports that would have paid farmers only when prices dropped below certain levels. He also took steps to relieve surpluses by increasing consumption, through such means as school lunch programs and overseas exports. These efforts failed to stop the growth of surpluses, however, and in 1956, the federal government began paying farmers to take land out of production.

The Agricultural Act of 1949, which initiated price supports, had no expiration date, so farm subsidies remained the law of the land for the next fifty years. Proponents offered up a number of justifications for continuing to provide taxpayer support for agriculture. "Farming, with the exception of national defense, is the only major sector of our economy that is subsidized by the government," pointed out one historian. "It has been considered a matter of public interest that farm income should keep pace with industrial income, that society should share some of the risks of farming, that the government should help buffer the fluctuations in supply and demand that make farming such an insecure form of livelihood" (Horwitz 1980).

In addition, many observers noted how difficult it was for the U.S. government to create a coherent farm policy. The agriculture industry enjoyed a great deal of political power over the years. Even though the states whose economies were based mostly on agriculture tended to be rural and sparsely populated, they still received equal representation in the U.S. Senate. Furthermore, every state in the Union possessed some sort of agricultural sector. Finally, many urban and suburban Americans—in addition to enjoying cheap and abundant food—had an emotional attachment to the idea of the family farm and the farming lifestyle and thus tended to support reasonable agricultural subsidies. Agriculture lobbyists used these advantages to ensure continued government support in the form of subsidies, tariffs, and import quotas (Gordon 2004).

Critics of agricultural subsidies, by contrast, argued that federal farm programs encouraged growers to maximize their production of the commodities that provided them with a guaranteed source of income, thus contributing to the surplus problem. They also claimed that subsidies made farmers increasingly dependent on the government, kept inefficient farmers on the land, and encouraged environmentally damaging land-use practices. Some observers complained about the sheer scope of agricultural subsidies, which sometimes constituted the majority of farmers' income. In 1995, for instance, net income from agricultural products averaged about $11,000 per farm in the United States, and government subsidies contributed another $24,000 per farm. An average farmer also earned over $39,000 that year from off-farm employment (Hurt 2002).

Perhaps the most damning criticism of U.S. farm policy, however, was that it tended to reward large-scale agribusiness enterprises with political clout rather than small-scale family farm operations. Over the years, a number of high-profile cases of government subsidies for wealthy farmers raised the ire of taxpayers. In 1985, for instance, the Food Security Act provided $20 million in government subsidies to J. G. Boswell of California, one of the nation's largest producers of cotton (Hurt 2002). By the turn of the twenty-first century, a full three-fourths of all commodity-related payments went to farms with sales over $100,000 per year (USDA 2005). Large producers also received benefits in the form of tax advantages for equipment purchases and exemptions from federal labor laws.

Critics claimed that government subsidies favoring large-scale agricultural enterprises aided in the consolidation and corporate control of American farming. Some analysts argued that, if trends continued, a handful of huge, multinational food companies would gain virtual control over U.S. food production. These companies would own millions of acres of farmland; develop and sell the majority of seeds; and produce, process, distribute, and market most food. A report by the National Commission on Small Farms entitled "A Time to Act" acknowledged that federal farm programs historically benefited large farms, even though these farms did not offer significant efficiencies over small farms in producing crops. "The pace of industrialization of agriculture has quickened," the report noted. "The dominant trend is a few large . . . firms controlling the majority of food and fiber products in an increasingly global processing and distribution system" (Casa 1999).

In 1996, Congress decided to take action to reduce government support programs for farmers and apply a free market model to U.S. agriculture. By that time, farmers were getting 21 percent of their income from federal subsidy programs, and the government was paying for 23 percent of the nation's cropland to remain idle (Hurt 2002). Congress tried to address the issue by passing the Federal Agriculture Improvement and Reform Act (FAIR), also known as the Freedom to Farm Act. This measure, which marked the first major change in farm policy since 1949, gradually reduced federal payments over a seven-year period while also lifting restrictions on the types of crops that farmers could plant. When the seven years were up, the government planned to make no further support payments for agriculture, regardless of surplus levels or market prices.

At first, many farmers welcomed the new policy. Even though it gradually eliminated subsidies, some farmers felt that they could take advantage of the seven-year window to plant as many acres as possible while continuing to receive price supports. Unfortunately, the increased production of commodities coincided with the collapse of

Asian financial markets and an associated reduction in international demand for grain. This situation created huge surpluses and depressed prices to thirty-year lows. Farmers immediately began lobbying for the reinstatement of price supports and other forms of government assistance. Since the FAIR act had not repealed the Agricultural Act of 1949, Congress was able to authorize emergency payments to the agricultural sector. These payments provided about half of net farm income for 1998, and 80 percent of this money went to large and medium-sized farms.

Some analysts viewed the government's quick retreat from the FAIR act as a missed opportunity to enact significant reforms to agricultural policy. According to Brad de Vries of the Sustainable Agriculture Coalition:

> There was a real opportunity for the Department of Agriculture and farmers to explore different systems that would get them off the roller-coaster of boom-and-bust commodities prices, to find ways to connect more directly with consumers or find alternative crops that would reduce their costs and increase their returns rather than producing corn yet again and taking whatever price they give you at the elevator. Unfortunately, one thing we've seen is the [USDA] and the commodity organizations continue to encourage people to do the same thing over and over again—to continue with corn and soybeans. (quoted in Casa 1999)

Government farm supports were back in the news in 2000, when it was revealed that about $27 billion in emergency subsidies went to just 10 percent of farm owners, including several wealthy members of Congress, media mogul Ted Turner, professional athletes, and real estate developers. In 2002, Congress finally repealed the Agricultural Act of 1949 by passing the Farm Security and Rural Investment Act. The act eliminated the original legislative foundation for farm subsidies, but it also allocated $190 billion to agricultural interests over ten years. Critics claimed that the bill would give 60 percent of subsidies to farms ranking in the top 10 percent by size (Hurt 2002). One analyst predicted that "finding a way to reduce and then eliminate the subsidies and protection will be one of the biggest political problems to solve as the world moves more and more to an integrated global economy" (Gordon 2004).

Agriculture's Impact on the Environment

The cultivation of plants for human consumption has always carried an environmental impact, from clearing forests to create arable land to diverting water sources to irrigate crops. In the modern era, however, the environmental impacts of agriculture have spread far beyond the traditional issue of land use to include unsustainable withdrawals of freshwater, degradation and loss of fertile soil, pollution of land and water resources with toxic chemicals, and concerns about human and ecosystem health stemming from the cultivation of genetically modified organisms (GMOs). Some critics claim that the consolidation of small family farms into large-scale agribusiness enterprises has exacerbated the environmental impact of modern farming: "A strong case against the large industrial corporate farm is that the investor, unlike the small farmer who hopes to pass his land on to his children, is interested only in short-term economic gains and has little concern with preserving the soil for the use and profit of the next generation" (Horwitz 1980).

Many observers have expressed concern about unsustainable withdrawals of freshwater from major river systems and underground aquifers for agricultural irrigation, particularly in the arid West. According to the U.S. Geological Survey, agriculture accounts for more total freshwater withdrawals (at 42 percent) than any other sector of the American economy, including power generation (39 percent) and industrial use (8 percent) (USGS 1997). In the dry climates of the West, farmers withdrew 45.6 trillion gallons of freshwater for irrigation in 1990, which represented 71 percent more water than was withdrawn for all other human uses. The sheer scale of modern farming has contributed to fears that water withdrawals might overwhelm availability; the overall amount of irrigated land in the United States has increased from 1.5 million hectares (more than 5,790 square miles) in 1890 to 21 million hectares (more than 81,000 square miles) in 1995 (MacDonnell 1999).

Soil conservation has concerned agriculturalists in North America since early tobacco and cotton farms were established in the seventeenth century. Although the most memorable examples of soil degradation and loss occurred during the Dust Bowl years of the 1930s, significant erosion of topsoil has also taken place during the modern era—most notably during the dust storms that hit the Great Plains in 1977 and in the problems that have plagued areas of wet-

The 1930s Dust Bowl covered this Texas farm and millions of other acres in the Great Plains under a smothering blanket of dirt. (Library of Congress)

lands that have been converted to agriculture in Florida. Although no-till farming methods and crop-rotation schemes have led to improvements in some areas, concerns remain about the salinization of irrigated farmland in the arid West.

The use of chemical fertilizers, pesticides, and herbicides is another source of environmental concern related to the agriculture industry. The application of such chemicals increased steadily during the postwar decades, from an average of 6.6 million tons per year between 1930 and 1939 to 13.6 million tons between 1940 and 1949, 22.3 million tons between 1950 and 1959, and 32.4 million tons between 1960 and 1969 ("History of American Agriculture" 2005). By the 1970s, however, Americans began to doubt whether the gains in agricultural efficiency these chemicals offered were significant enough to balance out potential threats to human health and the environment. Critics claimed that the use of chemical pesticides and herbicides on farm fields polluted groundwater and created foods that were harmful to eat. Such concerns launched a movement toward low-input sustainable agriculture—also known as natural or organic farming—to reduce the chemicals in produce and other farm products. In the 1990s, federal legislation established new guidelines for the reduction of chemical applications in agriculture.

Many observers credit Rachel Carson, the author of *Silent Spring*, with raising American consciousness of the environmental impact of agricultural chemicals. Carson's 1962 study alerted the public to the dangers of DDT, a potent pesticide that was developed during World War II and introduced for agricultural pest control in the United States in the 1940s. For many years, DDT was spread widely in swamps and fields to kill mosquitoes, ticks, and other disease-bearing insects. It was credited with saving millions of human lives around the world by halting the spread of insect-transmitted diseases such as malaria, typhus, and encephalitis. By the 1960s, however, scientists found that DDT killed not only pests but also beneficial insects and also that the toxin invaded water supplies and persisted in the body tissues of all kinds of organisms. *Silent Spring* showed that the pesticide moved through the food chain to negatively affect the reproductive capacity of birds, leading to precipitous declines in raptor populations throughout North America. DDT was subsequently banned for agricultural use.

In another high-profile case from the 1960s, Vietnam War veterans suffered a range of health problems following their exposure to the herbicide Agent Orange, which the U.S. military used to deforest large areas of Southeast Asia during the conflict. Agent Orange contained dioxin, a known carcinogen that caused genetic, reproductive, and neurological damage in humans. Vietnam veterans eventually filed class-action lawsuits against the U.S. government, seeking compensation for the range of health problems they suffered as a result of their exposure to the herbicide. Such high-profile cases not only raised concerns about the widespread application of chemical fertilizers, pesticides, and herbicides on agricultural fields but also created an atmosphere of skepticism that persisted during the introduction of genetically modified foods in the 1980s.

Biotechnology and Genetically Modified Organisms

Biotechnology emerged as an important component of the American agriculture industry in the 1980s, after U.S. patent law was extended to cover newly developed plant varieties and life-forms under the Plant Variety Protection Act of 1970. This idea was affirmed by the U.S. Supreme Court in its 1980 ruling in *Diamond v. Chakrabarty,* which said that the U.S. Patent Office could not deny a patent to inventors of new microorganisms simply because their inventions were alive. Once the law protected developments in the field, more companies began seeking profits in biotechnology and genetic engineering. They sought to develop plant strains that would resist insects and diseases, withstand applications of herbicides, and retain their appearance and nutritional value longer on grocery store shelves. The science was also applied to ranching, as companies produced hormones to increase meat and milk production and antibiotics to prevent the spread of diseases in livestock.

Perhaps the most controversial application of biotechnology to agriculture has involved the development of GMOs. Proponents of GMOs claimed that the introduction of new genes into plant species could produce superior crop strains that would lead to vast improvements in agricultural efficiency and help solve the problem of world hunger. From the beginning, however, many observers have expressed concerns about the safety of GMOs. Some critics worry that artificially introduced genes could have unintended effects on the environment, perhaps by spreading out of control or by cross-pollinating with native species. Other opponents worry about the safety of foods made with GMOs, arguing that the technology could reduce the nutritional value of foods, lead to an increase in food allergies, or contribute to the evolution of antibiotic-resistant bacteria. In addition, some critics claim that the widespread adoption of genetically modified plant strains could reduce the biodiversity of seeds and thus make crops more vulnerable to new pests and diseases. Finally, some consumers simply feel that GMOs were placed in the nation's food supply too quickly, with insufficient testing, to understand all the potential drawbacks of the technology.

In several cases, the cultivation of GMOs has had unintended consequences on the natural world. For instance, one of the most highly touted early GMOs was Bt corn—corn that was modified to include a gene from *Bacillus thuringiensis* (Bt), a naturally occurring bacterium that made the corn indigestible for corn borers. In 1999, however, scientists at Cornell University and the University of Iowa discovered that pollen from Bt corn was toxic to monarch butterfly larvae, which commonly feed on milkweed plants found around the

Genetic modification of corn and other crops remains controversial, but it has become standard operating practice for most U.S. growers. (Monsanto U.K.)

edges of cornfields. The following year, consumers roundly rejected Bt corn. The U.S. Food and Drug Administration had approved the Starlink brand of Bt corn, developed by Aventis, for livestock feed but not for human consumption. When Starlink corn accidentally got mixed in with corn used to produce taco shells for Kraft Foods, it led to a massive recall. Even though studies by the Centers for Disease Control found no evidence that Bt corn was harmful to humans, the high-profile case convinced the Department of Agriculture to remove all Bt corn from the market, at a cost of $20 million.

Despite concerns among consumers and environmentalists, the cultivation of GMOs increased rapidly during the 1990s. By 2000, 44.5 million hectares (almost 170,000 square miles) of GMO crops had been planted worldwide, with 68 percent of this land area in the United States (Pretty 2001). Among the crops most likely to include genetically modified elements were soybeans, corn, cotton, and potatoes. Yet some major food-processing companies—including Frito-Lay, Gerber, and Archer Daniels Midland—were concerned enough about a potential consumer backlash that they stopped buying genetically modified ingredients in the twenty-first century. The controversy over GMOs grew particularly intense in Europe, where a number of governments either banned genetically modified foods or instituted strict labeling requirements.

Although many American consumers support the idea of labeling foods that contain genetically modified ingredients, the high penetration of such products into the marketplace has made it very difficult to undertake such an initiative. By 2003, it was estimated that 60 to 70 percent of the processed foods in U.S. grocery stores contained some genetically modified ingredients (Jager 2004). Some critics claim that biotechnology companies took advantage of a friendly regulatory environment in the United States to introduce GMOs to the market very quickly, and thus "render a battle over GMO food obsolete before it could fully begin" (Jager 2004).

Like mechanization, biotechnology has contributed to the concentration of agricultural production among large-scale enterprises. The chemical companies that develop genetically modified seeds to be resistant to an herbicide, for example, are usually the same companies that produce the herbicide. Farmers that cultivate the seeds thus become a captive market, dependent on the chemical company for their livelihood and vulnerable to changes in corporate policy and pricing. Some critics question whether farmers and consumers attain any benefits from biotechnology or whether the main benefits take the form of profits gained by agribusiness:

> Sober critics wonder: Is this to be a global experiment with the health of the planet and the world's food supply? Who authorized that? Who supervises it? And who benefits from GMOs? And they answer: not the consumer, not the world's poor, occasionally the agribusinessman; but it is very certain that many corporations benefit enormously, those that produce and patent and sell the seeds and the herbicides, such as Monsanto, Novartis, Dont, Syngenta, Dow, and others. (Jager 2004)

Societal Impact of the Loss of Family Farms

The decline in the number of small, family farms across the United States produced many changes in American society. As more and more people left farms for the cities and suburbs, many small towns withered away, and numerous rural businesses and schools closed. As one analyst explained:

> The loss of millions of family farmers has undermined rural and small town economies, which depend for their vitality and survival on local farmers who buy locally, spend locally, and have a compelling interest in local social and political life.When their land is taken over by large corporate farming ventures with absentee owners who acquire their supplies elsewhere, local merchants cannot survive. For every six family farms that sell out, one small-town business folds. (Horwitz 1980)

Yet some observers argue that the transition from a rural to an urban economy is part of a natural—and desirable—process. In fact, some claim that there are still too many inefficient small farms in the United States and that efforts to protect family farms are based in an emotional attachment to the past.

> An inordinate amount of sentimental twaddle about the imminent demise of the family farm has been perpetrated by well-meaning but naive people who have been badly misled by official statistics. . . . Some city people who dislike changes in the countryside have disguised their true intent by using "the family farm" as a shibboleth. They know little and care less about farming; they would rather deify than define what they mean by a family farm because they realize that it is a more potent political ploy to prattle about preserving the family farm than it is to try to get people exercised about preserving pleasant rural landscapes. (Hart 1991)

Nevertheless, a number of experts have weighed in with advice about saving the remaining family farms. Some argue that the federal government should stop directing subsidies to large-scale agricultural conglomerates at the expense of small farmers and change the tax code so that farmers are exempt from inheritance taxes, thus allowing future generations to continue family farming operations. Others want the government to apply antitrust legislation to agribusiness so that the same handful of companies would not be allowed to control such broad areas of food production. Some observers claim that local governments should support small farming enterprises by passing zoning ordinances that require open spaces around suburbs and providing tax incentives for keeping land in agricultural use. Others see forging connections with the local community as a key to the survival of small farms. They encourage farmers to market their crops directly to local consumers and devise innovative ways of filling community needs, whether by welcoming people to "U-pick" fields and orchards, opening roadside produce stands and greenhouses, or planting corn mazes.

Given the growing public concerns about GMOs and the use of chemical fertilizers, pesticides, and herbicides, some supporters of small farms argue that such operations can succeed by offering organic produce to local consumers through farmers' markets or community-supported agriculture arrangements. They point out that concerned citizens can help local farmers by changing their purchasing habits. Although agricultural free trade agreements have led to inexpensive imported foods, buying these items reduces the local market available to family farms. Instead, they encourage consumers to make a commitment to buy fresh, seasonal produce from local farmers whenever possible.

Meatpacking in the Modern Era

The American meatpacking industry is responsible for converting live farm animals—beef cattle, hogs, sheep, and poultry—to packaged meat products. Slaughtering and butchering animals for human consumption is a huge business: the industry shipped $60.6 billion worth of meat products in 2001, and per capita meat consumption in the United States exceeded 200 pounds ("Meat Packing Plants" 2004). The meatpacking industry has undergone a number of changes in the modern era, some of which mirror those taking place in other areas of agriculture. The industry has consolidated its operations, for instance, so that a few large-scale producers tend to dominate each area of meat processing. The trend toward consolidation has also affected the raising of livestock, which is increasingly done on controversial "factory farms." Like farmers, meat producers have faced constant pressure to reduce costs and increase volume, as the price of meat for consumers has remained stable or declined over time. These pressures have exacerbated long-standing problems concerning working conditions in meatpacking plants. Finally, meatpackers have become subject to increasingly stringent government regulations in an effort to prevent dangerous pathogens from entering the U.S. food supply.

Chicago served as the center of the U.S. meatpacking industry for decades, thanks to its location at the hub of the various railroads leading from the premier livestock-raising areas of the Midwest. Like most other industries, meatpacking became increasingly mechanized after the turn of the twentieth century. Conveyor belts were installed to move animal carcasses through factories, and machines performed some of the routine processing functions. Meatpacking never became fully automated, however, because it was difficult to build machines that could adjust to the inherent differences in animal shapes and sizes.

The 1980s saw slaughterhouses disperse to the areas where livestock were raised. Placing processing plants closer to feedlots eliminated the need to transport animals over long distances in crowded railcars and trucks, thus reducing stress levels and injury rates. It also allowed meatpackers to locate their operations in rural areas that did not have a strong union tradition and presence. Around this time, consumer eating habits in the United States began to shift toward a diet that included less beef, which had a high saturated fat content and was viewed as less healthful than poultry. The decrease in demand led to the elimination of many smaller and less efficient meatpacking plants, accelerating the trend toward consolidation of meat processing among a few large companies, including Tyson, ConAgra, and Cargill. According to the USDA, there were 930 federally inspected meatpacking plants in 1998. Nearly 35.5 million cattle were slaughtered for food that year, and four packers combined to process 82 percent of the beef. In addition, 101 million hogs were slaughtered, and three packers processed 35 percent of the pork ("Meat Packing Plants" 2004).

According to the Bureau of Labor Statistics (BLS), U.S. meatpacking plants employed 520,000 people as of 2001, making it the largest employer in the overall food industry ("Meat Packing Plants" 2004). The slaughtering and butchering of animals is a dirty and often dangerous job, and working conditions within the meatpacking industry have often come under criticism from labor organizers and human rights activists. The most famous exposé of the working conditions in the slaughterhouses is Upton Sinclair's novel *The Jungle*, which raised public awareness of the situation and led to increased union activity as well as significant government regulatory actions in the first half of the twentieth century. As a result, workers in meatpacking plants received higher wages than the average paid in manufacturing industries for many years. This situation began to change in the 1980s, however, when the meatpacking industry consolidated. Facing economic pressures to control costs, the major processors responded by ending union contracts, cutting benefits, and reducing wages, until industry workers earned 30 percent less than the manufacturing average by 2000. The BLS reported that the average hourly wage received by packers—adjusted for inflation—went from $19.37 in 1970 to $19.45 in 1980, $12.63 in 1990, and $12.01 in 2000 (Kawar 2005).

Despite government regulations, working conditions in U.S. meatpacking plants remained dangerous in the 1980s and 1990s. Packers endured long exposure to cold temperatures in refrigerated plants, used sharp knives to dismember carcasses, and dragged heavy carcasses across slippery floors. As a result, 36 percent of meatpacking employees suffered injuries on the job each year—the highest rate of any U.S. industry ("Meat Packing Plants" 2004). They also suffered from a higher rate of cumulative stress disorders from repetitive motions than workers in any manufacturing industry. These figures are alarming enough, but critics claim that many on-the-job injuries in meatpacking plants go unreported. The industry employs a large number of immigrants from Mexico, Latin America, Eastern Europe, and Asia—some of them illegal—because they are the only workers willing to accept the low wages and dangerous working conditions. These immigrants are less likely to report injuries, for fear of job loss or deportation.

In 2005, the nonprofit watchdog group Human Rights Watch released a report entitled "Blood, Sweat, and Fear: Worker's Rights in U.S. Meat and Poultry Plants," which criticized the meatpacking industry for its high injury rates, resistance to labor unions, and exploitation of immigrant labor. According to that report:

> Meatpacking work has extraordinarily and unnecessarily high rates of injury, musculoskeletal disorders (repetitive stress injuries), and even death. . . . The inherent dangers of meatpacking work are aggravated by ever-increasing line speeds, inadequate training, close-quarters cutting, and long hours with few breaks. To reduce the extensive and systematic violations of the basic human rights standards in the industry,

we need new federal and state laws to reduce line speed, establish new ergonomics standards, devise stricter injury reporting, reduce under-reporting of industries, and honor workers' rights to organize. (quoted in "U.S. Meatpacking under Fire" 2005)

"A century after Upton Sinclair wrote *The Jungle,* workers in the meatpacking industry still face serious injuries," added Human Rights Watch spokesperson Jamie Fellner. "Public agencies try to protect consumers from tainted meat, but do little to protect workers from unsafe conditions" (quoted in Swanson 2005).

Federal inspection of meat products and processing plants began in 1906, prompted in part by publication of *The Jungle,* but it was not until the 1950s that the industry made major improvements in plant sanitation and packaging. Meatpacking operations came under increased media scrutiny in the late 1980s and 1990s, following several highly publicized outbreaks of *E. coli* and *Listeria* infections associated with contaminated meat products. In 1996, the Food Safety and Inspection Service (FSIS) implemented the Pathogen Reduction and Hazard Analysis and Critical Control Points rule, which marked the first major revision of meat inspection methods since the 1950s. When the rule took effect in 2000, all raw meat and poultry products were required to undergo inspections using methods capable of detecting invisible pathogens. The FSIS reported a 78 percent reduction in meat contamination from 2002 to 2004, and the U.S. Centers for Disease Control noted a 42 percent drop in *E. coli* infections from 1996 to 2004 (Clayton 2005). Additional safeguards were put in place across the industry following the discovery of the first case of bovine spongiform encephalopathy (better known as mad cow disease) in North America in 2003. Meatpacking plants increasingly began using source verification to track livestock throughout their lives, washing and pasteurizing hides to remove pathogens before beginning to process the meat, and employing microbiologists to help find ways to reduce the potential for contamination.

The small profit margins associated with meat production and processing have also led to significant consolidation in livestock-raising operations. According to the American Meat Institute, there were about 1.25 million livestock operations raising beef cattle, hogs, and sheep for human consumption in the United States in the 1990s, down from more than 2 million in the 1970s and more than 1.5 million in the 1980s. Until the 1970s, most of these animals were raised on family

farms that also grew crops, and so the farmers found it easy and economical to recycle the manure as fertilizer in their fields. By the 1980s,
however, farmers faced severe pressures to reduce costs. Many small
farms and ranches went out of business, and the larger operations that
remained began producing cattle, hogs, and poultry under contract for
major meat processors. These operations employed a number of methods—many of them controversial—in an effort to produce as much
meat as they could at the lowest possible cost.

The largest of this new breed of livestock-raising businesses became known as confined animal feeding operations (CAFOs), or factory farms. A typical CAFO would raise thousands of animals in a
relatively small area. Rather than roaming freely and grazing as in the
ranching days of old, these animals would spend their entire lives in
confined quarters. Since close confinement lowers the animals' resistance to diseases, they are routinely given antibiotics to prevent illness from wiping out whole herds. They also receive hormone injec-
tions in order to promote growth and minimize the amount of feed
needed.

Proponents argue that factory farming produces large quantities of
food at a low cost; critics claim that such operations entail environmental and human health costs that far outweigh the benefits. For example, raising thousands of animals in a confined area creates an ex-
cess of manure, which is then generally placed into holding ponds or
lagoons. Seepage from these facilities often pollutes groundwater,
and storm runoff can contaminate surface water. In 1995, for instance, 25 million gallons of raw animal waste spilled from a CAFO
lagoon in North Carolina, killing an estimated 10 million fish and
closing 364,000 acres of coastal wetlands for shellfishing. Air quality
is another concern, for the air pollution associated with factory farms
has contributed to health problems among nearby residents. Finally,
these massive operations have accelerated the loss of small, family
farms and ranches by reducing meat prices to a level where independent livestock operations cannot compete.

Sources

Casa, Kathryn. 1999. "Playing with the Big Boys." *National Catholic Reporter,*
    February 12.

Christison, Bill. 2000. "The Impact of Globalization on Family Farm Agriculture." *In Motion,* August 1. Available on-line at www.inmotionmagazine. com.

Clayton, Chris. 2005. "Meatpacking Refined." *Omaha World-Herald,* August 1.

Evans, Craig. 2001. *A New Look at Agriculture.* Boca Raton: Florida Stewardship Foundation.

Fite, Gilbert. 1964. *American Agriculture and Farm Policy Since 1900.* New York: Macmillan.

Gold, Mary V. 1999. *Sustainable Agriculture.* Washington, DC: U.S. Department of Agriculture, Agriculture Research Service.

Gordon, John Steele. 2004. "We Reap What He Reaped." *American Heritage,* August–September.

Hanson, Victor. 2001. "Giving Farms a Hand." *Country Living,* November.

Hart, John Fraser. 1991. *The Land That Feeds Us.* New York: W. W. Norton.

"History of American Agriculture, 1776–1990." 2005. Available on-line at http://inventors.about.com/lib/inventors/blfarm1.htm.

Horwitz, Elinor Lander. 1980. *On the Land: The Evolution of American Agriculture.* New York: Atheneum.

Hurt, R. Douglas. 2002. *Problems of Plenty: The American Farmer in the Twentieth Century.* Chicago: Ivan R. Dee.

Jager, Ronald. 2004. *The Fate of Family Farming.* Hanover, NH: University Press of New England.

Kawar, Mark. 2005. "Meatpacking Plant Wages Have Fallen behind the Pay in Other Jobs." *Omaha World-Herald,* January 10.

MacDonnell, Lawrence J. 1999. *From Reclamation to Sustainability: Water, Agriculture, and the Environment in the American West.* Niwot: University Press of Colorado.

"Meat Packing Industry Not Like It Used to Be." 2002. *Business Wire,* December 3.

"Meat Packing Plants" 2004. *Encyclopedia of American Industries.* Farmington Hills, MI: Gale Group.

Olsson, Karen. 2002. "The Shame of Meatpacking." *Nation,* September 16.

Pretty, Jules. 2001. "The Rapid Emergence of Genetic Modification in World Agriculture." *Environmental Conservation* 28, no. 3.

Schiavo, Christine. 2005. "Farmers Grow Imaginative to Survive along Suburbs." *Philadelphia Inquirer,* October 17.

Sheets, Kenneth R. 1996. "A Bumper Crop of Troubles." *U.S. News & World Report,* August 18.

Swanson, Al. 2005. "Analysis: Is Meatpacking a 'Jungle'?" *UPI Perspectives,* January 26.

U.S. Department of Agriculture (USDA), Economic Research Service. 2005. "Structural and Financial Characteristics of U.S. Farms." March.

U.S. Environmental Protection Agency (EPA). 2005. "Ag 101: Demographics." Available on-line at www.epa.gov/agriculture/ag101/demographics.html.

U.S. Geological Survey (USGS). 1997. "Estimated Use of Water in the United States in 1995." Washington, DC: U.S. Department of the Interior.

"U.S. Meatpacking under Fire." 2005. *Industrial Engineer,* April.

Index